D1570445

MOZART'S REQUIEM

MOZART'S REQUIEM
ON PREPARING A NEW EDITION

by

RICHARD MAUNDER

CLARENDON PRESS · OXFORD
1988

Oxford University Press, Walton Street, Oxford OX2 6DP

Oxford New York Toronto
Delhi Bombay Calcutta Madras Karachi
Petaling Jaya Singapore Hong Kong Tokyo
Nairobi Dar es Salaam Cape Town
Melbourne Auckland

and associated companies in
Berlin Ibadan

Oxford is a trade mark of Oxford University Press

Published in the United States
by Oxford University Press, New York

British Library Cataloguing in Publication Data
Maunder, Richard
Mozart's Requiem : on preparing a new
edition.
1. Mozart, Wolfgang Amadeus
I. Title
783'.092'4   M410.M9
ISBN 0-19-316413-2

Library of Congress Cataloging in Publication Data
Mozart's Requiem : on preparing a new edition / Richard Maunder.
Bibliography: p. 219
Includes index.
1. Mozart, Wolfgang Amadeus, 1756–1791. Requiem, K. 626, D minor.
2. Music—Editing.   I. Title.
ML410.M9M3   1988   783.2'1—dc19   87-31320
ISBN 0-19-316413-2

Set by Pentacor Ltd., High Wycombe, Bucks
Printed in Great Britain
at the University Printing House, Oxford
by David Stanford
Printer to the University

PREFACE

This book is intended as a companion volume to the score of my new edition of Mozart's Requiem (published by Oxford University Press). It contains a detailed commentary on the new version, with some introductory chapters on the historical background, and on the authenticity or otherwise of the traditional Süssmayr completion.

Books and articles are referred to simply by the author's name, with the date of publication added in brackets where necessary for identification purposes. Translations of quotations originally written in German are my own throughout, with the original texts reproduced in the Endnotes. Exceptionally, however, quotations from Blume and from Einstein are taken from the published English translations, which both appeared in print before the original German versions.

Apart from quotations from the Requiem itself and from Süssmayr's *Ave verum corpus* (published by Oxford University Press), all the necessary musical examples in the first nine chapters are included. It should be noted, though, that as a rule instrumental or vocal lines not relevant to the argument are omitted. From Chapter 10 onwards I have assumed that anyone who wishes to follow the commentary in detail will have access to the various versions of the Requiem and of other works of Mozart to which reference is made; hence almost no musical examples are included. This may cause the reader a little inconvenience; but to have included all the relevant examples would have unreasonably increased both the length and the price of this book.

It is a pleasure to thank Peter Evans, Christopher Hogwood, Julian Rushton, Stanley Sadie, Richard Trame, and Alan Tyson for many helpful suggestions and stimulating discussions. I am most grateful also to I. Kecskeméti of the National Széchényi Library, Budapest, for kindly supplying photocopies of Süssmayr manuscripts, to the Gesellschaft der Musikfreunde, Vienna, for a microfilm of Gassmann's Requiem, and to Messrs Breitkopf and Härtel, Wiesbaden, for permission to quote from their edition of Michael Haydn's Requiem in C minor.

R.M.

Cambridge
April 1987

CONTENTS

1
Introduction

For almost two hundred years Mozart's Requiem has been one of the best-loved works in the choral repertoire. Most musicians would rank it with Bach's B minor Mass and Beethoven's *Missa solemnis*; indeed, it is probably the most widely performed of the three works. The Requiem is unique among them, however, in having been left incomplete at its composer's untimely death, and subsequently finished by a rather obscure musician who would otherwise long since have been forgotten. The curious circumstances of the commissioning of the Requiem, too, have attracted such a fog of legends and speculations that it has become very difficult to remain objective and distinguish between what is historical fact and what is merely romantic fiction or even just wishful thinking. Many of the legends have been repeated so often that they have acquired a respectability quite unjustified by the meagre nature of the evidence on which they are based. Perhaps the most persistent of these concerns Süssmayr's part in the affair, where received tradition has it that Mozart frequently discussed the Requiem with him, and gave him detailed instructions on how to complete it after his (Mozart's) death. If this story were true, the movements missing from Mozart's autograph would to some extent be genuine, despite the fact that they contain some technical mistakes presumably made by the relatively inexperienced Süssmayr. But exactly how much in the additional movements is Mozart, and how much is Süssmayr, has been hotly debated ever since the Requiem was first published in 1800.

One school of thought, that Mozart's part in these movements is very small or even non-existent, can be traced back to Süssmayr himself, who stated in 1800, in a letter to Breitkopf and Härtel, that he alone completed the 'Lacrymosa', and 'composed afresh' the Sanctus, 'Osanna', Benedictus, and Agnus Dei. In modern times Alfred Einstein, in his entry for K 626 in the Köchel catalogue, has with few reservations accepted Süssmayr's claim:

The controversy over which parts of the Requiem are genuine or otherwise would have been unnecessary if Süssmayr's explanation of his part in the work . . . had been accepted as true. There is hardly any reason to doubt Süssmayr's truthfulness and honesty; he would have done Constanze a great service if he had been able to represent his own contributions as being of the most trifling nature. The often-repeated assertion of his absolute inferiority as a composer, leading to the conclusion that all of the Lacrimosa, the Benedictus, and the Agnus Dei could originate only from Mozart himself, would have to be founded on a more exact investigation of Süssmayr's church music than it has been to date.[1]

The contrary opinion, that Süssmayr was not sufficiently talented to have made a very significant contribution of his own to the extra movements, which therefore are substantially by Mozart, has just as respectable an antiquity. An anonymous reviewer in the *Allgemeine Musikalische Zeitung* (1 October 1801) considered that 'Mr Süssmayr's previously known compositions justify a rather severe criticism of the assertion that he played a substantial part in this great work'.[2] In 1829 Vincent Novello was more specific:

The 'Sanctus', 'Benedictus', 'Angus Dei' and 'Dona eis requiem' bear such internal proofs of their having been written by Mozart that I never for a moment believed they could have been produced by another composer, especially such an obscure writer as Süssmayr of whom nothing whatever can be shown as having the least resemblance to the style of Mozart's Requiem. (Medici and Hughes, pp. 129 f.)

More recently, Friedrich Blume has attacked what he calls Einstein's 'credulity' in accepting Süssmayr's own statement, and takes much the same line as Novello: 'At least the *Lacrimosa*, the Benedictus, and the Agnus reveal the hand of a master of Mozart's rank—who could it have been, if not Mozart himself?' (Blume, p. 154.) Indeed, Blume firmly believes that the onus of proof lies not with those who doubt that the additional movements are Süssmayr's unaided work, but on the contrary:

The assumption operative up to now, according to which Süssmayr is to be considered the composer of the missing portions as long as nothing can be proved to the contrary, seems today less justified than the assumption that the independent composition of the closing portions cannot be ascribed to Süssmayr so long as the doubts concerning his talent . . . are not resolved by demonstrating a corresponding accomplishment of his own from his pen. As long as no church compositions by Süssmayr can be brought forward that at least imitate faithfully the master's style . . . it is . . . irresponsible to attribute the later movements of the Requiem to the unproved pupil as his own compositions. (Blume, p. 156.)

Given that two scholars of the standing of Einstein and Blume disagree so fundamentally, and that they cannot both be right, what is the truth of the matter? Should Süssmayr's completion of the Requiem be treated with reverence as being faithful to Mozart's intentions and containing much of genuine Mozart? Or does Süssmayr's version have no special standing? Are his contributions good enough, or would it be better to remove his work altogether and make the best we can of Mozart's incomplete autograph?

Blume's case depends very much on the non-existence of church music by Süssmayr of comparable style and quality to the additional movements in the Requiem, for otherwise his assertion that pieces existing only in Süssmayr's hand, and stated by him to be his own compositions, should be ascribed to Mozart unless proved otherwise would be contrary to all logic. There must be *prima facie* evidence of *some* sort before serious consideration can be given to the suggestion that Mozart, not Süssmayr, was the composer of these movements. As it happens, though, there does exist a piece of Latin church music by Süssmayr, written moreover at exactly the time when he was working on his completion of the Requiem, that appears to refute this part of Blume's argument. This is his setting of *Ave verum corpus*, which, like Mozart's, was written for Stoll in Baden, and which is dated 9 June 1792, only a year later.[3] Süssmayr's setting will be discussed in detail in Chapter 3; suffice it to say now that it shows just the same combination of a certain talent for superficial imitation of Mozart with a lack of technical expertise as does, for example, the Sanctus in the Requiem.

It is, naturally, difficult to judge the additional movements objectively, since their very familiarity, and their traditional association with the name of Mozart, all too easily induce the suspension of normal critical faculties unless one is extremely careful to rid one's mind of prejudice. It is essential first to be clear about Süssmayr's status: what was his relationship to Mozart? What did Mozart think of him as a musician? Is it likely that Mozart wished him to finish the Requiem, discussed the work with him, and gave him instructions about its completion? Or is this merely a legend that grew up after the event?

It will be shown in Chapter 2 that all the available firsthand evidence points unmistakably to the conclusion that Süssmayr can barely be counted as a formal pupil of Mozart's, and that he was absent from Vienna during some of the time when Mozart was working on the Requiem. Mozart seems to have had very little regard for Süssmayr's musicianship, though he may have used him as a copyist during his work on *Die Zauberflöte*. This makes it difficult to believe that Mozart would have chosen Süssmayr to complete the Requiem; in any case, Mozart apparently did not until the last day or two of his life expect his illness to be fatal, and so had no reason until then to wish to give instructions to anyone at all, whether or not Süssmayr. However, Constanze Mozart said that, at the very last moment, Mozart told Süssmayr to repeat the Kyrie fugue for the 'Cum sanctis'. Shortly after Mozart's death, Constanze asked Joseph Eybler to complete the Requiem. Eybler was a musician of whom Mozart had a high opinion; he had, moreover, helped to nurse Mozart during his final illness, and so would have been at least as available as Süssmayr if Mozart had wanted to say anything about the Requiem. After orchestrating some movements, Eybler found that the work was taking more time than he could afford, and returned the score to Constanze. She then approached several other musicians before finally turning to Süssmayr.

These facts imply that Süssmayr's additional movements for the Requiem do not have Mozart's authority, and so need not be accorded any special status. The same holds for his orchestration of those movements in which Mozart wrote down the voice parts and figured bass, but gave only brief indications otherwise. It is obvious enough that Süssmayr had no instructions on this matter, for where Eybler had already completed the orchestration Süssmayr either copied his work or substituted a manifestly inferior version of his own. Many conductors have criticized Süssmayr's poor orchestration, including Richard Strauss, Benjamin Britten, and Bruno Walter, who is quoted by Hausner (p. 16) as having said 'Süssmayr was a good musician, but I have no respect for his orchestration.'[4] A revised version of Süssmayr's orchestration has been made by Franz Beyer (1971).[5]

On the face of it, therefore, there is no more Mozart in the Requiem than is in his incomplete autograph. However, the situation is not quite so straightforward, because Constanze said many years later that she had given Süssmayr a few of Mozart's papers, which might have contained preliminary material for the movements Süssmayr said he wrote himself. If they did, can some genuine Mozart be identified in them after all?

Since these hypothetical sketches have not survived (except for one sheet which Süssmayr did not use), any answer to this question must be based solely on internal evidence. It is all too easy, though, to convince oneself on vaguely stylistic grounds that an agreeable piece of dubious provenance must be by Mozart; so it is essential to use a much more objective test. Such a test is provided by the basic grammar of counterpoint, which in suitable cases is sufficient to show with near certainty that a doubtful piece cannot be genuine, if it contains a high density of what Mozart regarded as elementary technical blunders. The rules of Mozart's counterpoint will be reviewed in Chapter 3, and in the following three chapters the test will be applied to the 'Lacrymosa' completion, the Sanctus, 'Osanna', and Benedictus, to show that there can be no genuine Mozart in these movements, and hence Süssmayr's claim to have written them must be correct. For the Agnus Dei, however, the 'technical blunders' test fails, though of course this failure does not of itself prove that it was written by Mozart. Yet the music really does, for once, seem too good to be Süssmayr's, not merely in its general impression, but also in its highly ingenious yet simple construction, and above all in its relationship to the rest of the Requiem and its near-quotation of material from earlier Mozart masses. It seems very probable therefore (though in the absence of further evidence not certainly established) that a fairly complete draft of the Agnus Dei must have been among the papers that Constanze gave Süssmayr.

The rest of this book is concerned with the reconstruction work in making a performing version of the genuine Mozartian material, in a way that remains as faithful as possible to what can be deduced of the composer's intentions. A slightly revised Agnus Dei is retained, but the Sanctus, 'Osanna', and Benedictus are omitted as being wholly by Süssmayr; like the C minor Mass K 427, the Requiem must remain a torso. Similarly, Süssmayr's completion of the 'Lacrymosa' has been replaced by a new version based as far as possible on Mozartian material, which leads to a completion of the 'Amen' fugue exposition written out by Mozart on a sketch rediscovered by Wolfgang Plath about twenty-five years ago.[6] The Kyrie fugue is repeated for the 'Cum sanctis', and the traditional reuse of part of the 'Requiem aeternam' for the 'Lux aeterna' is a natural corollary. The orchestration has been reworked throughout.

As an introduction to the work, the models Mozart used, perhaps subconsciously, in writing the Requiem are surveyed in

Chapter 8, and this is followed in Chapter 9 by a study of Mozart's orchestration in works for voices and orchestra dating from 1791, especially *La clemenza di Tito, Die Zauberflöte*, and *Eine kleine Freymaurer-Kantate* K 623. This investigation reveals not only general principles but also detailed clues, for Mozart was evidently thinking about these works and the Requiem at roughly the same time. As a result, a passage in the Requiem is quite often sufficiently similar to something in the other works that almost the same instrumentation can be used.

The subsequent chapters are devoted to each movement of the Requiem in turn, and there is a final chapter on performance practice. Full details are given of the problems that arise, of analogous passages in other works, and of the reasons for the suggested solutions. These solutions are frequently compared with those of Eybler, Süssmayr, and Beyer; though the new edition should not be regarded as in any sense a revision of their work. On the contrary, the aim was to base a new version solely on what Mozart left at his death, and on a thorough study of Mozart's late style. Obviously no one can hope to reconstruct Mozart's intentions exactly, but perhaps the new edition comes a little closer than its predecessors to what Mozart might have written if he had lived to finish the Requiem.

2

The Genesis of the Requiem

On 14 February 1791 Countess Anna von Walsegg, wife of the minor Austrian landowner and industrialist Count Franz von Walsegg, died at her home, Schloss Stuppach, 'in the prime of her life';[1] and so was set in motion one of the strangest sequences of events in the history of music. According to Anton Herzog, one of Walsegg's musicians, the grieving Count

wished to give [the Countess] a twofold memorial, of an exceptional kind. He instructed his agent, the Vienna advocate Dr Johann Sortschan, to order a monument from one of the leading Vienna sculptors, and a Requiem from Mozart, to which, as usual, he would retain the sole rights.

The former cost about 3000 fr . . .

The Requiem, however, which was to be performed every year on the anniversary of the Countess's death, failed to appear for a long time, for death overtook Mozart in the middle of this famous work . . .

After Count von Walsegg had received the score of the Requiem, in his usual way he immediately made a fair copy of the score in his own hand, and passed it, movement by movement, to his violinist Benard for him to copy the parts.

During this work I often sat for hours at a time at Benard's side, and followed the progress of this distinguished piece with mounting interest; for at that time I had heard all about the previous history of the Requiem from the senior official Mr Leitgeb, whose job it was to see to the payment of the fee for it, from the gypsum warehouse in Vienna.

When all the parts had been copied, preparations for the performance of the Requiem were immediately set in hand. However, since not all of the appropriate musicians could be mustered in the neighbourhood of Stuppach, it was arranged that the first performance of the Requiem should take place in Wiener Neustadt. The musicians were chosen with a view to the solo and other most important parts being taken by the best musicians available; thus it happened that the solo parts were assigned to the castrato Ferenz of Neustadt, the contralto Kernbeiss of Schottwein, the tenor Klein of Neustadt, and the bass Thurner of Gloggnitz. The rehearsal took place in the evening of 12 December 1793 in the choir of the Cistercian Collegiate and Parish Church in Wiener Neustadt, and at 10 o'clock on 14 December an office for the dead was celebrated in the same church, at which this famous Requiem was first performed, such being its intended purpose.

Count von Walsegg himself conducted.[2]

As Herzog explained, Count Walsegg was an enthusiastic amateur musician who played the cello and the flute. He also wished to pass himself off as an accomplished composer, and to this end

contracted with many composers, but always anonymously, to supply him with works of which he was expressly to retain sole ownership, and for which he paid well. In particular, Mr Hoffmeister supplied many flute quartets, in which the flute parts were quite straightforward, but the three other parts were unusually difficult, so that the players had to work hard at them, which made the Count laugh.

. . . He usually copied these secretly acquired scores in his own hand, and then passed them on for the parts to be written out. We never got to see an original score. The quartets were then played, and afterwards we had to guess the composer. Usually we guessed that it was the Count himself, for he had in fact composed a few trifles occasionally; he smiled then, and was glad that he had, as he thought, mystified us; but we laughed because he thought us so credulous.

We were all young people, and considered that we were giving our Count a harmless pleasure. And in this way the mutual deception continued for several years.[3]

The commission from Count Walsegg must obviously have been sent to Mozart some time after the death of the Countess on 14 February 1791. It is not known for certain just when Mozart received it, or whether it was Sortschan or Leitgeb who, in delivering it, became the 'grey messenger' of popular legend. Constanze Mozart said that the commission arrived 'a few months'[4] before Mozart's death. Niemetschek, who knew the Mozarts well, acted as guardian for Carl Mozart for some years in the 1790s, and obtained much of his information directly from Constanze, said:

before Mozart received the commission to go to Prague, an unknown messenger delivered to him an unsigned letter, which inquired whether Mozart would be willing to compose a Requiem . . . Mozart, who was not in the habit of taking even the most trivial decisions without consulting his wife, told her all about this strange commission.[5] (Niemetschek, p. 48.)

If Niemetschek is correct, the commission arrived before Mozart's journey to Prague for the production of *La clemenza di Tito*, at the end of August; and Mozart's discussion with Constanze implies that it was not between 4 June and 12 July, when she was in Baden. Nowak (1965) has suggested that Mozart's petition at the end of April to the Vienna City Council for the post of assistant Kapellmeister at St Stephen's [6] shows that Mozart was becoming increasingly interested in church music at this time, and that this interest was a result of the Requiem commission. However, the latter conclusion does not necessarily follow, for Mozart never forgot his Salzburg masses: he asked his father to send him the scores on several occasions in the 1780s,[7] reported a performance of one of them in 1790,[8] and himself conducted performances of K 275 in Baden and Vienna in July 1791.[9] Moreover Tyson (1981) has shown that Mozart made several abortive attempts at masses during the period 1787–91. Probably all that can be deduced from Mozart's petition is that the Requiem commission arrived at a time when he already felt a desire to write a large-scale piece of church music.

One can only guess, then, that the Requiem commission arrived some time in the spring or summer of 1791. Mozart probably did not have time to start work on it immediately, for his own *Verzeichnüß* lists completed works frequently until the end of April, and most of the next three months must have been taken up by work on *Die Zauberflöte*, which was finished (apart from the Overture and the Priests' March) during July. Mozart's letters to Constanze during June and July mention his work on *Die Zauberflöte* frequently, but contain no reference whatever to the Requiem, which therefore he had presumably not yet started. He must surely have spent most of August writing *La clemenza di Tito* (though he may have written a few numbers such as 'Non più di fiori' some time before);[10] and then the visit to Prague for the first performance occupied the period from the end of August until shortly after 15 September.[11] Niemetschek (p. 50) said that Mozart did not start work on the Requiem until immediately after his return from Prague.[12]

There cannot, however, have been much time for work on the Requiem during September. During the fortnight between the return from Prague and the first performance of *Die Zauberflöte* on

30 September, Mozart wrote the Overture and Priests' March, and the Clarinet Concerto K 622, and must obviously have been busy with rehearsals for *Die Zauberflöte*. He probably had more time in October and November: the Clarinet Concerto was finished on 7 October,[13] so that afterwards he can have been working only on the Requiem or *Eine kleine Freymaurer-Kantate* K 623 (finished on 15 November). His letters to Constanze show that he was still working hard at the time: 'This morning I worked so hard that I was delayed until 1.30 . . . Straight after lunch I went back home and worked until it was time for the opera.'[14] (Mozart to Constanze, 8 and 9 October 1791.)

It seems very probable, then, that the bulk of Mozart's work on the Requiem was done during October and November, before he took to his bed on or a little after 20 November.[15] This is confirmed by the single extant page of sketches for the Requiem,[16] which has a four-bar sketch for the Overture to *Die Zauberflöte* at the top, followed by sketches for the 'Amen' and 'Rex tremendae' in the Requiem itself. The Overture to *Die Zauberflöte* was not finished until 28 September (and Mozart had already started and abandoned an earlier version): hence even this preliminary draft for the 'Rex tremendae' must date from the end of September at the earliest. Mozart's own expected completion date (1792) on the first page of his autograph score of the Requiem also supports the hypothesis of a late start.

On the other hand Nowak (1965), following Schnerich (pp. 14 f.), has drawn attention to the fact that Mozart's score of the Requiem is written on two types of paper, and suggests that the break between the two papers may have coincided with Mozart's visit to Prague. But this guess is not consistent either with the post-Prague date of the 'Rex tremendae' sketch, or with Tyson's conclusion that the paper on which Mozart *started* the Requiem, recognizable by the printed vertical lines at the beginning and end of each stave, was used by him in other works only after his return from Prague.[17]

Apart from any interruptions caused by the completion, rehearsals, and performance (on 18 November[18]) of K 623, work on the Requiem may have been interrupted during October because Constanze, alarmed at Mozart's deteriorating health and spirits, took the score away from him. This well-known legend goes back to Niemetschek (pp. 50 f.):

When one day she took him for a drive in the Prater, to cheer him up and amuse him, and they were sitting alone together there, Mozart began to talk of death, and maintained that he was writing the Requiem for himself . . . 'I feel very much', he continued, 'as if I have not long to go: surely someone has poisoned me! I can't rid myself of this idea.' This speech affected his wife very deeply, for she was hardly in a position to comfort him by proving his melancholy imaginings to be groundless. Thinking that he might well be sickening for an illness, and that the Requiem was preying on his sensitive nerves, she called the doctor, and took away the score.

In fact his condition improved somewhat, and during this improvement he was able to write a short cantata [K 623] that had been commissioned by a society for a celebration. His spirit gained new strength from the good performance of this work, and the great applause with which it was received. He became more cheerful, and wished once again to continue and complete his Requiem. His wife found no reason then not to give him back the score.[19]

Niemetschek could have had this story only from Constanze herself; but perhaps one should be sceptical of such hearsay evidence, which in any case does not quite square with Mozart's being confined to bed only two days or so after the performance of K 623 (not to mention doubts about the 'poisoning' legend). On the basis of meteorological records, Bär (p. 103) shows that such an outing to the Prater could have taken place only on 20 or 21 October.

Niemetschek's story touches on a familiar account of Mozart's last weeks, which has it that he was already mortally ill and working feverishly on the Requiem, convinced (according to more lurid versions of the legend) that Walsegg's agent was an emissary from the other world who had told him to write it for his own funeral. There is, however, very little evidence in support of this piece of romantic fiction. On the contrary, Mozart's own letters of October 1791 paint a picture of a man in cheerful spirits and apparently good health, relishing the success of *Die Zauberflöte*:

Although Saturday is always a bad day, the opera was performed to a completely full house with the usual applause and encores . . . I have just been enjoying an expensive piece of sturgeon, which Primus (my faithful valet) brought me—and since I have a rather big appetite today I have sent him out for something more . . . During Papageno's aria with the glockenspiel ['Ein Mädchen oder Weibchen'] I went behind the stage, because I had an urge to play it myself today. For a joke, when Schikaneder

had a rest I played an arpeggio—he was startled—looked into the wings
and saw me—at the repeat I didn't do it—he stopped and absolutely
refused to continue—I guessed what he was thinking and played another
chord—then he hit the glockenspiel and said 'shut up'—everyone laughed
then . . . Next Sunday I'll certainly come over [to Baden]— we'll all go to
the casino together and then home together on Monday . . .
NB I think you must have sent 2 pairs of yellow winter breeches to the
cleaners', for Joseph and I looked for them in vain.[20] (Mozart to
Constanze, 8 and 9 October 1791.)

   Yesterday . . . Hofer and I went to fetch Carl. We ate there, then drove
back, and at 6 o'clock I collected Salieri and Cavalieri in the coach and took
them to my box. Then I hurried back to get your mother and Carl, who in
the meantime had been at Hofer's. You can't believe how civil they both
[Salieri and Cavalieri] were—how much they liked not only my music, but
also the libretto and everything else. They both said it was an opera worthy
to be performed at the most important festival, before the greatest of
monarchs . . . Afterwards I had them driven back home, and had supper
with Carl at Hofer's. Then I drove home with him, where we both slept
very well. I've pleased Carl no end by taking him to the opera . . . On
Sunday morning I'll bring him over to you—he can either stay with you,
or I could take him back to Hecker after dinner on Sunday.[21] (Mozart to
Constanze, 14 October 1791.)

Towards the end of November, however, Mozart was certainly
ill enough to be confined to bed. According to Bär he was suffering
from rheumatic fever, of which there was an epidemic in Vienna at
the time. It does not necessarily follow, though, that Mozart's
illness lasted more than two weeks and therefore that he was ill
before he succumbed to the epidemic. Neither, it must be stressed,
does it follow that Mozart realized he was dying. It is all too easy
with hindsight to assume, as perhaps Niemetschek did, that Mozart
knew he had only a short time left to live; but the account by
Constanze's sister Sophie suggests on the contrary that he fully
expected to recover:

Now when Mozart was taken ill we both [Sophie and her mother] made
him a nightshirt, which he could put on from the front, since he could not
turn over because of the swelling. And since we did not know how serious
his illness might be, we also made him a quilted dressing gown (for both of
these his good wife, my dearest sister, gave us the material), so that when
he got up he would be well looked after. And so we visited him diligently
and he was ever so pleased with the dressing gown. I went to the town
every day to visit him. And when I went once on a Saturday Mozart said to

me, 'Now, dear Sophie, tell your mother that I am getting on very well, and that I will be sure to call and congratulate her on the octave of her name-day.' Who was more pleased than I to be able to bring my mother such a happy piece of news, which was hardly to be expected? I hurried back home, therefore, to set her mind at rest, for he seemed to me to be really very cheerful and well.[22] (Sophie Haibel to the Nissens, 7 April 1825.)

Sophie remembered this Saturday as being only two days before Mozart died, that is, 3 December. But her mother's name-day (her name was Cäcilie) was 22 November, so that, as Bär (pp. 31–2) suggests, perhaps it was the previous Saturday, 26 November.

The end seems, in fact, to have come quickly. On the afternoon of 4 December, only a few hours before he died, Sophie called again, when Constanze said to her:

'Thank God you have come, dear Sophie, he got so bad last night that I thought he would not survive today. Just stay with me today, for if he is the same today he will die tonight. Go to him for a bit and see how he is doing.' I tried to compose myself, and went to his bed, where he at once said to me, 'I'm glad you are here, dear Sophie, you must stay here tonight and see me die.' I tried to be confident and talk him out of it, but he only answered to everything, 'I already have the taste of death on my tongue, and who will look after my dearest Constanze if you don't stay here?' 'Yes, dear Mozart, only I must go back to our mother to tell her that you want me to stay today, or else she will think I have had an accident' . . . My poor sister came after me and cried, 'For God's sake go to St Peter's and ask for a priest' . . . Then I ran to my anxiously waiting mother. It was already dark . . . I ran back as fast as I could to my inconsolable sister, there was Süssmayr by Mozart's bed, the well-known Requiem lay on the coverlet and Mozart was explaining to him how in his opinion he should complete it after his death.[23] (Sophie to the Nissens, 7 April 1825.)

There is also a story that a rehearsal of the completed part of the Requiem took place that same afternoon:

Even on the afternoon before he died he had the score of the Requiem brought to his bed and himself sang the alto part (it was about two o'clock in the afternoon); Schack, the friend of the family, as he had always done before, sang the soprano part, Hofer, Mozart's brother-in-law, the tenor, and Gerle, later of the Mannheim theatre, the bass. When they got to the first bars of the Lacrimosa, Mozart began to weep violently, and laid the score aside. Eleven hours later, at one in the morning, he passed on.[24]

This account of Schack's must be treated with caution, since it was not published until 1827, at second hand, in his own obituary notice (he had died on 11 December 1826). It is difficult to believe that Schack, a professional tenor who was the first Tamino in *Die Zauberflöte*,[25] should have attempted the soprano part instead of Constanze, who was still of a sufficiently professional standard in 1795 to sing in public.[26] How could Schack have managed, in falsetto, the high *a*″s, and even the top *b*♭″ that occurs in bar 41 of the Kyrie?

After Mozart's death on 5 December 1791, Constanze first asked Joseph Eybler to complete the Requiem. Eybler made a formal undertaking on 21 December:

> The undersigned acknowledges hereby, that the widowed Mrs Constanze Mozart has entrusted the Requiem begun by her late husband to him for completion; the same declares that he will finish it by the middle of the coming Lent, and moreover affirms that it will neither be copied, nor given to anyone other than the above-named widow.[27]

Easter Sunday 1792 fell on 8 April, so 'the middle of the coming Lent' means mid-March 1792.

According to his own autobiographical sketch, in the *Allgemeine Musikalische Zeitung* (24 May 1826), Eybler was born in 1765 in Schwechat, where his father, a choirmaster and schoolteacher, had been a boyhood friend of Michael Haydn. Later, he said,

> I went . . . to Vienna, to the same school where the famous men Albrechtsberger, Joseph and Michael Haydn, and others had formerly been educated. There I received, besides a grounding in general knowledge, also training in singing, instrumental playing, and thorough bass. My patron, observing my progress, had me taught the elements of composition by the excellent Albrechtsberger in the years 1777–9 . . . I had the good fortune to enjoy his [Mozart's] constant friendship until his death; so that even in his painful final illness I helped to lift him up, lay him down, and wait upon him . . . When Mozart wrote the opera *Così fan tutte*, and had not yet finished the orchestration, so that time was pressing, he asked me to hold the vocal rehearsals, and especially to coach the two female soloists Fer[r]arese and Villeneuve . . . In 1792 I applied for the position of choirmaster at the Parish Church of the P. P. Carmelites.[28]

Mozart had therefore known Eybler for several years.[29] He had a high opinion of his abilities:

> I, the undersigned, certify hereby that I have found Mr Joseph Eybler to be a worthy pupil of his famous master Albrechtsberger. He has a

thorough knowledge of composition, is equally skilled in both the church and chamber styles, is fully experienced in the art of singing, and is also an accomplished organist and pianist. In short, I have found him to be a young musician of whom it is to be regretted only that so few are his equal.[30] (Mozart's testimonial for Eybler, 30 May 1790.)

It is therefore perfectly reasonable that Constanze should first have asked Eybler to complete the Requiem. Many years later, though, she had forgotten that he had actually done some work on it:

That I proposed to Eybler that he should complete [the Requiem] came about because I was (I do not know why) angry with Süssmayr, and Mozart himself had thought highly of Eybler, and I thought he would be a suitable man to complete those parts where the main ideas were all written out. And so I had Eybler come to me, and told him what I wanted; but since he immediately gave me a smooth-tongued refusal, he did not get it.[31] (Constanze to Stadler, 31 May 1827.)

(She explained her mistake to Vincent Novello on 3 August 1829 by saying that 'she was so agitated and confused at the time that she has not the least recollection of the circumstances' (Medici and Hughes, p. 215).)

Eybler worked on the orchestration of the Sequence as far as the end of the 'Confutatis', and added two bars of soprano to the incomplete 'Lacrymosa', to the words 'huic ergo parce Deus'. All of his work was written on Mozart's incomplete autograph score. At this point, however, Eybler returned the score to Constanze, perhaps because his new job as choirmaster at the Carmelite Church left him too little spare time.

It seems that Constanze then approached several other musicians, before finally turning to Franz Xaver Süssmayr. This is made clear by his own account, in a letter he wrote to Breitkopf and Härtel on 8 February 1800, in reply to an enquiry suggested by Constanze:[32]

Your kind letter of 24 January gave me the greatest pleasure, for I see from it that you are too concerned for the esteem of the German-speaking public to mislead it with works that cannot be entirely ascribed to my late friend Mozart. I owe too much to the teaching of that great man to allow myself to remain silent when a work whose greater part is mine is published as his, for I am firmly convinced that my work is unworthy of that great man. Mozart's compositions are so unique, and I venture to assert so unattainable by most living musicians, that any imitator, and particularly any deliberate counterfeiter, would come off worse than the raven who adorned himself with peacock feathers. That the completion of the Requiem, which has occasioned our correspondence, was entrusted to me, happened in the following way. Mozart's widow could probably forsee that her husband's posthumous works would be sought after; death overtook him while he was working on this Requiem.

The completion of this work was therefore offered to a number of masters; some of them could not undertake it because of pressure of work, others however did not wish to compromise their talents with Mozart's. Eventually the matter came to me, for it was known that I had often played and sung through the completed sections with Mozart during his lifetime, that he had very frequently discussed the realization of this work with me, and that he had explained to me the principles and practice of his orchestration. I can only hope that I have been fortunate enough, at least, to have worked sufficiently well that connoisseurs may here and there find some traces of his unforgettable teaching.

In the 'Requiem [aeternam]', together with Kyrie—'Dies irae' [i.e Sequence]—'Domine Jesu Christe', Mozart completely finished the 4 vocal parts and the figured bass, but gave only brief indications of the orchestration here and there. In the 'Dies irae', the last line he set was 'qua resurget ex favilla', and [thus far] his score was in the same state as in the previous sections. I completed the 'Dies irae' from the line 'judicandus homo reus'.

The Sanctus, Benedictus, and Agnus Dei were composed afresh by me; I only allowed myself, in order to give the work more unity, to repeat the Kyrie fugue at the words 'cum sanctis'.

I should esteem it greatly if I have been able to render you a small service with this communication.[33]

He had, it seems, told much the same story to Niemetschek as early as 1794: 'The published version [of the Requiem] was completed by Süssmayr, whose work started at the Sanctus. Süssmayr himself told me this, while he was staying with me 17 years ago.'[34] (Niemetschek to A. Kühnel, 10 August 1811.)

Süssmayr's letter appears clear and specific, and, together with Sophie Haibel's recollection of the deathbed discussion between Mozart and Süssmayr, is the basis of the traditional legend that Mozart gave Süssmayr full instructions on how to complete the Requiem, which he faithfully carried out after Mozart's death. The legend is, to some extent, supported by Constanze:

When he [Mozart] foresaw his death, he spoke to Mr Süssmayr . . . and told him that if he were really to die without finishing it, he should repeat the first fugue, as is anyway normal practice, for the final movement. He also told him how he should finish off where the important ideas were already worked out here and there in the parts.[35] (Constanze to Breitkopf and Härtel, 27 March 1799.)

Thirty years later, she repeated this account to the Novellos, in almost the same words. Mary Novello said Constanze told them that Mozart

called Süssmayr to him and desired that if he died before he had completed the work, that the fugue he had written at the commencement might be repeated and pointed out where and how other parts should be filled up that were already sketched. (Medici and Hughes, p. 126.)

Vincent Novello's version of Constanze's account reads:

finding his death approaching, [Mozart] gave directions (as his widow distinctly and decidedly asserted to me that he did) to Süssmayr to fill up the mere *remplissage* of the leading features which Mozart himself had indicated: that he also told Süssmayr to repeat the Fugue at the end . . . (Medici and Hughes, p. 130.)

The last sentence in Constanze's letter to Breitkopf and Härtel has sometimes been taken to mean that Süssmayr was given advice on how to use Mozart's sketches for missing movements,[36] rather than merely told how to complete the orchestration where Mozart had 'given only brief indications here and there'—though even this much seems rather unlikely, for Süssmayr often copied Eybler's orchestration, and when he did not his version is usually inferior to Eybler's. That the second interpretation is the correct one is clarified by Vincent Novello's 'mere *remplissage*', and also by Constanze's letter to André of 26 November 1800 to assure him that, despite rumours to the contrary, the Requiem was substantially genuine:

in the 'Dies irae', 'Tuba mirum', 'Rex tremendae', 'Recordare', and 'Confutatis', Mozart had written all the important parts, but little if anything of the inner parts: these were completed by another . . . The Sanctus . . . is in the handwriting of the man who wrote this movement and the remainder . . . That is, the Sanctus is entirely by the composer of the completion.[37]

Notice that Constanze uses very similar wording here ('allen Hauptstimmen') to refer explicitly to movements of the Sequence, to that used ('die hauptsache hie und da in Stimmen') in her apparently more ambiguous letter of the previous year to Breitkopf and Härtel.

How reliable is Süssmayr's own statement? Certainly there are details in his letter that are not quite right: for example Mozart completely orchestrated the 'Requiem aeternam', and also set the line 'judicandus homo reus'. And as we have just seen, according to Constanze the idea of repeating the Kyrie fugue for the 'Cum sanctis' was Mozart's, not Süssmayr's. By no stretch of the imagination can the 'greater part' of the Requiem be ascribed to Süssmayr.

Süssmayr's statement that Mozart 'had very frequently discussed the realization of this work' with him seems suspicious too, for it would presuppose a relationship between the two men that went further than one would normally expect of master and pupil. The available evidence strongly suggests, however, that this was far from being the case.

It is not known when Mozart and Süssmayr first met,[38] though obviously it must have been after the latter's arrival in Vienna in July 1788, at the age of twenty-two.[39] The first mention of Süssmayr in Mozart's letters occurs on 7 June 1791, when he wrote to Constanze: 'Yesterday I had lunch with Süssmayr at the Ungarische Krone.'[40] In the twenty extant letters from Mozart to Constanze during 1791, Süssmayr is mentioned by name in seven of them (probably in another three, though the name has been crossed out by Nissen), and by nickname in another five; but he is not mentioned at all in the eight or nine extant letters from Mozart to Constanze during 1790. This strongly suggests that Mozart had not met Süssmayr before his return from Frankfurt in November 1790. Indeed, the first meeting could have been as late as May 1791 (the reference to Süssmayr in Mozart's letter of 7 June appears to imply that Constanze had met him before she went to Baden on 4 June). Probably, then, Mozart and Süssmayr were acquainted for only a few months; possibly as much as a year.

It is rather doubtful, therefore, whether Süssmayr could have been a formal pupil in the same way as Thomas Attwood, say, who worked with Mozart through a detailed and comprehensive course in harmony, counterpoint, orchestration, and composition, over a period of some eighteen months.[41] Süssmayr himself described Mozart only as a 'friend', although he acknowledged Mozart's 'unforgettable teaching'. Certainly Constanze, in her letter to

André of 1 January 1826, described Süssmayr as Mozart's 'friend and pupil'[42] (although she was discussing and quoting Süssmayr's letter to Breitkopf and Härtel at the time, which may have put the idea in her mind). But a year later she said:

when he [Mozart] felt ill, however, Süssmayr and I often had to sing through with him what he had written, and in this way Süssmayr received formal instruction from Mozart. And I can still hear Mozart saying, as he often did to Süssmayr, 'There you stand like a duck in a thunderstorm again; aren't you ever going to understand?'; then took his pen and no doubt wrote down ideas that were plain enough for Süssmayr.[43] (Constanze to Stadler, 31 May 1827.)

Two years later still, she told Vincent Novello (Medici and Hughes, p. 130) that 'although Süssmayr had a few Lessons from Mozart . . . he was also a pupil and friend of Salieri's'.[44] This rather suggests that Süssmayr had few, if any, proper lessons from Mozart, but merely picked up some general advice as a result of taking part in rehearsals of completed sections of the Requiem. And the impression that Mozart found Süssmayr rather slow-witted is reinforced by his letters to Constanze during 1791:

I will answer Süssmayr by word of mouth—I would rather not waste paper on him.[45] (25 June 1791.)

NB Greetings to Snai—how is he getting on?—like a blockhead, he ought to copy hard so that I get my things back.[46] (end of June or early July 1791.)

   Please tell that ass Süssmayr to send me my score of the first act [of *Die Zauberflöte*], from the Introduction to the Finale, so that I can orchestrate it. It would be convenient if he could get it together today, so that it can go on the first coach tomorrow morning, and then I will get it by midday.—Just now a couple of Englishmen called, who didn't want to leave Vienna without meeting me—but that's a lie—they wanted to meet the Great Man Süssmayr, and only called on me to find out where he lives, because they had heard that I have the good fortune to have some small influence with him.—I told them to go to the Ungarische Krone, and wait there until he comes back from Baden!—Snai!—They want to employ him as a lamp-cleaner.[47] (2 July 1791.)

Süssmayr is to send me my manuscript of Nos. 4 and 5—also everything else I wanted, and is to lick my arse for me.[48] (5 July 1791.)

Presumably, therefore, Mozart was using Süssmayr as a copyist while he was working on *Die Zauberflöte*. Quite what the rather unmerciful ragging implies is difficult to determine, since Anton Stadler, for example, also came in for some of this treatment, although Mozart had enough respect for him as a musician to write the Clarinet Quintet and Concerto for him. What is certainly clear from Mozart's letters, however, is that Süssmayr was in Baden, not Vienna, for parts of June, July, and October 1791 [49]—the latter period when Mozart was almost certainly working on the Requiem itself. One begins to wonder when, if ever, Süssmayr's 'frequent discussions' can have taken place.

It is often stated that Süssmayr accompanied Mozart and Constanze to Prague in August for the first performance of *La clemenza di Tito*, and indeed that he wrote the secco recitatives for that opera. But the evidence for this statement is pretty meagre,[50] and one can almost see the legend growing in front of one's eyes. In December 1791 a newspaper reported that 'only the arias and choruses were written by [Mozart], the recitatives were by another'.[51] Seven years later, Niemetschek (p. 112) expanded this a little: 'The few accompanied recitatives are by Mozart, all the others—much to be regretted—are by a pupil'.[52] After another thirty years the legend had grown still further, for Nissen, who otherwise took this part of his book almost word-for-word from Niemetschek,[53] added on p. 558 that Mozart 'had his pupil Süssmayr complete the secco recitatives'.[54] Nissen seems, however, to have been unsure about the identity of the 'pupil', for on p. 131 of his *Anhang* the latter statement is amended to: 'one of his pupils completed the secco recitatives'.[55] Of course, there can be little doubt that Mozart himself did not write the secco recitatives in *La clemenza di Tito*; but the only other supporting evidence for Süssmayr's authorship appears to be that a draft of a clarinet concerto by him, the later fair copy of which is dated 1792, is written on the same Prague paper that Mozart used for the parts of *La clemenza di Tito* he wrote there.[56] Thus Süssmayr *might* have been in Prague at the time; if so, this would strengthen the case for his having written the recitatives.

Whatever is the truth about Süssmayr's part in *La clemenza di Tito*, it is clear that Mozart had a low opinion of his abilities, which again makes Süssmayr's 'frequent discussions' difficult to believe. Indeed, it is just not credible that Mozart would ever have discussed 'work in progress' with anyone at all. Moreover, until the last day or two Mozart seems to have expected to recover from his illness, so it would not have occurred to him that there was any need to tell anyone how to finish the Requiem. Right at the end, though, when at last he realized he was dying, he might well have wanted to pass on some last-minute thoughts, as Sophie and Constanze apparently overheard. Even then, why Süssmayr and not Eybler? Possibly Süssmayr just happened to be present at Mozart's bedside on 4 December 1791, when Mozart urgently needed to tell someone?

What of the rehearsals of completed sections of the Requiem, from which Süssmayr could have learned a good deal, particularly if Mozart himself accompanied them? Süssmayr's statement that 'I had often played and sung through the completed sections with Mozart' is, on the face of it, supported by Constanze's remark in 1827 that she and Süssmayr had 'often had to sing through with him [Mozart] what he had written'.[57] However, in conversation with the Novellos in July 1829 (Medici and Hughes, pp. 126 and 128) she described only 'one occasion', 'a short time before his death', on which 'some of the passages so excited him that he could not refrain from tears, and was unable to proceed'. This sounds suspiciously like Schack's account, which Constanze had no doubt recently read (it is quoted in Nissen's biography). It should also be remembered that Constanze had long been familiar with Süss-mayr's letter to Breitkopf and Härtel, and it is understandable that her memory in the 1820s of events of thirty-five years before was a little erratic; what she wrote *c*.1800 should obviously be given more weight than her later reminiscences, which often show signs of having been influenced by the writings of others. In any case, it is difficult to see how Constanze, Mozart, and Süssmayr could have sung music that is nearly always in four parts. Schack's account, on the other hand (if it can be relied upon), explicitly names singers other than Süssmayr and Constanze as participants at these hypothetical rehearsals.

Although it is reasonable that such rehearsals may have taken place, then, their existence is supported only by rather contradictory evidence, some of which suggests that Süssmayr did not take part in them. Once again, therefore, Süssmayr's statement must be regarded as dubious, and the likelihood is that the only knowledge of Mozart's intentions he may have had direct from him was the last-minute deathbed instruction to repeat the Kyrie fugue for the 'Cum sanctis'.

It is possible, however, that Süssmayr might have learned more of Mozart's intentions indirectly, if he had got hold of any of the composer's sketches. Indeed, according to Stadler (p. 16), 'Mozart's widow told me that, after his death, a few scraps of music turned up on his desk, which she gave to Mr Süssmayr. What they contained, and what use Süssmayr might have made of them, she did not know.'[58] At first sight, it is surprising that Constanze did not give these papers to Eybler on 21 December 1791, but she had probably not yet found them: as she later explained in her letter to Stadler of 31 May 1827, 'One thing one can reproach Mozart with is that he was not very tidy with his papers.'[59] There is no other supporting evidence for the existence of the 'few scraps of music',[60] and, as Constanze herself pointed out, they may not have contained any Requiem sketches at all.[61] Nevertheless it is known that Mozart made extensive use of sketches, many of which still survive.[62] There must surely have been other preliminary material for the Requiem than the single extant sheet, and it is surprising that more has not been discovered, unless Constanze, who was very careful with Mozart's manuscripts, did indeed give such papers to Süssmayr; if they contained sketches for the movements that he afterwards claimed to have written himself, he would presumably have destroyed them when he had finished with them.

To sum up, then, it is possible that Süssmayr had access to some of Mozart's sketches, in the papers given to him by Constanze, in addition to Mozart's specific instruction to repeat the Kyrie fugue at the end. His claims to have had discussions with Mozart about the Requiem, and to have taken part in rehearsals of completed sections, look very doubtful, however; and it is even less likely that Mozart actually wanted Süssmayr to complete the Requiem after his death. Even Süssmayr's own account makes it clear that Constanze turned to him only after first approaching Eybler and then several other musicians.

Süssmayr used the already complete score of the 'Requiem aeternam' and Kyrie,[63] but made a new copy of the rest of Mozart's autograph, since Eybler had already used it for his work. It is not known when Süssmayr finished his completion,[64] but the first performance (nearly a year before Walsegg's) was arranged by Gottfried van Swieten for Constanze's benefit on 2 January 1793.[65]

What did those most in a position to know the facts think of Süssmayr's claims? Constanze accepted his statement that he had written the movements missing from Mozart's autograph, in 1800 (letter to André quoted above) and again in 1802 (letter to Breitkopf and Härtel, 2 June):

everything up to the start of the 'Dies irae' is entirely by Mozart . . . and this autograph of his is in the possession of the anonymous client [Walsegg], as I myself saw last year. Everything else composed by Mozart himself and hence written down by him is in my custody and is my property. Süssmayr was kind enough to give it to me unexpectedly some time ago; for it did not occur to me that he must have had it. This manuscript goes as far as the end of the 'Confutatis'. Most of the inner parts, and perhaps occasionally a little more, are not by Mozart; but everything not by Mozart has been ringed in pencil, as in any case would be clear to a good handwriting expert . . . I must also tell you that Süssmayr, who clearly wished to return to me *only* Mozart's work, and could have thought that he perhaps owed me the return *only* of this, also gave me the Sanctus, in which not a single note or word is in Mozart's hand.[66]

('Sanctus' presumably includes also the 'Osanna', Benedictus, and Agnus Dei.) Niemetschek's opinion in 1811 was the same: 'Süssmayr's work consists of the Sanctus which, pretty as it is, conflicts intensely with the divinely serious style of the other, genuinely Mozartian, movements. No true connoisseur of Mozart will fail to notice this.'[67] (Niemetschek to A. Kühnel, 10 August 1811.) In 1826 Stadler (pp. 12 f.), having quoted Constanze's report that she had given Süssmayr the papers she had found on Mozart's desk, nevertheless still accepted Süssmayr's claim that he 'himself composed the Sanctus, Benedictus, and Agnus Dei'.[68] Perhaps as a result of her correspondence with Stadler, and the reminder of the existence of the papers she had given to Süssmayr, Constanze herself began to have small doubts at this time, though as usual one should compare her apparently unequivocal statements of twenty-five years before. She wrote to André on 1 January 1826:

everything in the autograph is his [Mozart's] . . . what if anything in the remainder is his will remain uncertain for ever. It is plausible, naturally, that Süssmayr used those ideas that Mozart . . . may have passed on to him together with his express instruction. Süssmayr hoped . . . in his letter to Breitkopf to have left *traces* of them. How complicated would it have been to have given details? And *where* might this have happened?[69]

There appears to be no more documentary evidence that throws any light on the extent of Süssmayr's contributions. The only way to make further progress is to examine the music itself, to see how far its craftsmanship measures up to Mozart's rigorous standards.

3
Mozart's Counterpoint

Any attempt to use internal evidence to discover which parts of the 'doubtful' movements were written by Süssmayr must proceed with extreme caution, for what is known as 'stylistic analysis' is usually too subjective, and can far too easily be made to yield any desired conclusion. It is essential, therefore, to use only the most rigorously objective tests, and one such is provided by checking whether the counterpoint is, in Mozart's terms, grammatical. It should be borne in mind here that, as the sketches for the 'Rex tremendae' and the 'Amen' show, even the most fragmentary of Mozart's preliminary versions of four-part vocal music are usually written in the full four parts; moreover, although even Mozart very occasionally corrected himself, there is no evidence from his surviving sketch material to suggest that his first versions are in any way grammatically careless. Thus if a passage contains grammatical mistakes it is almost certain that it did not originate even from a sketch by Mozart.

What Mozart regarded as 'correct' can be established very conveniently from Thomas Attwood's notebooks.[1] Mozart spent some time teaching Attwood counterpoint, and in the course of the lessons he gave his interpretation of the rules in Fux's famous *Gradus ad Parnassum*.[2] The most basic of Fux's rules can be summarized as follows.

1. No two parts may proceed from an octave or fifth to another octave or fifth respectively.
2. Indeed, no two parts may approach an octave or fifth by similar motion (a breach of this rule constitutes a *hidden octave*, or *hidden fifth*).

Clearly Rule 1 is only a special case of Rule 2 (except for 'consecutives by contrary motion'); but it is nevertheless useful to state them separately, since Fux made it clear that Rule 1 is an absolute prohibition, whereas Rule 2 may sometimes be broken: it must be strictly followed in two parts, but in three or more parts occasional unavoidable exceptions are allowed, for example at cadences, where if more than two parts have the tonic in the final chord it is obviously impossible to avoid a hidden octave.

Of course, every eighteenth-century composer knew that consecutive fifths and octaves were forbidden, and so it is too much to expect that a piece of bogus Mozart will reveal itself by being full of such mistakes. Where composers did, however, differ in their personal opinions was on the extent to which consecutives could be saved (or created) by various standard devices. For example, Fux stated that consecutive octaves are not saved by suspending the upper part to make a ninth (Ex. 3.1) but that consecutive octaves or fifths are saved, even in two parts, if one part moves by a skip of at least a fourth (a third is allowable in three or more parts) on the weak beat (Ex. 3.2). Mozart, on the other hand, made it clear to

Ex. 3.1

Ex. 3.2

Attwood that his standards were considerably stricter than Fux's. He agreed with Fux that hidden octaves or fifths are not allowed in two parts, but might occasionally be excused in more parts if really necessary. In his opinion, however, consecutives are *never* saved by a moving part, and indeed such a moving part may well create consecutives. On page 54 of the Attwood Studies it is stated that an octave in any part of one bar followed by an octave at the beginning of the next constitutes consecutive octaves; similarly for fifths. This remains the case even in more than two parts: thus on page 123 Mozart twice corrected Attwood for violating the rule in the following ways:

Ex. 3.3

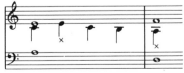

Of course, it would be unreasonable to take the world 'bar' too literally in this strict rule of Mozart's, for there may in practice be many changes of harmony within one bar. Probably the most sensible interpretation of Mozart's rule is to say that consecutives occur when two parts have an octave or fifth, followed by another octave or fifth respectively at the next change of harmony. To illustrate this point, consider Ex. 3.4. At first sight, Mozart's rule

Ex. 3.4 'Tuba mirum', bars 60–1.

- cu - - rus?

says that the alto and bass have consecutive octaves, even though the alto moves to the third on the fourth beat. However, this movement of the alto coincides with the change of chord from $^6_4$ to $^6_3\,^5_2$, so that the octave B flat between alto and bass occurs only at the next-but-one change of harmony.

Another good test is provided by the way in which $^6_4$ chords are used. According to Fux, a $^6_4$ may occur as a passing chord on a weak beat, but if the chord is on a strong beat the fourth must be properly prepared and resolved. On the face of it, Mozart was slightly less fastidious than Fux on this point, for he said to Attwood of the $^6_4$ that it could be used 'senza che sia preparato, e la quarta può risolversi in ogni maniera'. This presumably allows an unprepared 'appoggiatura' $^6_4$, for example at a cadence (though such unprepared fourths are rather uncommon in Mozart). But even though Mozart allows the fourth to be resolved 'in ogni maniera', it does still have to be resolved somehow. In practice this means that the resolution of the fourth by stepwise descent may be transferred (as in Ex 3.4), or may be ornamented or delayed in some way, for example as in Ex. 3.5, where the soprano *d″* is transferred to the tenor and back again, and does not resolve for two bars. But if the fourth in an accented $^6_4$ never resolves at all, as in Ex. 3.6, one should be very suspicious.

Ex. 3.5 'Requiem aeternam', bars 44–6.

Ex. 3.6 'Lacrymosa', bar 12.

Of course, it is necessary to check that Mozart actually obeyed the rules in his own music, and did not merely regard them as a guide for students. His horror of outright consecutives, even by contrary motion, is neatly demonstrated by a very rare example of a correction in his autograph score of the Requiem, in bar 74 of the 'Domine Jesu', where, to avoid consecutive fifths by contrary motion between alto and bass, he altered Ex. 3.7 to Ex. 3.8. The most convincing way to check Mozart's strict rule that consecutives can never be saved by a moving part is, again, to examine the counterpoint in his vocal parts in the Requiem itself. An exhaustive search in four selected movements ('Requiem aeternam', Kyrie, 'Dies irae', and 'Rex tremendae') shows conclusively enough that Mozart really did stick to his rule. There are only four breaches in these movements: between alto and tenor in bars 27–8 of the 'Requiem aeternam', between tenor and bass in bar 6 and between soprano and tenor in bars 30–1 of the Kyrie, between soprano and tenor in bars 5–6 of the 'Dies irae', and with none at all in the 'Rex tremendae'. In all four cases there are *two* notes (or one note and a

Ex. 3.7

Ex. 3.8

rest) between the two octaves or fifths; in no case do the consecutives occur between the two outer parts.

It must be admitted that Mozart did sometimes allow a breach of the 'consecutives' rule in operatic arias, but nevertheless carefully avoided it in the more strict 'church' style. In arias it is quite common at a main cadence for the soloist to have the dominant followed by the tonic, so that there are consecutive octaves with the bass: this is illustrated by Ex. 3.9 from *Die Zauberflöte*. This form of cadence was clearly recognized by Mozart, though, as being a lapse from the strict rules appropriate in church music.

Ex. 3.9 K 620, 'Alles fühlt der Liebe Freuden', bars 19–21.

The conclusion from the Attwood Studies, that Mozart agreed with Fux that hidden octaves or fifths were undesirable but occasionally unavoidable, is amply confirmed by the first three movements of the Requiem. Excluding breaches of the rule at cadences, there are only six examples of hidden octaves or fifths in the 'Requiem aeternam': two of them (soprano and alto, bar 12; tenor and bass, bar 11) occur merely as a result of decoration of what would otherwise be unexceptionable, and one (soprano and tenor, bar 39) happens simply because the parts move to a different position of the same chord. The remaining three examples (alto and tenor, bar 47; tenor and bass, bars 12 and 31) are unavoidable for various reasons, and in any case none of these six examples involves the outer two parts. The same care is shown in the Kyrie: there is only one breach between soprano and bass (bar 13), but this hidden fifth results merely from the decoration of what is otherwise a sustained a'' in the soprano part. In the 'Dies irae' hidden octaves and fifths are very rare, probably because they are more easily avoided in a 'homophonic' movement: apart from cadences, there is one hidden octave between soprano and bass in bars 12–13, and really only two other breaches of the rule (soprano and tenor, bar 6; tenor and bass, bar 26).

Thus Mozart obeyed these grammatical rules in his own music, lapses being very rare indeed. It follows that a passage containing breaches of the rules is almost certainly not genuine Mozart. Even hidden octaves or fifths, at least in any great number, are enough by themselves to make authenticity highly suspect.

It is very instructive at this point to examine Süssmayr's *Ave verum corpus*, dated 9 June 1792.[3] This appears to be the only piece of Latin church music by Süssmayr written at the time when he was working on his completion of the Requiem,[4] and so provides a uniquely valuable 'control' for the contrapuntal tests.

Rather surprisingly, there are several outright consecutives in Süssmayr's setting. In bars 5–6 oboe I and violin I are in consecutive octaves with the bass; and in bars 7–8 the alto and tenor are in unison, heavily reinforced by oboe II, horn I, and violin I. The unison between oboe II and horn I in bars 8–10 is perhaps excusable, but the wind parts in bars 14–21 contain many elementary mistakes. In bars 14–15 there are simultaneously consecutive octaves between horn II and bass and unisons between oboe II and horn I; in bars 15–16 the unison between oboe II and horn I is reinforced by adding horn II as well. After the blatant consecutive fifths between the horns in bar 16 (reminiscent of Mozart's *Ein musikalischer Spaß* K 522), horn II now goes in unison with oboe II into bar 17, and then continues in octaves with the bass to bar 18. From bar 19 to bar 20 oboe II and horn I are in unison, while horn II is in octaves with the bass as far as bar 21. There are consecutive octaves again between violin II and bass in bar 27, and soprano and bass are in octaves at the cadence in bars 28–9, just as in Mozart's conventional 'operatic' cadence: perhaps Süssmayr did not realize that this lapse was not allowed in the church style?

On the other hand hidden octaves and fifths are not very numerous. Excluding cadences, there are only four instances in the vocal parts: a hidden octave between alto and bass in bars 4–5, a hidden fifth between tenor and bass in bars 5–6, another between soprano and alto in bar 27 (approached from a diminished fifth), and a hidden octave between tenor and bass in bar 37.

Apart from these breaches of the contrapuntal rules, there are other small infelicities worth noting. In bar 3 the tenor c' is doubled by horn II and violin II, though without proper preparation. In several places, for example in bars 21 and 29, the orchestra is left with a bare fifth, and in other places (bars 17 and 38) Süssmayr adds the seventh to the dominant triad without indicating it in the figuring. This failure to distinguish different forms of dominant harmony is very characteristic of Süssmayr, and occurs often in his completion of the Requiem. A similar inconsistency in the figuring occurs in bars 15 and 36, on the last beat of each of which Süssmayr writes 5, whereas the correct figuring is 7 (bar 15) and $\frac{6}{5}$ (bar 36). In bar 31 the resolution of the appoggiatura d'' in the soprano is anticipated by horn II.

Otherwise the vocal parts are not too bad, if rather pedestrian and lacking in inspiration. The form is kept reasonably clear, and there is even some attempt at imitation in bars 21–5, with inversion in bar 34 (very reminiscent of bars 15–16 of the Benedictus in the Requiem, it should be noted). The approach to the cadences in bars 15–18 and 36–9 is quite effective, though the use of IV7 may be thought to contribute a touch of saccharine (again, these bars are very reminiscent of the Requiem, this time of bars 9–10 of the Sanctus; note also how the incomplete figuring 5 on the last beat of bar 36 corresponds exactly to the last quaver of bar 9 in the

Sanctus). The touch of chromatic harmony in bar 13 makes a characteristically Mozartian effect, being a (deliberate?) near-quotation of bars 5–7 of the Sanctus of K 317.

On the other hand the orchestration is distinctly clumsy. Many technical mistakes, particularly in the wind parts, have already been noted; it is worth drawing attention also to the insensitive sforzandi in the horn parts in bars 22 and 32 (reminiscent of the fortissimo in bar 18 of the Benedictus in the Requiem), and the generally too low tessitura of the oboe parts.

One is left with the impression of a pretty mediocre and unmemorable piece, by a composer obviously trying to imitate Mozart's own setting, but lacking both inspiration and technical expertise. It is easy to see why Mozart had a poor opinion of Süssmayr's capabilities.

A final word of warning: although the contrapuntal tests may be used in suitable cases to show almost conclusively that a piece is not genuine Mozart, the absence of 'mistakes' does not prove the converse. The tests will be sufficient to show beyond reasonable doubt that Süssmayr truthfully claimed the 'Lacrymosa' completion, the Sanctus, 'Osanna', and Benedictus as his own work; but the opposite conclusion in the case of the Agnus Dei, which seems likely to have been extensively sketched by Mozart himself, will have to be established by other methods, and so cannot be regarded as quite so certain.

4
The 'Lacrymosa' Completion

The first eight bars of the 'Lacrymosa' (except for the orchestral parts in bars 3–8) are in Mozart's autograph score, and so are unquestionably genuine. But what of the rest? Is it entirely by Süssmayr, as he himself claimed, or did he have some help from Mozart in the form of preliminary sketches that may have been included in the papers Constanze gave him? If such sketches did exist, how extensive were they, and is it possible to make a reasonable attempt at reconstructing them? Obviously such sketches would have been no more complete than Mozart's autograph score, and hence would not have contained any but the briefest indications of the instrumentation. Thus almost all the orchestration must be Süssmayr's, and it is only in the vocal parts and figured bass that the authorship can be in any doubt.

Let us, therefore, check from bar 9 for breaches of Mozart's grammatical rules. The first occurs in bar 9 itself, where there is a hidden octave between tenor and bass from the sixth to the seventh quaver. One might, by analogy with bars 8 and 10 of the 'Domine Jesu', regard the 'real' bass in bar 9 as two beats of $c\sharp$ followed by two beats of d, but this would by no means excuse the mistake because the hidden octave would then become an explicit consecutive. But what is supposed to be the bass on the fourth beat of bar 9? If it is A, the harmony is an unconventional $\frac{6}{4}$; if it is d, then why is the bass not $c\sharp$ on the second beat? There is a similar (though worse) confusion on the last beat of bar 10: the third beat has a poorly spaced seventh chord (with doubled major third) that resolves onto a $\frac{6}{4}$ (or is it supposed to be a $\frac{6}{3}$ on f?), that does not itself resolve. Notice also the extraordinary muddle between different forms of dominant harmony (very characteristic of Süssmayr, as noted in Chapter 3) on the first two beats of bar 10: the first beat has a diminished seventh, and the second beat has successively a dominant minor ninth (surely never used as casually as this by Mozart), a dominant seventh (but including the tonic(!) as a passing note, and thus containing neither the third nor the fifth), and then a plain dominant triad (in an attempt, presumably, to disguise the non-resolution of the alto g', which is substituted by a $c\sharp'$ that does not rise to the tonic).

These faults are surely sufficient by themselves to make Süssmayr's authorship of bars 9–10 perfectly clear. But, in addition, it is hard to see the point of repeating the words of bars 3–8 to much less effective music (oddly enough, this repeat seems to have been an afterthought on Süssmayr's part, for the facsimile of his autograph in Schnerich shows that in bars 9–10 the words were probably originally 'huic ergo parce Deus', which he afterwards altered to 'Lacrymosa dies illa'). Moreover, should not the dominant chord at the end of bar 8 be followed in bar 9 by the tonic (as in bars 15–16 of the 'Hostias'), or perhaps by a modulation (as in bars 14–15 of the 'Requiem aeternam'), rather than just another dominant chord?

Bars 11–14 are, if anything, even worse than bars 9–10. Hess (p. 105) and Marguerre (p. 173) have already drawn attention to the misuse of the Neapolitan sixth in bar 11 (as indeed did the review of the Requiem in the *Allgemeine Musikalische Zeitung* of 7 October 1801), which would possibly make a little more sense if the following bass note were $G\sharp$ rather than $A\flat$, although the resulting diminished third ($G\sharp$–$b\flat$) would be difficult to believe. Notice also the doubled $E\flat$ in the Neapolitan sixth chord, which is approached by soprano and tenor as a hidden octave, and vanishes completely on the fifth quaver of bar 11. Bar 12 has already been quoted (Ex. 3.6) as an example of a highly suspicious mishandling of $^6_4$ chords; moreover the soprano e'' in bar 12 clashes with the anticipated resolution in the tenor. Marguerre (p. 173) points out the absurdity of the break in the imitation in bar 14, where the expected soprano part fails to materialize (one wonders why not: there are plenty of a''s in the soprano elsewhere in the Requiem); in any case the pattern of the imitation in bars 12–14 seems pretty confused.

So much for bars 11–14, though again there is additional supporting evidence:

1. bad underlay in bars 11–12 (Marguerre, p. 173);
2. sudden appearance of figures in the bass in bar 11 (why?);
3. tenor and bass parts cross in bars 13 and 14 (Hess (p. 105) suggests that the octaves in the bass should be the other way up in bars 11–14, but this would produce even worse crossing).

It has been suggested by Fischer (p. 72), following Abert (ii:

873), that the use in the bass in bars 11–14 of a rising chromatic scale analogous to the soprano in bars 7–8, below imitative treatment of the soprano phrase of bars 3 and 4, is a development of previous material that can be ascribed only to Mozart. But the idea does not seem particularly clever, and in any case the execution is very faulty; it is surprising, too, that the imitation makes no use of the characteristic rising sixth in bar 3.

Fischer (p. 12) has also pointed out that bars 15–17 appear to be based on bars 26–31 of the 'Recordare'. But comparison of the two passages serves only to show how clumsy and unimaginative these bars of the 'Lacrymosa' are. The alto and tenor parts are completely static (Marguerre, p. 173), and the progression from db ' to $d\natural$ ' in the bass in bars 16–17 is illogical (Hess, p. 105). The continuation in bars 17–19 is full of grammatical mistakes. In bar 17 the alto and tenor cross in a crude attempt to conceal the consecutive fifths with the soprano (though the result is hidden octaves between soprano and alto in bar 17 and between tenor and bass into bar 18); even worse are the consecutive octaves between soprano and bass in bars 18–19, which according to Mozart's strict 'consecutives' rule are not saved by the interpolation of the notes bb ' and g' in the soprano. These consecutive octaves are similar to those at the cadence in bars 28–9 of Süssmayr's *Ave verum corpus*. All these mistakes, together with the curious seventh leap in the bass in bars 17–18 and the doubled seventh on the last beat of bar 18 (Hess, p. 105), show that bars 15–19 are again pure Süssmayr.

Bars 19–20 are a near-repeat in the orchestra of bars 17–18, complete with consecutive octaves at the cadence. Then bar 21 modulates back to D minor in preparation for a recapitulation of bars 3–4. This recapitulation makes a certain sense musically, perhaps, but in relation to the text it is utterly absurd, for it occurs not at the start of a new verse, or at the repeat of a previous one, but *in the middle of a sentence*. The actual notes in bars 22–3 are, of course, Mozart's; but in any case they do not suit the new words (Marguerre, p. 174).

Bars 24–8, seen by Abert (ii: 874) and Fischer (p. 15) as a truly Mozartian answer by inversion to bars 5–6, are unfortunately still too full of mistakes to be taken seriously; and even Fischer cannot bring himself to accept these bars without modification in his revised version of the 'Lacrymosa'. There is a bad hidden fifth between tenor and bass in bar 25, and a hidden octave into bar 26.

The alto part in bars 25–6, in Mozart's phrase, 'non è cantabile',[1] and the separation of the instrumental and vocal bass in bars 24–5, with the oddly doubled E♭ on the first beat of bar 25 (and with the alto below the tenor) all seem most implausible (Marguerre, p. 174). Süssmayr seems to have made a mistake in the figuring in bar 26: ⁶₆ on the first beat should read ⁶₃.

Curiously, though, the soprano in bars 26–7 quotes the main theme of the Requiem, first stated in bars 1–2 of the 'Requiem aeternam'.[2] Indeed, if one imagines an *a'* on the last beat of bar 24, the soprano part combines successively the inverted, retrograde, and original versions of the theme (presumably Fischer did not notice this, for he changed the *e'* in bar 26 to *e♭'* in his version). This is probably only an accidental coincidence: for after all the soprano part consists merely of a descending scale and a standard cadential cliché; and if the quotation were deliberate one might have expected it to play a part in the 'imitation' in bars 24–5. There is a trace of it in the tenor in bars 25–6, but the alto is just a clumsy 'fill-in', and the imitation between bass and soprano stops just where the bass might have begun the retrograde version of the theme.

Despite this odd coincidence, then, there is every reason to ascribe bars 24–8 solely to Süssmayr. The final bars 29–30 are certainly spurious, because Mozart intended a double fugue in D minor for the 'Amen'; he might well have ended the 'Lacrymosa' itself with a plagal cadence, but the final chord would have been A major, not D major: compare the last bar of the 'Requiem aeternam'.

To sum up, all of the 'Lacrymosa' completion from bar 9 to bar 30 was written by Süssmayr, and there is no evidence whatever for the existence of any Mozart sketches[3] or, for that matter, even oral instructions. Süssmayr simply did his best to complete Mozart's eight-bar start by using material from it, together with a few bars from the 'Recordare'.

Before leaving the 'Lacrymosa', it is worth saying a little more about Fischer's revised version. Fischer argues that Süssmayr must have worked from Mozart's sketches, so that the 'Lacrymosa' is substantially genuine, but that the piece is without form, and so needs lengthening. It has already been shown, however, that almost every bar is so faulty technically that Mozart can have had nothing to do with it. As for the form, one can only agree that

Süssmayr got it wrong, as his superfluous repeat of the first three lines of the text and his absurd attempt at a recapitulation in bars 22–3 show; but it is equally wrong to postulate a full-scale sonata-like movement comparable with the 'Dies irae'. In other settings of the Requiem that Mozart may have known and used as models (see Chapter 8), at least the first three lines of the text are clearly regarded as just a continuation of the preceding 'Confutatis' section; indeed, bar 40 of Mozart's 'Confutatis', with its modulation back to D minor and the instruction 'segue',[4] makes it pretty clear that Mozart thought of the 'Lacrymosa' in the same way. Since he also set half of the text in the first eight bars, there is no reason to suppose that he intended anything but a short section, leading from the 'Confutatis' to a probably fairly extensive 'Amen' fugue. Süssmayr's completion is therefore too long already, and so Fischer's attempt at extending it is misconceived. Unfortunately Fischer did not correct any of Süssmayr's mistakes (indeed, most of them are repeated because of the lengthening), and introduced a few new ones of his own, such as the consecutive octaves between tenor and bass in his bar 23, or the 'modulation' between bars 34 and 35 (Ex. 4.1). Fischer says of the latter that it is 'ganz im Geiste Mozarts', but it is difficult to see on what evidence he bases this assertion.

The new completion of the 'Lacrymosa' will be described in Chapter 16.

Ex. 4.1

5

The Sanctus and 'Osanna'

The repeat of the 'Osanna' in B flat shows at once that there is something wrong with the key of at least one movement in the Sanctus—'Osanna'—Benedictus sequence: for it is quite inconceivable that Mozart would have repeated a whole movement transposed down a major third. Indeed, it is improbable that Mozart intended the Sanctus to be in D major, which in itself shows that no Mozart sketch for the Sanctus is likely to have existed.

In the Sequence, the keys of the individual sections are as follows:

'Dies irae':	D minor
'Tuba mirum':	B flat major
'Rex tremendae':	G minor (but ends in D minor)
'Recordare':	F major
'Confutatis':	A minor (but ends in F major)
'Lacrymosa':	D minor.

All these keys are related in the closest possible way, so that the new tonic chord of each section has two notes in common with the tonic chord of the previous section (note particularly how the 'Rex tremendae' and 'Confutatis' end in different keys so as to preserve this relationship). The same key relationship holds between the 'Domine Jesu' (in G minor) and 'Hostias' (in E flat major), although it is somewhat obscured by the G major chord at the end of the 'Domine Jesu'. If, as is likely, the 'Amen' was meant to end with a D major chord, this would lead naturally as the dominant to the G minor of the 'Domine Jesu', in exactly the same way that the 'Hostias' leads back to the repeat of the 'Quam olim Abrahae' fugue.

Thus the key relationships in the authentic parts of the Requiem are exceedingly close: even closer, for example, than in the C minor Mass K 427. Of course, this is very characteristic of Mozart: fond though he was of exploring the most distant modulations within a movement, he did not normally put successive movements in remote keys, as for example Haydn did in his Piano Sonata in E flat major of 1794 (Hob.XVI.52), whose slow movement is in E major.

It seems very unlikely that Mozart would suddenly have abandoned the close key relationships at the end of the second 'Quam olim Abrahae' fugue, and gone straight from G minor (or rather, what sounds like the dominant of C minor) to D major for the Sanctus, and almost incredible that he would have immediately followed the 'Osanna' in D major by the Benedictus in B flat major. It must be admitted, though, that there is an example of just these changes of key in *Die Zauberflöte*, where 'Ach ich fühl's' in G minor is followed by the chorus 'O Isis, und Osiris, welche Wonne!' in D major, and then by the trio 'Soll ich dich Teurer nicht mehr sehn' in B flat major. But the key relationships 'between successive movements in *Die Zauberflöte* are not nearly as close as those in the Requiem: both here and elsewhere in the opera Mozart allows remote changes of key after intervening spoken dialogue.

Moreover, the precedent in *Die Zauberflöte* does nothing to explain the purpose of the apparent modulation to C minor at the end of the 'Quam olim Abrahae' fugue, which at its first occurrence has the disadvantage of obscuring the closeness of key of the 'Hostias'. What did Mozart intend by these bars? They could of course be interpreted as a conventional plagal cadence with Tierce de Picardie, though it is not easy to find Mozartian precedents for such an ending to a fugue, and in any case Mozart's use of the dominant seventh of C minor makes the modulation sound convincing enough. Such an explanation does not seem adequate to explain the purpose of the coda, but it would make perfectly good sense, by analogy with the modulations at the ends of the 'Rex tremendae', 'Confutatis', and 'Hostias', if it were a preparation for the key of the succeeding Sanctus. One should compare

1. the end of the 'Qui tollis' of K 427, where a section in G minor similarly ends with a G major chord, to prepare for the succeeding 'Quoniam' in E minor (relative minor of G major); and

2. the end of the 'Quam olim Abrahae' fugue in Michael Haydn's Requiem in C minor[1] (written in Salzburg in 1771, and no doubt familiar to Mozart: see Chapter 8). Haydn's 'Quam olim Abrahae', like Mozart's, is in G minor but ends with what appears to be the dominant of C minor; his Sanctus then starts with a C

major chord, which afterwards turns out to be the dominant of F minor (C minor is restored after a few bars): see Ex. 5.1.

In what key, then, did Mozart intend his Sanctus? The possibilities appear to be E minor or B minor (the 'two notes in common' rule followed in the Sequence), or C major or minor (treating the chord of G major as the dominant). Of these, E minor or B minor seem far too remote from the original D minor, bearing in mind the narrow range of keys used elsewhere in the Requiem.

Ex. 5.1 M. Haydn, Requiem in C minor

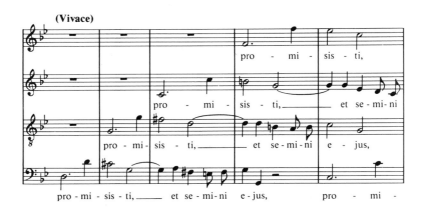

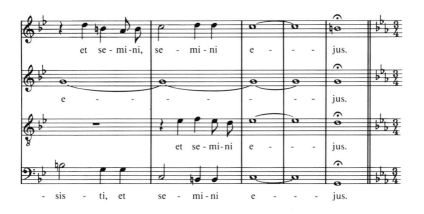

Andante

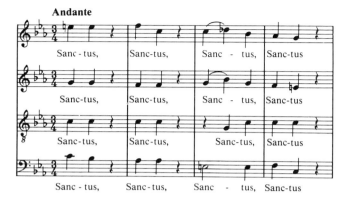

Of the remaining C minor or major, C major is possibly the more likely, being more closely related to D minor, although it might be argued that the minor mode would be more appropriate for the Sanctus in a requiem mass.[2] Perhaps Mozart would have followed Michael Haydn's ingenious solution, and started with a C major chord but used a different key for the movement itself?

Having decided, then, that the choice of the key of D major for the Sanctus makes authenticity doubtful, let us analyse it in detail. As Handke (p. 122) pointed out, the soprano part in bars 1–4 is more-or-less the same as the soprano part in the 'Dies irae', bars 1–7 (but omitting bars 5 and 6), put into the major; moreover the bass part corresponds roughly to that of the 'Dies irae' as well. It is odd, though, that both references to the main Requiem theme at the start of the 'Dies irae' (soprano, bars 5–6; bass, bars 1–5) are here completely removed. As Marguerre (p. 174) said, though, these cross-references do not prove anything, for it is perfectly possible that they represent merely Süssmayr's attempt to relate the Sanctus to earlier material in the Requiem. Moreover, although the soprano and bass parts are near-copies of those in the 'Dies irae', the inner parts have been altered, and as a result the soprano and alto have a bad hidden fifth in bars 1–2 and a hidden octave in bars 3–4 (notice how Mozart carefully avoids them in the 'Dies irae'). Süssmayr seems also to have misunderstood the function of the C♮ in the bass in bar 6 of the 'Dies irae': what is a passing note there (and is C♮ rather than C♯ because Mozart is using the descending melodic minor scale) becomes, in bar 3 of the Sanctus, part of a firm and convincing modulation to G major; but then the C♯ in the tenor in bar 4 is plainly a wrong note, because the modulation back to D major does not take place until the next bar (compare bar 7 of the 'Dies irae', where the C♯ in the tenor is correct because there has been no modulation away from D minor).

It will be noticed that bar 4, besides being modelled on bar 7 of the 'Dies irae', also closely resembles part of 'O Isis, und Osiris, welche Wonne!' in *Die Zauberflöte* (see Ex. 5.2). Again, though, comparison with genuine Mozart serves to show how poor this bar of the Sanctus really is: for Ex. 5.2 is preceded by the dominant of D major, not by the dominant seventh of G major, and Mozart does not add a superfluous fourth part to a descending scale in ⁶₃s.

Ex. 5.2 K 620, 'O Isis, und Osiris, welche Wonne!', bars 5–6.

Bar 5 appears also to be copied from 'O Isis, und Osiris, welche Wonne!': see Ex. 5.3. As usual, though, something has gone wrong in the copying process, for the tenor and bass are in consecutive octaves according to Fux's rule quoted in Chapter 3 (the intervening C♯ in the bass does not really make any difference).

Ex. 5.3 K 620, 'O Isis, und Osiris, welche Wonne!', bars 24–6.

Bars 6–10 have been criticized by Marguerre (pp. 174 f.) for their muddled and pointless modulations, but they are not without a

certain logic. The bass in bars 6–7 has of course the same descending scale as the bass in bars 3–4 (which in turn is transposed up a fifth in the soprano in bar 4, and down a fourth in the bass in bars 4–5); moreover the soprano in bars 7–8 has the descending chromatic scale of the bass in bars 1–4, transposed up a tone, and in bar 9 repeats bar 4. One might also regard the rhythm in bars 6–10 as a development of that of bars 4–5. There are even Mozartian precedents for the harmonic progressions: that of bars 5–7 can be found in Ex. 5.4. It also resembles the corresponding part of the Sanctus of K 194 (Ex. 5.5). Bars 9–10 appear to be modelled on 'O Isis, und Osiris, welche Wonne!' again (Ex. 5.6), though, as noted

Ex. 5.4 K 427, 'Gratias', bars 3–4.

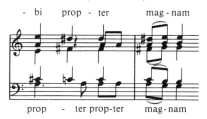

Ex. 5.5 K 194, Sanctus, bars 10–13.

Ex. 5.6 K 620, 'O Isis, und Osiris, welche Wonne!', bars 36–8.

in Chapter 3, they also closely resemble bars 36–8 of Süssmayr's
Ave verum corpus.

But it certainly does not follow that bars 6–10 are genuine
Mozart, for it has already been shown that the key of D major is
improbable, and that bars 1–5 appear to be a rather botched attempt
to relate both to the 'Die irae' and to 'O Isis, und Osiris, welche
Wonne!'. There are harmonic and contrapuntal errors in these bars,
too: in bar 7 the fourth quaver has no third, and there is a hidden
fifth between alto and tenor; in bar 8 the figuring on the third beat
should be $\frac{6}{3}$, not $\frac{6}{4}$, to avoid anticipating the modulation back to D
major (Marguerre, pp. 174–5); and in bar 9 there is a hidden octave
between soprano and alto (it is odd that the second note in the alto
should be *f♯* ' rather than *d″*: for *d″* would have avoided both the
hidden octave and the doubled fifth in the B minor chord).

Taking all the above arguments into account, it seems inescap-
able that the whole of the Sanctus is Süssmayr's work, and there is
no evidence for even the most incomplete Mozart sketch. But
credit is certainly due to Süssmayr for his attempt to relate to the
'Dies irae', and also to copy the style of 'O Isis, und Osiris, welche
Wonne!', which is by no means inappropriate here. The Sanctus is
perhaps the most successful of Süssmayr's attempts to include, as
he hoped, 'some traces of Mozart's unforgettable teaching'.

Let us now consider the 'Osanna' fugue, the theme of which was
considered by Handke (p. 123) to have been written by Mozart.
Handke's argument was that the themes of the Kyrie and 'Osanna'
fugues are both based on the falling seventh from the submediant to
the leading note (though the interval is filled in by a scale in the
'Osanna', as indeed it is in bars 3–4 of the Kyrie), and that the first
bar of the Kyrie and the first two bars of the 'Osanna' have the
same shape: thus one could consider the theme of the 'Osanna' to
be a 'development' of that of the Kyrie. Handke also pointed out
that the first two bars of the 'Osanna' are a sort of retrograde
version of the soprano in bars 9–10 of the Sanctus, and that bars 3–4
of the transposed 'Osanna' resemble the soprano in bars 48–50 of
the Benedictus, again retrograde; but these derivations do not seem
very convincing, and in any case prove nothing if the Sanctus and
Benedictus were written by Süssmayr. Handke's thematic relationships seem, as elsewhere, to be insufficiently distinguishable from
chance resemblances to constitute anything like a rigorous proof of
Mozart's authorship of the 'Osanna' theme: after all, many other

composers have used the falling diminished seventh characteristic of Mozart's Kyrie theme!

If Handke's attribution of the theme to Mozart is questionable, the rest of the fugue is so inept that there can be no doubt that Süssmayr was the composer. There is a suggestion of a modulation to A major in bars 6–7, though without a G♯; the appearance of G♯ is delayed until bar 9, that is, precisely at the point where the alto enters on d'! The harmony in bars 9–10 is truly amazing: in bar 9 there is a diminished triad on G♯ (in second inversion), with no third but doubled diminished fifth, followed on the first beat of bar 10 by a $^6_4$ whose fourth does not resolve (this mistake is repeated in bar 12). One should compare the 'correct' handling of this sort of fugal exposition in Ex. 5.7. In bar 13 what appears to be the third inversion of the dominant seventh proceeds in characteristic Süssmayr fashion just to drop the inconvenient seventh that would otherwise constrain the bass to move to F♯, which would make a hidden octave with the soprano.

Ex. 5.7 K 193, Magnificat, bars 106–10.

These mistakes make Süssmayr's authorship of bars 9–13 almost certain, and of bars 6–8 highly probable (notice also the clumsy partwriting in bar 6, where the bass note *B* has to be omitted from the voices since it does not fit the words). But this conclusion in turn implies that even the theme is most unlikely to be Mozart's: for he was not in the habit of sketching merely the theme of a fugue, rather than at least a partial exposition.

Having seen that the exposition of the fugue is Süssmayr's, it is almost superfluous to examine the rest in detail; not that very much remains once the exposition is over. The craftsmanship shows no sign of improvement: starting in bar 17, the bass absurdly has the tonally altered version of the theme, but at the original pitch; bars 18–23 are virtually a repeat of bars 10–15, with the parts exchanged (an ingenious way to avoid the labour of writing any more counterpoint!); and bars 24–5 have simultaneously a hidden octave between alto and bass and a hidden fifth between tenor and bass, while tenor and bass are in near-consecutive octaves in bars 25–6.

To sum up, there is a faint possibility that the theme of the fugue might be Mozart's (though Handke's arguments seem insufficient to outweigh the intrinsic implausibility of Mozart's having sketched only the theme of a fugue, and that in apparently the wrong key). The rest of the exposition contains many elementary mistakes and so must be by Süssmayr, as also must be the ridiculously short continuation (hardly more than a repeat of a part of the exposition) and the coda.

The second 'Osanna', transposed, slightly shortened, and with a few minor alterations, must obviously also be Süssmayr's work.

6

The Benedictus

Handke's detailed case for the authenticity of at least bars 1–18 and 28–50 (Handke, pp. 109-19) has been accepted by several writers, such as Blume[1] and the otherwise rather sceptical Marguerre (pp. 175–6). Even Einstein, who, in his entry for K 626 in the Köchel catalogue, on the whole accepted Süssmayr's claim to have written all the 'additional' movements, considered that in the Benedictus Süssmayr 'apparently [had] an indication of Mozart's intentions, in the form of six or eight measures in Mozart's manuscript' (Einstein, p. 354). Hussey (p. 262) stands almost alone amongst modern writers in his opinion that all of 'the Benedictus [may be] safely judged to be genuine Süssmayr'. This movement must therefore be analysed with the greatest possible care.

Handke begins his argument by showing that the theme, in bars 1–3, is similar to those used by Mozart in earlier settings of the Benedictus. The first half, which can plausibly be derived from the soprano in bar 3 of the 'Lacrymosa', is identical in rhythm to that of the theme of K 194 (Ex. 6.1). In K 259 there is a similar rhythm, now with a sixth leap as well (Ex. 6.2). Moreover the second half of the theme is similar in shape to corresponding places in, for

Ex. 6.1 K 194, Benedictus, bars 1–2.

Be - ne - dic - tus,   qui   ve - nit

Ex. 6.2 K 259, Benedictus, bars 9–10.

Be - ne - dic - tus

example, K 167 (Ex. 6.3). Handke suggests that there must have been a long, and perhaps subconscious, evolutionary process going

Ex. 6.3 K 167, Benedictus, bars 35–8.

on in Mozart's mind, which finally, after well over ten years, produced the theme of the Benedictus in the Requiem. Handke's case could perhaps be strengthened by the following points, which he seems to have overlooked.

1. The first five notes of the theme are identical, as was first noted by Lach[2] in 1918, with the first five notes of a theme set by Mozart in 1784 in an exercise for his pupil Barbara Ployer (Ex. 6.4).

Ex. 6.4

2. The second half of the theme closely resembles (indeed, the resemblance is much closer than in Handke's examples) a phrase in the Sanctus of K 337 (Ex. 6.5), which is used again at bar 14 of the 'Osanna' of K 337. It occurs also in the Act II Finale of *La clemenza di Tito* (Ex. 6.6).

Ex. 6.5 K 337, Sanctus, bars 5–6.

Ex. 6.6 K 621, Act II Finale, bars 5–7.

3. The counterpoint in the bassoons and viola in bars 2–3 is used similarly in 'Torna di Tito a lato' in *La clemenza di Tito* (Ex. 6.7). It is, moreover, used frequently in the Kyrie of the Requiem itself, being part of the countersubject.

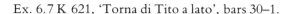

Ex. 6.7 K 621, 'Torna di Tito a lato', bars 30–1.

4. The orchestration, with the theme in the basset-horn doubled an octave higher by violin I, is reminiscent of the opening of 'Non più di fiori' in *La clemenza di Tito* (Ex. 6.8).

Thus the theme, and the counterpoint in bars 2–3, are assembled from fragments that are demonstrably Mozartian, although as it happens the originals have all been transposed. Does this represent, as Handke believed, the workings of Mozart's (possibly subconscious) mind, or is it Süssmayr's attempt to manufacture synthetic Mozart, or is it all nothing but coincidence? Let us now re-examine bars 1–3, this time to see what the evidence is *against* Mozart's authorship.

The first suspicious point is that violin I cannot make up its mind whether to double the basset-horn in unison or at the octave (compare the opening of 'Non più di fiori', where the doubling is consistently at the octave). This rather clumsy change of octave suggests that the violin I part is an addition by Süssmayr. Next, the viola is in consecutive octaves with the theme on the first two quavers of bar 2, which according to Mozart's rule is not saved by

Ex. 6.8 K 621, 'Non più di fiori', bars 1–4.

the intervening (sounding) *a'* in the basset-horn. Amusingly enough, these consecutive octaves are identical with some perpetrated by Mozart in *Ein musikalischer Spaß* (Ex. 6.9). Hence the viola part in bars 1–2 is not authentic. Again, violin II is in consecutive fifths with the bass in bar 3. The bass looks rather dubious anyway, for the emphatic repeated cadence in the first bar-and-a-half seems inappropriately final for the start of a movement

Ex. 6.9 K 522, 3rd mvt., bar 50.

(observe how Mozart carefully avoids it in Ex. 6.4). And the trombone and lower woodwind parts may easily be dismissed: note, for example, the unison between basset-horn II, bassoon I, and trombone I in bar 2.

It appears, therefore, that at most the theme and the counterpoint in bars 2–3 could possibly be authentic. But what is supposed to be the harmony on the first beat of bar 3? If the bass (*c*) is correct, the harmony is $\frac{7}{4}$; but Ex. 6.7 shows that the fourth should have been prepared (in bar 3 of the Benedictus, on the contrary, this fourth is approached via consecutive fourths with the bass!). The alternative (as happens in bars 5–7 of the Act II Finale of K 621) would be for the bass to be *A*, not *c*, so that the (sounding) *f′* in basset-horn I would be a sixth, not an unprepared fourth; but then the suspended *bb* in the bassoons would become a highly improbable minor ninth, and the *g* on the second semiquaver would make no sense at all. The only possible harmony on the first beat of bar 3 is a plain $\frac{6}{3}$ with *A* in the bass, hence without the counterpoint in the bassoons and viola. In fact this counterpoint, agreeable as it may sound on first hearing, is nothing very special in itself, for it is a standard cliché, specified by Mozart to Attwood[3] as one of the two possible cadential formulae in the third species of counterpoint (four notes against one). One cannot help suspecting that it was introduced by Süssmayr in order that bar 3 should have an appropriately ecclesiastical sound: he must have felt that counterpoint was called for, but probably lacked the necessary technique. Süssmayr's *Alleluia* for bass and orchestra[4] has an analogous example of his 'pseudo-counterpoint', where he seems to have hoped that a sequence of suspensions and resolutions would create the right effect: see Ex. 6.10.

There remains the theme. Yet the end still looks dubious, for it has to be altered slightly to fit the word 'Domini' three bars later: see Ex. 6.11. This appears to leave only the first phrase. It is very unlikely that Mozart would have written down this much and no more, and even less likely that Süssmayr had seen and copied Barbara Ployer's seven-year-old exercise book, so there is no good reason to doubt that he simply hit on this theme by accident. He was probably trying to imitate 'Non più di fiori', and added the bassoon part in bars 2–3 to give a 'churchy' flavour.

Bars 4–6 are essentially a repeat of bars 1–3, with the small change in the end of the theme necessary to make it fit the words,

Ex. 6.10 Süssmayr, *Alleluia*, bars 18–21.

Ex. 6.11

and the bass slightly altered. Observe, though, that as a result of the change of bass the consecutive octaves between violin I and viola become absolutely explicit.

Handke's case (p. 112) for bars 7–9 is that the phrases in the soprano are based successively on the intervals of a third, fourth, fifth, sixth, and seventh; this demonstrates, he says, 'a particular characteristic of Mozart's language',[5] analogous to Ex. 6.12. But the latter is a straightforward rising sequence, not a sequence of increasingly wider intervals, and so is not a close analogue. Moreover the rhythm in bar 8 on the word 'Domine' is faulty, and appears to be without precedent in Mozart's settings of the

Ex. 6.12 K 475, bars 86–9.

Benedictus in his earlier masses. It looks suspiciously as if the phrase was first written with a crochet *bb* ', which had to be broken up when the words were added afterwards. Thus, even if Handke's by no means convincing argument were accepted, there could have existed, in bars 7–9, nothing but a single-line sketch without words (the orchestral parts are obviously spurious: there are consecutive octaves between basset-horn and viola in bar 7, there is a bare fourth on the third beat of bar 7, and there are nonsensical parallel seconds between soprano and violin I on the last beat of bar 9).

Bars 10–11 are harmonically inept. There is nothing but an alternation of tonic and dominant, and, what is worse, the voices are harmonically incomplete most of the time (for example, bare fifth on the fourth beat of bar 10, and several bare fifths and octaves on the second half of main beats). These bars are totally empty, and will not stand comparison with Mozart's own treatment of this sort of idea: see Ex. 6.13.

Ex. 6.13 K 257, Benedictus, bars 23–7.

Handke (p. 115) observes that the arpeggio motif used in bars 12–13 occurs in a roughly similar context in the *Romanze* of K 525; he might have added that the phrase also occurs in the Sanctus of K 194 (Ex. 6.14). But the counterpoint here is so faulty that there can be no question of Mozart's being the composer. After a hidden fifth between soprano and bass on the second beat of bar 12, every

Ex. 6.14 K 194, Sanctus, bar 5.

(Sanc) - - tus — Do - (minus)

statement of the motif ends with consecutive octaves, thinly but inadequately disguised by the movement of one part by a skip of a third: these consecutives occur between alto and bass (last beat of bar 12 to first beat of bar 13), soprano and bass (second to third beats of bar 13), and tenor and bass (last beat of bar 13 to first beat of bar 14). Clearly, therefore, these bars are pure Süssmayr.

The rising chromatic scale in thirds in bar 14, as Handke (p. 111) points out, resembles a similar scale in the *Romanze* of K 525; also a rising chromatic scale (though without the thirds) is set to the same words in K 257 (Ex. 6.15). Handke apparently overlooked a precedent for the descending scale in §s in the second half of bar 14, in K 192 (Ex. 6.16). But these observations do not prove anything,

Ex. 6.15 K 257, Benedictus, bars 72–4.

in   no - mi - ne Do   -   mi - ni.

Ex. 6.16 K 192, Gloria, bars 135–7.

Je - - su Chris - - te.

Je - - su Chris - - te.

Je - - su Chris - - te.

Je - su Chris - - te.

for rising or descending (chromatic) scales are amongst the most common clichés in the works of every eighteenth-century composer. There are curious inconsistencies between bar 14 and the corresponding bar 42, the most noticeable being the *e'* in the tenor in bar 14 but the *ab'* in bar 42. But there are also inconsistencies in the underlay: for example the alto's problem of singing a repeated *a'* to the same syllable in bar 14 is avoided in bar 42. Like bar 8, bar 14 gives the impression of having been written first without words, which were afterwards added in a none-too-skilful way.

Bars 15–18 make a plausibly 'Mozartian' sound at first hearing, but will not bear close examination. The use of the dominant ninth in bar 16 recalls both bar 38 of the 'Domine Jesu' and a phrase in Mozart's *Ave verum corpus* (Ex. 6.17), but the effect of the passing

Ex. 6.17 K 618, bars 24–5.

notes in the alto and tenor is to produce a very odd $^9_4$ chord (with doubled fourth) instead of the correct $^9_7$. Immediately afterwards, there are blatant consecutive fifths between tenor and bass into bar 17. It is true that the tenor and bass in the first half of bar 16 make an agreeable effect, but the phrase closely resembles bar 34 of Süssmayr's *Ave verum corpus* (see Chapter 3), so that, even if there were no technical mistakes in bars 16 and 17, the arguments used by Handke would tend to suggest that the composer was Süssmayr, not Mozart. One curiosity should be noticed (it is probably only a coincidence): the soprano's final phrase in bars 17–18 is essentially a retrograde version of the original theme in bar 1.

To summarize the conclusions about bars 1–18, then, the only places where Mozart sketches might possibly have existed are bars 1–3 (a single line), bars 7–9 (again a single line, without words), and bar 14 (without words). In each of these places, however, there are good reasons for doubt; thus there does not seem to be enough evidence even to make the existence of sketches look probable. In any case, it hardly matters who wrote these fragments, for it would be impossible to reconstruct a whole movement from such slender material.

The rest of the movement can be dismissed more briefly. The middle section, from bar 18 to bar 27, was considered even by Handke (p. 115) to be Süssmayr's work: the fortissimo passage from bar 18 to bar 27, obviously a garbled version of bars 43–4 of the 'Requiem aeternam', is totally out of place in this movement, and shows the same sort of insensitivity that allowed Süssmayr to write sforzando brass chords in the middle of his *Ave verum corpus*. Bars 21–2 consist of an aimless meandering in no particular key, and are followed by five bars of utter banality. It is worth observing, though, that Süssmayr has the wit in bars 23–6 to (mis)quote bars 15–17 of the 'Requiem aeternam', although not without introducing a hidden fifth immediately followed by a hidden octave between soprano and alto in bars 25–6.

Bar 27, which as Marguerre (p. 175) remarks would be more appropriate in a Strauss waltz, leads back to the recapitulation, in which, according to Marguerre, there are 'exchanges of parts such as only late Mozart could undertake'.[6] But one cannot transmute Süssmayr into Mozart merely by exchanging parts; and it hardly needs a flash of genius to transfer the soprano and alto in bars 4–9 to the tenor and bass at the recapitulation. Moreover the modulation to E flat major in bars 32–3 is much too abrupt (and the new tonic is anticipated at the start of bar 32). Bars 33–4 are just as empty as bars 10–11. Bars 35–7 correspond to bars 12–13, except that what was imitative there (but was full of consecutive octaves) now becomes just a continuous bass line! The firm modulation to F major at the first beat of bar 38 is absurd, for this is the wrong key for what follows, which is yet another repeat of bars 10–11 (though with some new mistakes, such as the bare fifths on the first beats of bars 39 and 40). There is a half-hearted attempt in bar 41 to recapitulate bars 12–13 (already more-or-less repeated in bars 35–7); the consecutive octaves are still present, but now are made quite explicit between tenor and bass. Bar 42 is like bar 14, except for the *ab* ′ in the tenor, and the (accidental?) omission of the appoggiatura from the alto *bb* ′ on the fourth beat. There follows a recapitulation of bars 15–18, with the dubious ninth chord omitted this time, and with the consecutive fifths between tenor and bass replaced by a hidden octave. Bars 46–7 are frankly boring, and are rhythmically wrong, because they force the final cadence to occur on the first beat of bar 50 instead of the third beat as in bar 18. Then bars 48–50 correspond to bars 17–18, but there are several new mistakes: a hidden octave between soprano and tenor in bar 48, a hidden fifth between soprano and alto into bar 49, and an incomplete chord on the third beat of bar 48. It is an odd coincidence, though, that the soprano in bars 48–9 is virtually a repeat of the bass in bars 13–14. Finally, the orchestral fortissimo of bars 19–21 is repeated, still out of phase with the bar-lines, and is followed by a conventional cadential formula.

Thus there is absolutely no evidence in bars 18–53 for the existence of any new authentic material, and the conclusion must remain as it was after the first eighteen bars, namely that the only places where one might possibly accept Handke's argument are in bars 1–3, 7–9 (but only a single line), and perhaps bar 14. But Handke's case has serious weaknesses (and he failed to notice some of the closest thematic resemblances) and cannot be regarded as convincing. Indeed, throughout the whole of the Benedictus, and for that matter the 'Lacrymosa' completion, the Sanctus, and the 'Osanna', there is such an absence of the miracles that one almost takes for granted in Mozart, and such an unrelieved display of technical incompetence, that it is difficult to see why anyone should want to convince himself that Mozart had any part in such poor music.

7

The Agnus Dei

Straightforward tests of technical competence have shown that the 'Lacrymosa' completion, the Sanctus, the 'Osanna', and the Benedictus are almost certainly spurious. But, in the absence of autograph material, there is no way of showing with such confidence that the Agnus Dei is in essence genuine. However, comparison with earlier Mozart masses, and analysis of the form of the Agnus Dei and its relation to the rest of the Requiem, will show at least that Süssmayr very probably based this movement on a Mozart sketch, presumably given to him by Constanze.

Many writers have observed that the bass in the first nine bars consists of the theme that starts the 'Requiem aeternam', extended upwards to the dominant (Ex. 7.1). There are in fact many uses of

Ex. 7.1

this theme in the Requiem after the 'Requiem aeternam', for example the first six bars of the 'Dies irae', and the subject (by inversion) of the 'Amen' fugue sketch. This observation would not by itself, of course, prove that the first nine bars are genuine, for in several other places Süssmayr reused material from earlier movements. What is remarkable about these bars, however, is that, not only does the bass have the Requiem theme, but at the same time all four vocal parts are a near-quotation of sections of the Gloria of K 220, in which the words are almost the same. Bars 39–43 of this Gloria, transposed down a tone, run as follows·

Ex. 7.2

qui tol - - lis pec - ca - ta

It will be seen that this is identical with bars 2–6 of the Agnus Dei, apart from an exchange of inner parts in the first two bars to produce a spacing of the diminished seventh chord that, to judge from bar 52 of the 'Hostias', Mozart evidently preferred in 1791. Then bars 6–9 of the Agnus Dei closely resemble bars 78–81 of the Gloria of K 220, this time transposed up a tone (Ex. 7.3). It might

Ex. 7.3

mi - se - re - re   no - bis

be objected that Mozart is known to have had perfect pitch, and is therefore unlikely, even unconsciously, to have reused earlier ideas at a different pitch. But in the Gloria of K 220 Ex. 7.2 is not associated with any particular key, for it first appears in E minor, is then transposed down to D minor in bars 53–6, and is transposed again to E flat major/C minor in bars 67–71. Indeed, bars 53–5 are an exact transposition of bars 39–41, and so coincide precisely with bars 2–4 of the Agnus Dei, except for the minor exchange of inner parts.

There are other, though not quite so close, resemblances between this section of the Agnus Dei and Mozart's settings of similar words in earlier masses: see Exx. 7.4 and 7.5.

There are of course two possible explanations for the nearly exact quotations of sections of the Gloria of K 220 in bars 2–9 of the Agnus Dei. Either they represent Süssmayr's attempt, as parts of the Sanctus may have done, to construct synthetic Mozart out of genuine pieces; or else Süssmayr was here using a Mozart sketch, in which Mozart was reworking earlier ideas, perhaps suggested to him by the words, in the same way that he reused his own and other composers' ideas elsewhere in the Requiem (see Chapter 8 for a discussion of Mozart's borrowings). (It seems out of the question that the close resemblances here are only coincidence, for the quotations from K 220 are of a different order of magnitude from

Ex. 7.4 K 317, Gloria, bars 78–86.

Ex. 7.5 K 192, Gloria, bars 87–91.

the short thematic fragments noted elsewhere by Handke and others.) It is impossible to be absolutely certain that the former hypothesis is wrong, but the following points show that it is highly improbable.

1. For Süssmayr to have written these bars unaided, he would have to have known K 220, and realized that bars 39–43 of the Gloria could be transposed down a tone so as to fit the Requiem theme in the bass. It is, unfortunately, impossible to know whether Süssmayr could have had access to the score of K 220;[1] but it seems very unlikely that he would have noticed the remarkable coincidence that the bass in the Gloria of K 220 actually quotes the main

Requiem theme, though transposed up a tone. No one else seems to have noticed this, during almost two centuries.

2. Even if Süssmayr had known and copied K 220, there would have been no point in his exchanging the alto and tenor parts in the first two bars: why not copy these bars exactly? On the other hand it is perfectly plausible that Mozart might have forgotten the precise details of the inner parts after over fifteen years, and have automatically substituted his currently preferred spacing of the diminished seventh chord.

3. There are no contrapuntal mistakes in these bars. One might at first sight question the hidden octaves between soprano and tenor into bar 4, and between soprano and alto into bar 9, but in both cases the alternative would have been a diminished fifth followed by a perfect fifth, and hence hidden fifths. The progression here corresponds exactly to that in bars 52–3 of the 'Hostias', which shows that Mozart must have preferred the hidden octave as the lesser of two evils in this context. Of course, the absence of mistakes is not by itself conclusive evidence, although one should compare the Sanctus, for example, in which almost every bar contains an elementary blunder even when Süssmayr is apparently basing his work on the 'Dies irae' or *Die Zauberflöte*.

Thus there seems every reason to believe that Süssmayr possessed a Mozart sketch for the first nine bars of the Agnus Dei, containing the four vocal parts. What of the orchestral parts: were there any indications of these in the sketch? There is a precedent in K 192 for an Agnus Dei in D minor, accompanied by semiquaver figuration in the violins and repeated quavers in the lower strings; moreover there are even thematic resemblances to the Agnus Dei in the Requiem, and the characteristic progression from the dominant of D minor straight to F major occurs prominently: see Ex. 7.6. (One is tempted to think that, despite the quotations from K 220, it was the Agnus Dei of K 192 that really served Mozart as a model here, in much the same way that he seems to have reworked his *Sancta Maria, mater Dei* K 273 in the *Ave verum corpus* K 618.) Not only is the general style of the accompaniment in the Agnus Dei of the Requiem similar to that of K 192, but the violin figuration in bar 1 is itself derived from the main Requiem theme, by inversion and retrograde motion (Ex. 7.7). It seems quite possible then that, like the autographs of the 'Lacrymosa' and 'Hostias', the sketch also contained at least the violin and bass parts in the introductory bar 1.

Ex. 7.6 K 192, Agnus Dei, bars 4–7.

Ex. 7.7

Probably they continued no further, and the wind parts were missing altogether.

Let us now consider bars 10–14. The progression straight from the dominant of the tonic minor to the relative major was one of Mozart's favourite devices for resolving the tension of the dominant triad, while generating a new phrase and avoiding the finality of a perfect cadence. There are plenty of precedents besides Ex. 7.6: for example bars 14–15 of the 'Requiem aeternam', bars 8–10 of the 'Dies irae', and Ex. 7.8. The same progression, but with no intervening chord, occurs in *Die Zauberflöte* (Ex. 7.9).

Ex. 7.8 K 427, Benedictus, bars 20–1.

Ex. 7.9 K 620, 'Bewahret euch vor Weibertücken', bars 15–19.

Handke (p. 122) has noted that the soprano part in bar 12 closely resembles the soprano in bar 11 of the 'Requiem aeternam' (with the same words, 'dona eis'). Bars 11–14 are also very like bars 3–8 of the Agnus Dei of K 275 (Ex. 7.10), which anticipate the soprano

Ex. 7.10 K 275, Agnus Dei, bars 3–8.

line, the rising chromatic scale in the tenor, and the somewhat unusual approach to the cadence via the minor (not diminished) seventh on IV♯. It looks very much, in fact, as if the Agnus Dei of K 275, which Mozart performed twice in July 1791, was the model for the 'dona eis requiem' sections here. There is another precedent for the minor seventh on IV♯ as an approach to a perfect cadence in F major, this time from November 1791, in *Eine kleine Freymaurer-Kantate* (Ex. 7.11). Moreover the cadence itself in bars 13–14, with

Ex. 7.11 K 623, 'Lange sollen diese Mauern', bars 93–6.

the alto and tenor parts crossed and the falling sixth in the tenor, is almost identical with that in bars 135–7 of the Gloria of K 192 (Ex. 6.16).

The situation here, then, is very similar to that in bars 1–9: again the music consists of near-quotations—it might almost be called a distillation—of earlier material, mainly from the Agnus Dei of K 275, which is nevertheless closely related to the 'Requiem aeternam'. The same argument therefore applies: either these bars are a piece of very clever forgery, or else they are genuine Mozart. It is not quite so easy this time to dismiss the former hypothesis, for it is quite possible that Süssmayr heard one of the performances of K 275 in July 1791. On the other hand bars 10–14 seem to provide a 'resolution', in Rosen's sense, of the long-range tension set up by the main theme in the 'Requiem aeternam'. This resolution, which occurs to the most appropriate possible words, is accomplished by making the last statement of the Requiem theme, in bars 1–9 of the Agnus Dei, more inconclusive than before by extending it to the dominant, and then giving a satisfying answering phrase, in a way that had been hinted at long before, for example in bars 11 and 14–15 of the 'Requiem aeternam' and bars 8–10 of the 'Dies irae', but never previously carried anywhere near a full conclusion. This procedure was one of Mozart's chief ways of imparting a sense of inevitability to a large-scale structure. A well-known example of its use occurs in the Andante of the Piano Concerto in G major K 453, where the inconclusive opening solo phrase, ending on a dominant chord, is repeated several times, but only on its last appearance, when the new chromatic harmony in the woodwind makes it even more inconclusive, is it given a truly satisfying answer by the piano. In the Andante of K 453, of course, the long-range tension and resolution spans only a single movement, whereas in the

Requiem it is a unifying principle over the whole of a large-scale work with many contrasting sections. One would think that it would take a greater composer than Süssmayr to extend the classical 'resolution' principle so far.

The sense of large-scale structure perhaps explains why Mozart should have sketched the 'Amen' fugue exposition and also, conjecturally, the Agnus Dei, before starting work on the details of the earlier movements (on the sketch sheet, the 'Amen' exposition comes before an early draft of the 'Rex tremendae'). For the whole of the Requiem can be conceived of as a sort of extended sonata form, in which the 'Requiem aeternam' is the exposition and the Agnus Dei starts the recapitulation; the mid-point of the 'development' was no doubt intended to be the 'Amen' fugue, whose subject is the inversion of the main theme. If this view of the structure is correct, it is quite natural that Mozart should first have sketched out its main outlines in the 'Amen' and Agnus Dei.

Bars 14–16 are a repeat by the woodwind of bars 11–13, though it is odd that, on the last beat of bar 16, basset-horn I uses the obviously wrong cadential figure that Süssmayr gave to violin I in bar 13. The low C in bassoon II is, in addition, too obtrusive. It is probable that this repeat, plausible enough here but nonsensical in bars 31–3 (and impossible after bar 45) was Süssmayr's idea: perhaps he was thinking of bars 49–52 of 'O Isis und Osiris' in *Die Zauberflöte*? He seems to have liked echoing a final vocal phrase in the orchestra, for he did it also in bars 19–21 of the 'Lacrymosa'.

The section from bar 17 to bar 24 is rhythmically identical to bars 2–9. It starts and ends appropriately enough (Marguerre (p. 176) has surely misunderstood the key-scheme of this movement: his suggested replacement for bars 17–24, ending on the dominant of C minor, is not at all convincing), but goes very wrong in the middle. The chord on the third beat of bar 19 cannot be right: the *a* in the vocal bass produces an unresolved $^6_4$ as well as an awkward seventh leap (Marguerre, p. 176) and the unison between soprano and alto makes the worst possible approach to the hidden fifth in bar 20. Then the key of C major, to be used in bars 25–31, is firmly anticipated in bar 21 (Marguerre, p. 176). (Note the absence of triads in root position and the avoidance of F major in bars 5–8.) One is tempted to conjecture that, as in so many of Mozart's preliminary sketches,[2] there was a section missing here. On the other hand, the chord at the end of bar 19 is so pointlessly faulty that it is hard to see how even the most incompetent composer could have written it. Why on earth go to the trouble of moving the soprano down to *f'* and the bass up to *a* when the obvious procedure would have been to keep the soprano at *a'* and move the bass down to *d* in unison with the instrumental bass? A possible explanation, if it does not seem too far-fetched, is that Mozart's sketch continued, but was illegible in at least bar 19. Perhaps Süssmayr imagined that he could see the chord he supplied on the last beat of bar 19, and accepted it uncritically without considering whether it made sense?[3] Süssmayr's bad chord in bar 19 may therefore, paradoxically, be corroborative evidence for the existence of a Mozart sketch.

There seem to be no very close precedents for bars 25–31, although the figure used in the imitation is closer to the soprano in bar 11 of the 'Requiem aeternam' than was the soprano in bar 12, and bars 30–1 resemble a cadence in K 317 (Ex. 7.12). But it is

Ex. 7.12 K 317, Gloria, bars 34–6.

surely inconceivable that these bars are not genuine. They are a typically Mozartian 'expansion' of bars 10–14, and serve to reinforce the sense of resolution. Bars 10–14 were the perfect answer to bars 1–9, but were insufficient by themselves to resolve satisfactorily the long-range tension set up originally in the 'Requiem aeternam' and maintained throughout the work. The expanded answer creates much more of a feeling of repose, though without being over-conclusive, for after all there is still a repeat of the words and a whole final section to come. It is remarkable that these bars also act as a recapitulation and resolution of the final bars of the 'Quam olim Abrahae' fugue. The craftsmanship is impeccable, particularly in the handling of chromatic harmony with complete assurance and without the least trace of vulgarity. One might perhaps at first sight question the hidden fifth between soprano and bass in bar 30 (approached from a diminished fifth), particularly when Mozart normally preferred a hidden octave in this context. But it is hard to see how the progression could have been avoided, and there is in any case an excellent precedent in (where else?) the Gloria of K 220 (Ex. 7.13).

Ex. 7.13 K 220, Gloria, bars 50–3.

Bars 31–3 are another instrumental repeat of bars 11–13, now transposed to C major. They make no sense here, and may be confidently dismissed. Bars 34–41 again have the same rhythm as bars 2–9, and, like those bars, closely resemble part of the Gloria of K 220 (bars 53–7), transposed down a tone (Ex. 7.14). (Bars 53–5 in

Ex. 7.14

Ex. 7.14, remember, are almost identical at their original pitch with bars 2–4 of the Agnus Dei.) There is now a strong feeling, very much akin to that around bars 23–8 of the 'Hostias', that the music is heading for a flat major key, though just which one remains in doubt until the start of the 'Lux aeterna', where the answer is, of course, the same B flat major that took the place of the dominant in the 'second subject' of the 'Requiem aeternam', starting at bar 20. As before, the counterpoint is faultless: the resolution of the dominant seventh onto the $^6_4$ on the same bass is standard in Mozart (compare bars 5–6 of the 'Tuba mirum', or bar 35 of the 'Confutatis'), and the resulting doubled fourth on the last beat of

bar 39 even contrives to resolve simultaneously in bar 41 without consecutive octaves.

One slightly odd feature of the three settings of the same words in bars 2–9, 17–24, and 34–41 may be noticed: the top note of the phrase never occurs at quite the same point. But a glance at, say, the Agnus Dei of K 275 shows that no consistency is to be expected.

The key sequence from bar 41 onwards is quite remarkable in maintaining the uncertainty about the key aimed at for the 'Lux aeterna'. By analogy with bars 9–10 and 24–5, one would expect a bar's gap, and then 'dona eis requiem' in G flat major (this is a powerful reason why, *pace* Marguerre, bar 24 had to have the dominant of A minor). But the appearance of G flat major is delayed, by another typically Mozartian 'expansion', to bar 47, where it appears seemingly inevitably as an elaboration of a standard approach to a half close in B flat minor, in preparation for the B flat major of the next movement. Who else but Mozart could have devised such a deceptively simple conclusion, so obvious with hindsight, to a sequence of modulations that started in bar 38, where, it should be remembered, the Gloria of K 220 was still being quoted?

Since bar 41 continues without the expected change of key, no bar's gap is necessary this time. Bars 41–4 are an exact transposition up a fourth of bars 10–13, except for the alto and tenor on the last beat of bar 44, but lead now to an interrupted cadence in bars 44–5. This most surprising and inconclusive form of interrupted cadence, with the expected tonic triad replaced by the diminished seventh on IV$\sharp$, was used quite often by Mozart. It occurs in a very similar context in K 275 (Ex. 7.15). (This Agnus Dei seems to have been

Ex. 7.15 K 275, Agnus Dei, bars 23–4.

the model for bars 10–14, which have just been repeated.) The same interrupted cadence can be found in *Die Zauberflöte* (Ex. 7.16). It also occurs in *La clemenza di Tito* (Ex. 7.17). In each of these three

Ex. 7.16 K 620, Act II Finale, bars 347–8.

Ex. 7.17 K 621, Act I Finale, bars 151–2.

examples, however, the diminished seventh chord is in *root*
position, instead of the first inversion as in bar 45 of the Agnus Dei.
But in bar 58 of the Gloria of K 220 essentially the same
progression occurs in 'German sixth' form: the dominant seventh
in bar 57 (quoted in Ex. 7.14 as a precedent for bar 38 of the Agnus
Dei) is immediately followed by the German sixth on VIb.[5]
(Mozart explained to Attwood[6] that he regarded the German sixth
on VIb as 'the same chord' as the first inversion of the diminished
seventh on IV♯, but with the bass displaced a semitone downwards.) There has to be a good reason why the diminished seventh
in bar 45 is not in root position, which would have allowed a
complete chord on the last beat of bar 44 (compare Ex. 7.15). But if
the hint from K 220 is borne in mind, and the Gb expected in bar
42 but delayed to bar 47 is taken into account, bar 45 makes
perfectly good sense *provided the G in the bass is changed to a Gb*. In
this way bars 45–9 become another 'expansion', this time of the
identical German sixth on the last beat of bar 49. There is a very
similar progression, complete with the same unconventional
harmonization of the Neapolitan Cb, in bars 100–4 of the Adagio

of the Violin Sonata in E flat major K 481, which, transposed up a
tone and in outline, run as shown in Ex. 7.18.

Ex. 7.18.

A glance at any of Mozart's sketches, for example the single sheet
for the Requiem, shows that he almost always omitted clefs and
key-signatures, and very frequently accidentals, in rapid jottings
intended only for his own use. He might well, therefore, have
omitted the flat before the G in the bass in bar 45. Indeed,
Süssmayr's G♮ makes so little sense that, as in bar 19, the only
plausible explanation seems to be that he copied it from Mozart's
sketch without asking himself whether there was a missing flat.

There are two apparent oddities in the counterpoint in bars 44–5:
the dominant seventh at the end of bar 44 has no third, and soprano
and alto have a perfect fifth followed by a diminished fifth. But the
missing third is a necessary consequence of the choice of chord in
bar 45, and may be compared with the missing third in the second
diminished seventh chord in Ex. 7.15; in any case, Mozart seems to
have regarded a dominant chord with missing third as acceptable,
provided the seventh is present to prevent the sound of a bare fifth.
As for the fifths between soprano and alto, they are less
theoretically objectionable than the opposite progression that had
to be explained in bars 29–30, because there is no hidden fifth;
moreover they occur in exactly the same way, though between
soprano and bass, in Ex. 7.15. In any case, the harmonic ambiguity
of the German sixth chord makes it unclear whether the alto has *e'*
or *fb'*; in the latter case the interval between alto and soprano is an
augmented fourth rather than a diminished fifth.

Bars 46–51 continue the amazing modulation scheme to the half
close in B flat minor in preparation for the 'Lux aeterna', and so
perform the same function as the ends of the 'Rex tremendae' and
'Hostias', the resemblance to bars 46–53 of the 'Hostias' being
particularly striking. Note that bars 47–9 are an exact transposition
to G flat major of bars 17–19, and that the main Requiem theme has

not been lost sight of: both soprano and bass have inversions of its first half. Of course, we do not know for certain what key Mozart intended for the 'Lux aeterna', since the traditional version is only Süssmayr's makeshift repeat of part of the 'Requiem aeternam'. But it is difficult to see what would have been more appropriate than B flat major, which Mozart used consistently as a 'substitute dominant' in the Requiem, not only in the 'Requiem aeternam' itself but also in the 'Tuba mirum', which could be regarded as the 'second subject' of an overall sonata form for the whole Requiem. Moreover if bars 50–1 are accepted as genuine, it would follow anyway that Mozart intended the 'Lux aeterna' to be in B flat major. Perhaps Mozart himself suggested the repeat of part of the 'Requiem aeternam' as well as the Kyrie fugue?

One last possible objection might be that it is most unusual for a movement to start in one key (D minor), and then to abandon it permanently after only a few bars. Unusual, perhaps, but not unprecedented: the 'Rex tremendae' behaves in a similar way, as also does the Agnus Dei of K 192, which has already been cited as a model here (though admittedly there is a brief return to D minor at the end). In any case, the Agnus Dei should not be thought of as a self-contained movement, but as the start of a large-scale recapitulation that includes also the 'Lux aeterna' and 'Cum sanctis', in which there is such an extensive restatement of D minor that it would have been superfluous—indeed, premature—to dwell on that key in the Agnus Dei.

To sum up, then: the vocal parts throughout the Agnus Dei, apart from bars 19 to 21 or 22, are almost certainly genuine, as also are the outer string parts in bar 1. This much was probably contained, therefore, in a sketch amongst the papers that Constanze gave Süssmayr, which was illegible in bars 19–21, and omitted the flat in the bass in bar 45. Süssmayr very likely added bars 14–16 and 31–3, misread or otherwise bungled bars 19–22, and completed the orchestration using bar 1 as a model. If these contributions of Süssmayr's are removed, what remains is very nearly as complete as most of the movements in Mozart's autograph score, and in its masterly construction is fully worthy to stand beside them.

At this point the investigation of the authenticity of the 'doubtful' movements is complete. The 'Lacrymosa' completion and the whole of the Sanctus—'Osanna'—Benedictus sequence may be dismissed as spurious, but the Agnus Dei is very likely to be substantially genuine. Most of the rest of this book is concerned with the problems of restoration, and to provide a background for this work the next chapter surveys Mozart's models in writing the Requiem.

8
Mozart's Models for the Requiem

It was shown in the last chapter that Mozart apparently used parts of his earlier masses, particularly the Agnus Dei of K 192, the Gloria of K 220, and the Agnus Dei of K 275, as models for the Agnus Dei in the Requiem. Indeed, it has been known for some time that Mozart often needed the stimulus of other music to get himself started. Dent described in 1907 some of the earlier settings of the requiem that Mozart probably knew, and drew attention in particular to the unfinished Requiem in C minor by Florian Gassmann (1729–74),[1] which appears to have provided a model for Mozart's 'Requiem aeternam'. Certainly there is a striking resemblance between the two settings of the opening words 'Requiem aeternam dona eis Domine: et lux perpetua luceat eis'. Gassmann's version is shown in Ex. 8.1.

Ex. 8.1 Gassmann, 'Requiem aeternam', bars 15–32.

Other movements in the two Requiems, while having no apparent melodic material in common, are nevertheless quite closely related in their designs. Gassmann's 'Confutatis' is very similar to Mozart's, not only in its construction, but also in its forceful opening vocal phrase and its contrasting setting of 'voca me cum benedictis': see Ex. 8.2. (As in Mozart's 'Confutatis', these contrasting sections are then recapitulated in different keys.)

Nowak (1965), following Abert (ii, Noten–Beilagen, 50 ff.), has also pointed out some similarities with other works, for example the often-quoted resemblance between the subject of Mozart's Kyrie and the chorus 'And with his stripes' in Handel's *Messiah*. It is, perhaps, of rather greater significance that Mozart had himself used an almost identical fugue subject (in the same key of D minor) in 1780: see Ex. 8.3. Mozart had also previously used the main theme of the 'Requiem aeternam' itself: it is the chief subject (again in D minor) of the *Misericordias Domini*, which Mozart sent on 4 September 1776 to Padre Martini for his approval as a 'test piece in counterpoint' (Ex. 8.4). (Notice also the anticipation in the tenor of the soprano part in bar 11 of the 'Requiem aeternam', which is an important source for the Agnus Dei.)

Ex. 8.2 Gassmann, 'Confutatis', bars 12–26.

Ex. 8.3 K 339, 'Laudate pueri', bars 1–9.

Ex. 8.4 K 222, bars 3–6.

Nowak has also drawn attention to the 'Te decet hymnus' in the 'Requiem aeternam' of Michael Haydn's Requiem in C minor. Haydn's setting uses the first phrase of the same plainsong melody (the Tonus Peregrinus) as Mozart's: see Ex. 8.5. It is interesting

Ex. 8.5 M. Haydn, 'Requiem aeternam', bars 26–8.

that Haydn liked this theme enough to use it again for his Benedictus (Ex. 8.6). Once again, though, the best precedent is in Mozart himself, for, as Abert (i: 288 f. and ii: 859) pointed out, it is used as a cantus firmus in *Betulia liberata* (1771): see Ex. 8.7.

Haydn's 'Requiem aeternam' resembles Mozart's in other ways: the first entry of the voices, though thematically different (or is it?—notice the tenor part), is very similar in effect, even to the accompaniment rhythm (Ex. 8.8). Moreover Haydn's setting of 'et lux perpetua' is if anything more like Mozart's than was Gass-mann's (Ex. 8.9).

Ex. 8.6 M. Haydn, Benedictus, bars 14–20.

Ex. 8.7 K 118, 'Lodi al gran Dio', bars 6–15.

Ex. 8.8 M. Haydn, 'Requiem aeternam', bars 11–15.

Ex. 8.9 M. Haydn, 'Requiem aeternam', bars 18–23.

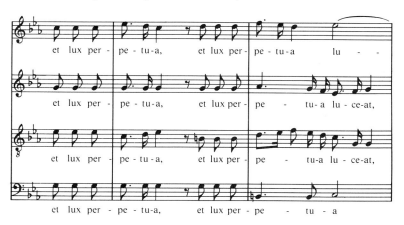

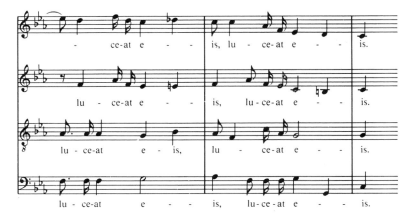

Haydn's Sequence, which he set as one continuous, almost monothematic movement, bears little resemblance to Mozart's more extensive treatment. In the 'Domine Jesu', however, the similarities are again quite striking. Haydn's settings of 'Rex gloriae' (Ex. 8.10), 'et de profundo lacu' (Ex. 8.11), and 'de ore leonis' (Ex. 8.12)—repeated a bar later, transposed up a minor third—are sufficiently similar to Mozart's to need no further comment, while the energetic 'ne absorbeat eas tartarus' and succeeding 'ne cadant in obscurum', although based on a different fugue subject, are obviously aiming at the same effect as Mozart's (Ex. 8.13).

Ex. 8.10 M. Haydn, 'Domine Jesu', bars 1–2.

Ex. 8.11 M. Haydn, 'Domine Jesu', bars 8–13.

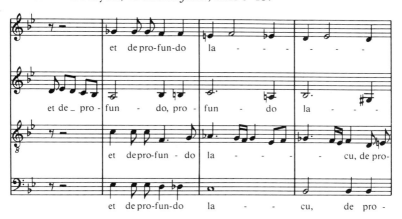

Ex. 8.12 M. Haydn, 'Domine Jesu', bars 16–17.

Ex. 8.13 M. Haydn, 'Domine Jesu', bars 20–32.

Moreover Haydn's 'Quam olim Abrahae' fugue subject (Ex. 8.14) is not unlike Mozart's. (The end of this fugue has already been

Ex. 8.14 M. Haydn, 'Domine Jesu', bars 49–55.

quoted as a precedent for the final bars of Mozart's: see Ex. 5.1.)
His 'Cum sanctis' subject, too, is not unfamiliar (Ex. 8.15).

Ex. 8.15

More surprisingly, it seems quite possible that Mozart also knew
the Requiem in F minor by Heinrich Biber (1644–1704).[2] This was
written towards the end of the seventeenth century, apparently for
Salzburg Cathedral, and may have been given an occasional
performance in Mozart's time, for there are similarities between
Biber's and Mozart's settings that seem too close for mere
coincidence. Biber's 'Quam olim Abrahae' fugue (Ex. 8.16) has the
same subject as Mozart's 'Requiem aeternam'. The two settings of
'ne cadant' in the 'Domine Jesu' are strikingly similar: Mozart's
bars 29–30 should be compared with Biber's version (Ex. 8.17). It
might, perhaps, be fanciful to find a precursor of Mozart's 'statuens
in parte dextra' ('Recordare') in Biber's (Ex. 8.18), but the latter's
'Oro supplex et acclinis' seems definitely to be aiming at the same
sort of striking harmonic effect as Mozart's (Ex. 8.19). Perhaps the
most remarkable of all is the similarity between Biber's setting of
the 'Lacrymosa' (Ex. 8.20) and both subject and countersubject of
Mozart's 'Amen' sketch. The resemblance is even more striking
with Mozart's first version of his countersubject (Ex. 8.21) which
he afterwards altered[3] to Ex. 8.22. (Mozart's 'Amen' subject is, of
course, the inversion of the main theme of the 'Requiem aeternam';
in Biber's Requiem this 'inverted' version occurs before its
appearance the other way up in the 'Quam olim Abrahae'.)

Ex. 8.16 Biber, 'Domine Jesu', bars 54–9.

Ex. 8.17 Biber, 'Domine Jesu', bars 33–6.

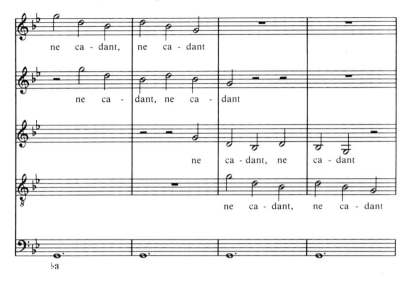

Ex. 8.18 Biber, 'Dies irae', bars 124–7.

Ex. 8.19 Biber, 'Dies irae', bars 131–5.

Ex. 8.20 Biber, 'Dies irae', bars 135–44.

Ex. 8.21

Ex. 8.22

Finally, there is another precedent for 'Oro supplex et acclinis', this time in Mozart's own *Regina coeli* (Ex. 8.23). It is quite remarkable that, probably twelve years before the Requiem, Mozart should have set very similar words in almost the same way, even to the orchestral accompaniment that he for once indicated fully in his incomplete score of the Requiem. The sustained woodwind, entering only with the voices and silent in the first bar, is worth especial notice, not least because Süssmayr so misunderstood Mozart's orchestration at the corresponding point in the Requiem that he added an extra bar of woodwind before the chorus entry.

Ex. 8.23 K 276, bars 68–76.

9

Some Notes on Mozart's Orchestration

This is clearly not the place for a comprehensive study of Mozart's orchestration. But it is an essential preliminary exercise, for work on those movements in the Requiem where Mozart wrote little more than the vocal parts and figured bass, to study the instrumentation of *Die Zauberflöte, La clemenza di Tito,* and *Eine kleine Freymaurer-Kantate,* in order to learn as much as possible about Mozart's methods, specifically when writing for voices and orchestra in 1791. This is not only because of a wish to make the new orchestration as 'correct' as possible in style, but also because, from what is now known about Mozart's working methods,[1] his autograph of the Requiem was in no sense a preliminary sketch or draft, but represents an unfortunately incomplete stage in the writing out of the final score. The orchestration of these movements ought therefore to be regarded less as an exercise in creative imagination than as an attempt to deduce, from the state of the autograph and from parallel passages in other comparable works of the time, what Mozart had already worked out in detail but had not yet committed to paper. In support of this point it is very instructive to compare the incomplete autograph (for basset–horn in G) with the final version of the first movement of the Clarinet Concerto K 622.[2] Mozart apparently altered nothing in the solo or bass parts (apart from the transposition), which strongly suggests that the earlier version was already virtually complete in his mind: for if he had not thought about the orchestration until writing out the later version, he would surely have had to make a few consequential alterations to the existing parts.[3]

Of course, the 'Requiem aeternam' is in some ways the best source of all, but it is insufficient by itself to solve all the problems that arise in orchestrating the following movements. In any case, it provides the best possible check that the principles deduced from other works still apply to the Requiem. For this reason a detailed analysis of the 'Requiem aeternam' is postponed to Chapter 10.

A glance at almost any Mozart score quickly shows that the orchestration often arises naturally from the harmony. Mozart is very careful to ensure that the harmony is always complete, and this principle will often fix the shape and the number of inner parts. For example, in the standard cadence V7–I, *five* parts are usually necessary to make both chords complete (Ex. 9.1). Hence the violas must be divided, or there has to be an extra wind part, normally for bassoon since it has the most appropriate range for an inner part. A good example of such an added bassoon part occurs in 'Se all' impero' in K 621 (Ex. 9.2); observe also how, to avoid a sudden increase in the number of parts, the bassoon has been doubling the bass for the last four bars. Occasionally, however, a dominant seventh may have no fifth, or—more rarely—no third, for example in the progression $\frac{7}{5} \frac{6}{4} \frac{5}{3}$ over the dominant. The same principle of completeness of the harmony means that string arpeggio patterns must be very carefully fitted, as for example in Ex. 9.3.

Ex. 9.1

Ex. 9.2 K 621, 'Se all'impero', bars 25–31.

Ex. 9.3 K 621, 'S'altro che lacrime', bars 17–20.

Other essentially harmonic rules determine the layout of some chords. Mozart is clearly not fond of the sound of a fifth (or fourth, for that matter) between a pair of identical instruments, unless it is approached by oblique motion, or unless it is unavoidable on brass instruments because of the limited range of notes available. Thus woodwind pairs nearly always avoid fifths or fourths, and in a common version of the standard $\frac{6}{4}\frac{5}{3}$ cadence the violin II and viola parts cross so that the violins can move in sixths, as in Ex. 9.4. Crossings of violin II and viola occur also in other places, to avoid fifths or fourths between the violin parts. Again, in a diminished seventh chord (and to some extent in other chords) Mozart never doubles the bass in a higher octave unless this is absolutely unavoidable on a brass instrument: the 'Donner, Blitz, Sturm' chord at bar 807 of the Act II Finale of K 620 is noteworthy in being laid out for full orchestra in twenty parts; the bass note (B♭) is given to cellos and basses, timpani, bass trombone, and horn II, but to no higher instrument except trumpet I. It should also be noted that the bass in this chord is given only to strings, brass, and timpani, not woodwind: nearly all the chords in the 'Ah che tumulto orrendo!' section of the Act I Finale of K 621 are laid out in this way.

Ex. 9.4 K 623, 'Lange sollen diese Mauern', bar 7.

Some other miscellaneous harmonic points are the following.

1. Dissonant passing notes are nearly always classifiable as some form of seventh (occasionally ninth) chord, often with a diatonic semitone clash, and are usually associated with a moving viola part: see Exx. 9.5 and 9.6, and, of course, bars 7–12 of the 'Recordare'.

Ex. 9.5 K 621, 'S'altro che lacrime', bar 34.

Ex. 9.6 K 623, 'Dieser Gottheit Allmacht ruhet', bar 43.

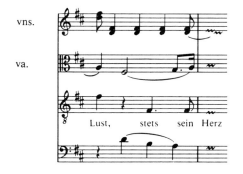

2. Appoggiaturas in a solo part (but not suspensions) may sometimes have their resolution anticipated if the accompaniment rhythm makes this necessary, as in Exx. 9.7 and 9.8. But if possible the clash is avoided, for example by omitting the first beat of the bar (Ex. 9.9), or by omitting the third of a dominant seventh (Ex. 9.10).

Ex. 9.7 K 620, 'Dies Bildnis ist bezaubernd schön', bar 10.

vns.

va.

Herz _____ mit neu -

Ex. 9.8 K 621, 'Ah grazie si rendano', bars 40–2.

vns.

vas.

se in   Ro - ma il   mio fa - to   si

Ex. 9.9 K 621, Act I Finale, bar 10.

vns.

va.

- cor,   coi

Ex. 9.10 K 620, Act I Finale, bar 403.

Mohr ver-lang-te

3. Orchestral parts may be freely doubled at the unison or octave, and even 'casual' consecutive octaves are acceptable between, say, viola and bass, or between a string and a wind instrument (Ex. 9.11). On the other hand consecutive fifths are

Ex. 9.11 K 620, 'Zu Hilfe! zu Hilfe!', bar 13.

bns.

va.

very rare indeed. In particular, a sequence of fourths cannot be doubled in another octave: this accounts for the different viola parts in bars 2 and 10 of 'Laut verkünde unsre Freude' in K 623 (Ex. 9.12): it will be seen that, if the violas in bar 10 were to double the second tenors at the octave, they would be in consecutive fifths with the first tenors. It must be admitted that Mozart very occasionally violates this rule in the case of a *solo* tenor part, which he perhaps regarded as sounding an octave higher than its actual pitch: see Ex. 9.13, where strictly speaking violin II is in consecutive fifths with the solo tenor. No doubt the fifths between violin II and bassoon I in bar 20 of the 'Requiem aeternam' may be similarly explained.

Ex. 9.12

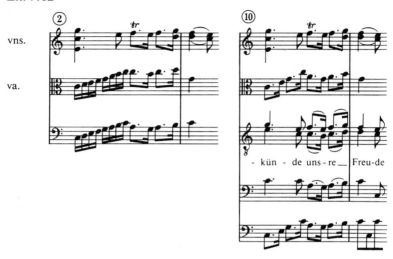

Ex. 9. 13 K 623, 'Lange sollen diese Mauern', bar 53.

4. A German sixth is frequently associated with a moving violin II part, and if it is followed by a dominant triad, then to avoid

consecutive fifths with the bass the German sixth must first be substituted by a plain Italian sixth (Ex. 9.14).

Ex. 9.14 K 621, Act I Finale, bars 44–5.

5. Mozart's treatment of 'false relations' is different from that recommended by most harmony textbooks. He seems on the whole to prefer to put a chromatically altered note in a *different* part, if possible with a short gap in which neither version of the note is heard (Ex. 9.15). However, this gap is apparently unnecessary if the chromatically altered note is part of a diminished seventh chord, as in Ex. 9.16.

Ex. 9.15 K 620, 'Du feines Täubchen', bars 13–14.

Ex. 9.16 K 620, 'Dies Bildnis ist bezaubernd schön', bar 32.

Some of Mozart's other, non-harmonic, principles in writing for different groups of instruments are worth particular notice. Strings are often used for more-or-less standardized accompaniment patterns (for example at the beginning of the 'Requiem aeternam'), which tend to be the more elaborate as the harmony becomes the more static, but are never, of course, used mechanically. Each such pattern has its own characteristic bass rhythm, and if the bass changes then so does the overall pattern (this observation is particularly helpful in completing the 'Tuba mirum': see Chapter 13). Strings are by no means always in four real parts, and in rapid forte passages are usually in only two. At other times the violas may double the bass, either at the unison or in octaves; on the other hand to keep the harmony complete it may be necessary to divide the violas (more rarely the second violins) for a few notes. This use of divided violas should be distinguished from the (comparatively rare) use of divided violas to double violin thirds or sixths at the lower octave, in which case the violas will probably be divided for most of the movement (Ex. 9.17). Divided violas may also be used

Ex. 9.17 K 620, Act II Finale, bars 252–6.

vns.

vas.

Wohl dir,   nun   kann sie mit dir gehn!   nun

tren - net euch kein Schick - sal __   mehr,

for long sustained notes (Ex. 9.8), though such sustained notes are just as often not divided, and in any case seem to be inappropriate near the beginning of a movement. Violin chords of up to four parts are common, though Mozart is always careful to allow sufficient time for recovery of the bow afterwards. The two violin parts either have the same chord or, more frequently, are 'dovetailed', so that the harmony is still complete when the violins are left holding the top one or two notes of their chords (Ex. 9.18). In fact Mozart seems to expect only the top note to be held in any but a short chord unless the notation explicitly specifies the contrary, as in Ex. 9.19. The violas are almost never given chords

Ex. 9.18 K 623, final bar.

Ex. 9.19 K 621, Act I Finale, bar 152.

of more than two notes, and the cellos never have chords at all. A final but important principle of Mozart's string writing, which also applies to some extent to wind, is that, when accompanying a chorus and on the face of it merely doubling them, there will be many minor rhythmic or melodic variations between the vocal and the string parts, and in particular the strings will have their own characteristic layout. A good example of this is provided by Ex. 9.20.

Ex. 9.20 K 621, 'Ah grazie si rendano', bars 22–6.

A few principles of Mozart's wind layout have already been noted. Unlike the strings, however, wind chords are not always complete, and may have the fifth or even the bass missing (to allow high bassoons, for example), if this is present in the strings. There will commonly be just one pair in thirds, or more frequently two pairs doubling the thirds at the octave (in which case sevenths of chords and leading notes are freely doubled). Woodwind 'dovetailing' is very rare, though is occasionally used for special effect, as in Ex. 9.21. Mozart's normal procedure in a full wind chord is to have the second of each pair in unison with the first of the next lower pair (Ex. 9.22). However, brass are sometimes dovetailed *with*

Ex. 9.21 K 620, 'O Isis und Osiris', bars 12–15.

Ex. 9.22 K 620, 'O Isis und Osiris', bars 1–4.

woodwind, as in Ex. 9.23, or, more rarely, with each other, as in Ex. 9.24. There are not nearly so many standardized accompaniment patterns for wind as there are for strings, but a version of a

Ex. 9.23 'Requiem aeternam', bar 43.

Ex. 9.24 K 620, Act I Finale, bars 1–5.

common cadence nearly always has two bars of sustained harmony (Ex. 9.25). If this cadence is approached via a sequence of suspensions and resolutions, these, too, are likely to be sustained by woodwind (Ex. 9.26). In other similar places sustained woodwind

Ex. 9.25 K 621, 'Se a volto mai ti senti', bars 18–20.

Ex. 9.26 K 621, 'Deh si piacer mi vuoi', bars 40–4.

sto du - bi - tar.

may be used; or they may be added only for a bar or two to reinforce a climax or particular harmonic point, as in Ex. 9.27. Woodwind instruments are frequently used to double solo voices for quite long stretches, although more often than not in a different octave, especially if the voice is doubled at the unison by strings (a solo tenor counting as sounding an octave higher): see Ex. 9.28. On the other hand, a voice may be doubled by several wind instruments in various octaves for just a few bars. This sort of 'multiple doubling' appears to have a definitely structural purpose, for it normally happens only at the end of a section, as in Ex. 9.29.

A few miscellaneous points concerning particular wind instruments (and timpani) are the following.

1. Basset-horns cannot articulate very crisply, so that other instruments must be added to provide rhythmic point (Ex. 9.30). Indeed, it is remarkable that in K 620 basset-horns are almost never heard by themselves, but are used almost exclusively for their blending qualities.

2. Bassoons are often used to double the violas, or of course to provide an extra inner part. They are also used, almost without exception, to support the cellos when the double basses are silent.

Ex. 9.27 K 621, 'Tu fosti tradito', bars 27–9.

Ex. 9.28 K 623, 'Lange sollen diese Mauern', bars 9–12.

Ex. 9.29 K 621, 'Non più di fiori', bars 25–8.

fl.

basset-
horn in F

bn.

vns.

va.

veg - - go la mor - - te ___ ver me a - van - zar.

Ex. 9.30 K 620, Act I Finale, bar 400.

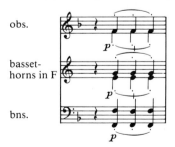

obs.

basset-
horns in F

bns.

3. Trumpets are hardly ever used melodically, even when this would be easily possible. A good example occurs in Ex. 9.31.

Ex. 9.31 K 620, Act I Finale, bars 374–6.

Es   le - be Sa-ra - stro, Sa - ra - stro soll le - ben!

Indeed, it is rare for trumpets to be sustained, except occasionally piano, so that they are quite likely to be given crotchets and crochet rests when most other instruments have minims: see Ex. 9.32.

4. If trombones are used to support the chorus (the normal procedure in eighteenth-century Austrian church music), then unlike other instruments they usually double the chorus exactly, their parts normally not being written out but indicated merely by 'trombone colla parte' or words to that effect. Occasionally, though, they have independent parts, for example in bars 143–5 and 149–51 of the Act I Finale of K 620, and now and again in the C minor Mass K 427. They also tend to be used independently (if they are used at all) with *solo* voices, and then the bass trombone is usually kept fairly low. The 'edge' may be taken off their tone by adding basset-horns, violas, or bassoons in unison, as in Ex. 9.33.

5. Timpani do not necessarily have to accompany the trumpets, but either instruments may be used separately for special effect, or because only the trumpets can play any of the notes of the chord. Rolls are rare, and generally rhythms are kept pretty simple. The end of K 621 (Ex. 9.34) has about as elaborate a part as can be found in Mozart.

Ex. 9.32 K 621, 'Che del ciel, che degli Dei', bars 6–7.

Ex. 9.33 K 620, 'O Isis und Osiris', bars 52–5.

Ex. 9.34 K 621, Act II Finale, bars 107–19.

Finally, a few points about Mozart's writing for full orchestra. A chord with a large gap between high and low wind instruments is acceptable, provided the gap is bridged by strings, often with (dovetailed) double stopping, as in Ex. 9.35. Treatment of repeats varies: a full recapitulation may be more-or-less exact, but if only a few bars are repeated, particularly if there is a change in dynamics, Mozart will normally take care to vary the instrumentation. Compare, for example, the two extracts from K 620 shown in Ex. 9.36. Nothing is ever done mechanically: Mozart clearly gave much thought to every note in every part, so that there will

Ex. 9.35 K 620, 'Dies Bildnis ist bezaubernd schön', bar 9.

Ex. 9.36 K 620, Act II Finale, (a) bars 330–2.

(b) bars 339–41.

continually be subtle modifications of the 'obvious' textures to achieve the best possible effect. Examples where the orchestra appears to be doubling the chorus have already been noted; but there are many other instances. A very instructive example is provided by the opening tutti of K 623, where violins I and II are in unison throughout the first five bars, except for just three notes in bars 2 and 3 where they diverge to make a four-part string chord at the start of bar 3. Sometimes Mozart almost imperceptibly transforms one texture into another, or exchanges instruments as if by magic. Some of the best examples are in K 621: for instance the almost undetectable substitution of viola for violin II in Ex. 9.37, or the extraordinary gradual metamorphosis of the accompaniment texture in Ex. 9.38.

Ex. 9.37 K 621, 'Ah perdona al primo affetto', bars 27–8.

- cen - ti del   mio   be - ne.

Ex. 9.38 K 621, 'Se all'impero', bars 91–7.

10

The 'Requiem aeternam'

This is the only movement in the whole of the Requiem that was quite certainly completely finished by Mozart himself. Before starting the reconstruction work on the incomplete parts, therefore, it is very helpful to analyse this movement in detail, to study the counterpoint carefully, but most of all to check that the orchestration is consistent with the principles established in Chapter 9.

The seven bars of orchestral introduction consist of a fugal exposition of the main theme on the four woodwind instruments, with an extra bar leading to the chorus entry. Meanwhile the strings, to point the rhythm, have one of Mozart's favourite accompaniment patterns. A particular problem posed by the choice of instruments in the Requiem is that, without the oboes of Mozart's 'normal' orchestra, there is no woodwind instrument capable of a crisp attack, and therefore the rhythm can be articulated clearly only by the strings (or trumpets and drums where their use is otherwise appropriate). Mozart characteristically turns this deficiency into a virtue, for the offbeat string rhythm becomes one of the most seminal ideas throughout the whole of the Requiem, and is subjected to all sorts of subtle variations, such as the figure ♪♫ in bars 8–14. The strings are in four parts throughout, this being maintained in bar 7 by giving double stopping to violin II when viola doubles the bass. The brass and drums are reserved to give maximum weight to the cadence into bar 8.

In bars 8–14 the chorus start with a fugal exposition similar to that in bars 1–5, though the entries are closer together and there is a longer continuation, in which the theme is first heard inverted (alto, bars 12–13) and retrograde (bass, bar 13). The woodwind double the chorus, though with a smoother rhythm: for the difference between, say, a crotchet and two repeated quavers on a basset-horn would be inaudible here. The strings are now in only two parts, since anything more elaborate would be lost against the chorus. Observe that the violins have what amounts to a fifth free contrapuntal part. Trumpets and drums are again reserved for the cadence, but this time are more elaborate than before. Notice that there is no C♮ anywhere in the orchestra on the fourth beat of bar 14 (despite the figuring), in accordance with Mozart's normal treatment of 'false relations'.

Bars 15–16 substitute an antiphonal homophonic exchange between chorus and woodwind for the previous four- or five-part counterpoint, as a result of which the chorus is unaccompanied for part of each bar. Once again the lack of clear articulation in basset-horns and bassoons is compensated for by the strings, now playing unison arpeggios (note the staccato markings). Bars 17–19 continue in the same vein, although the strings have now reverted to the accompaniment pattern of bars 1–7, but with added woodwind chords when appropriate to the dynamics, and a slightly more elaborate rhythm at the cadence. The woodwind in bars 18 and 19 have fragments derived from the main theme or its inversion. Two small subtleties should be noted: in the second half of bar 17 bassoon I stops doubling basset-horn I at the octave in order to support the cellos while the basses are silent; and bassoons are used to sustain the harmony in bar 18 (the violins are therefore kept low on the first two beats) because the basset-horns take over in bar 19 (in contrast to bar 1): this in turn is because the bassoons are wanted in bar 20 to double the violins. (This doubling, as noted in Chapter 9, produces consecutive fifths between violin II and bassoon I in bar 20.)

Bars 20–6 consist of a five-part contrapuntal passage involving much imitation (sometimes with inversion) at different intervals. The material appears at first sight to be new, but in fact the violin I part in bar 20 is derived from the inversion of the main theme, put into the major, so that when re-inverted as in bar 21 it becomes simply a major version of the original theme. The soprano cantus firmus is a version of the Tonus Peregrinus (Ex. 10.1, quoted from the *Liber usualis*). It will be noticed that Mozart has slightly altered this melody so that it contains, in bars 22–3, a strict inversion of the main theme of the Requiem. Notice that the characteristic string

Ex. 10.1

In   e- xi -tu Is - ra - el de Ae - gy -pto   do-mus Ja-cob de po-pu-lo bar-ba-ro. _

accompaniment pattern in bar 19 is 'smoothed out' into the violin II part in bar 20. From bar 26 to bar 31 there is a different setting of the same cantus firmus, with added vocal parts. As in bars 8–14, the strings have what amount to independent contrapuntal parts, but the more transparent vocal writing now allows four-part strings, so that the resulting texture is in seven real parts almost throughout. As always, the balance is very carefully judged: the sopranos are doubled by both basset-horns in unison, who as usual have a slightly more sustained version of the theme.

Bars 32–3 are a repeat in the minor (complete with fifths between violin II and bassoon I) of bars 19–20, with an added bassoon part in bar 32. A characteristic example of Mozart's great care for detail occurs in bar 32, where basset-horn II has a quaver rest to take a breath, while basset-horn I sustains a full crotchet before his crotchet rest. (This looks like an afterthought on Mozart's part, for in the autograph the tail of the quaver and the quaver rest in basset-horn II appear to be later additions.)

In bars 34–42 there is a recapitulation of bars 8–14, now in the form of a double-fugue exposition, the countersubject being an extension in the minor of the violin I figure in bar 20, which was itself derived by inversion from the main theme. The alto part in bars 34–5 thus combines successively the inverted, retrograde, and original versions of the subject. The violin accompaniment pattern of bars 8–14 is used again, but with the octaves the other way up, until the end of bar 36, by which time the bass can no longer continue in even crotchets, and anyway the contrapuntal texture has become so dense that a fifth part would be difficult to follow. The strings then double the voices, but with the rhythm characteristically broken up (in contrast to the woodwind instruments' smoother version). Small points worth particular notice are that only bassoon II doubles the basses in bars 34–5 (unlike bars 37–8) since bassoon I needs a rest; the violas have an independent part during the tenor rests in bars 37, 40, and 41; and in bars 40–1, where the soprano part is too high for basset-horn I, that instrument changes to the alto part while basset-horn II goes with the tenors (in unison with bassoon I).

Bars 43–4 correspond to bars 15–16, but the layout of the antiphonal parts is different. Since the strings are consequently not available to reinforce the articulation in the first half of each bar, their function is taken over by trumpets and drums. Notice the careful balancing of the full wind chords, with no doubling by the woodwind of the trumpet notes.

Finally, bars 45–8 form a coda leading to the Kyrie. As before the material is derived from the main theme, mostly by retrograde motion. The orchestra more-or-less doubles the voices, though as usual the strings have a more broken rhythm and the woodwind are smoother. The violin II and viola parts cross in bar 45 to prepare for Mozart's standard string layout (different from the choral layout) of the $^6_4$ $^5_3$ half close in bar 46. Note the characteristic trumpet and drum rhythm, and also that the woodwind play continuously in bar 45 so as to sustain the harmony. Although the woodwind are dropped at the piano marking in bar 46, the trumpets and drums are brought back in bar 48, as at other important cadences. Here, however, the trumpets have (very rare) sustained notes, to keep them quiet, and the drum part is carefully judged to point the rhythm without being too fussy.

11
The Orchestration of the Kyrie

Until recently it was taken for granted that the orchestral parts in the original manuscript of the Kyrie were written by Mozart himself: see for example Nowak (1965). However, serious doubts were later expressed, first by Beyer,[1] and afterwards by the editor of the Neue Mozart Ausgabe edition of the Requiem himself, Nowak (1973–4).

Beyer argues that examination of the handwriting in the orchestral parts shows it to be Süssmayr's, not Mozart's; this hypothesis is supported by the wrong accidentals in the basset-horns (flat and natural signs are used consistently in front of each f'', instead of naturals and sharps respectively), and by a few passages which Beyer says are uncharacteristic of Mozart, such as the consecutive octaves between basset-horn I and tenors in bar 41, the wrong notes in the trumpets and drums on the sixth quaver of bar 42, and the reduction of the woodwind to only three parts in bars 50–2. Nowak examines the handwriting again, and concludes that only the trumpet and drum parts were written by Süssmayr, the other orchestral parts being in the hand of F. J. Freystädtler.[2]

Nowak's argument about the handwriting seems reasonably convincing in the case of the trumpet and drum parts, though he perhaps attaches too much weight to the irregular placing of semibreve rests, for although they are certainly characteristic of Süssmayr they occur also in the autograph of the 'Requiem aeternam', where, although they might conceivably have been filled in by Süssmayr in bars left blank by Mozart, they are much more likely to have been written by Mozart himself. Nowak's case for Freystädtler is based on the shape of the natural signs, whose right-hand vertical stroke ends with a hook at the bottom: ♮. Mozart's usual natural sign is written with just three more-or-less straight pen-strokes ♮, and Süssmayr's with two L-shaped strokes: ♮; but the version with the lower right-hand hook is shown by Nowak to be characteristic of Freystädtler. However, neither Mozart nor Süssmayr is quite so consistent in this matter as Nowak suggests, for the facsimiles in the Neue Mozart Ausgabe edition of the Requiem[3] show that both of them occasionally used Freystädtler's form of natural sign (see for example Kyrie, bar 50, alto; and particularly 'Domine Jesu', bars 72–3, instrumental bass). Even if it is accepted that the handwriting is unlikely to be Mozart's, it is surely too much to identify Freystädtler with confidence merely from the shape of the natural signs.

It is difficult to imagine Mozart making mistakes in the accidentals in the basset-horn parts, but Beyer's conclusion that Süssmayr wrote them is questionable for two reasons, quite apart from Nowak's Freystädtler theory. First, the facsimiles in the Neue Mozart Ausgabe show that Süssmayr did not normally make such mistakes. Secondly, whoever wrote these parts knew that the effective upper limit of the basset-horn range was (written) d'''; on the other hand it is clear from bar 7 of the 'Dies irae' that when Süssmayr was orchestrating that movement he thought d''' was too high. It is puzzling that whoever wrote these parts apparently knew more about the basset-horn than Süssmayr did, and yet was capable of making elementary mistakes in transposition. It should be remembered, though, that eighteenth-century musicians were familiar with a wide variety of C-clefs, and so when writing out a part for basset-horn in F they would probably have mentally substituted the mezzo-soprano for the treble clef, rather than literally have calculated a transposition of a fifth. In the mezzo-soprano clef the top line represents b', not f'', so it would make sense to use naturals and flats instead of sharps and naturals respectively. Thus the consistently wrong accidentals can be explained as a minor oversight attributable to almost anyone, and do not necessarily imply that the scribe was musically illiterate.

The 'uncharacteristic' passages noted by Beyer are, with the exception of the wrong notes in the trumpets and drums in bar 42, perhaps not as uncharacteristic as he thinks. The consecutive octaves between basset-horn I and the tenors in bar 41 are surely excusable as being the same sort of 'casual' octaves as those for example (admittedly by contrary motion) between voice and viola in Ex. 11.1. Moreover the reduction of the woodwind to three parts in bars 50–2 cannot be ascribed to the incompetence of a beginner, who would surely have continued the 'obvious' doubling of the altos by basset-horn II. The layout here, on the contrary, is the result of careful balancing of the parts, for the alto a' is already doubled by trumpet I, so there would have been no point in giving

Ex. 11.1 K 621, 'Ah perdona al primo affetto', bar 11.

that note also to the relatively inaudible basset-horn II. The layout also avoids a bare fourth between the basset-horns in the final chord. As noted in Chapter 9, it is very characteristic of Mozart to make minor variations like these in instrumental parts that at first sight appear merely to be doubling the chorus.

Beyer did not comment on the occasional too-literal doubling of vocal parts, as for example basset-horn I in bar 32, which ought according to Mozart's normal practice to have a smoother rhythm, or violin II in bar 43, which should obviously have the original version of the theme, like the instrumental bass in bar 39. There are also bad consecutive octaves between basset-horn I and bassoon I in bars 48–9 (rather reminiscent of Süssmayr's *Ave verum corpus*).

There can be little doubt, then, that the orchestral parts are not in Mozart's handwriting, and there are certainly places where the craftsmanship is faulty. The accompaniment could therefore all be dismissed as spurious were it not for two nagging doubts.

The first doubt concerns the timing: since Constanze gave the incomplete autograph to Eybler on 21 December 1791, and passed it to Süssmayr only after Eybler had abandoned work on it, why did Eybler make no attempt at orchestrating the Kyrie? (The parts are certainly not in Eybler's handwriting.) If Eybler had all of Mozart's autograph from Constanze, he surely would not have started work only at the 'Dies irae' unless the Kyrie had already been completed. Possibly Constanze did not give him the first two movements—but what reason could there have been for this omission, other than that all the parts had already been filled in? In either case, how did it come about that the Kyrie was complete only sixteen days after Mozart's death?

The second doubt concerns the layout of the wind instruments in bars 50–2. As discussed above, the balance appears carefully considered; moreover the decision to put basset-horn II in unison with bassoon I depends on, and hence must have been taken after, the decision to use trumpet I to double the altos. It follows that the trumpet and drum parts must have been filled in (by Süssmayr?) *before* the other wind and string parts (by Freystädtler, according to Nowak's theory). What is the explanation of this apparently perverse order of working?

It is possible to invent two hypotheses to explain these difficulties, but neither can be supported by positive evidence, and neither of them seems entirely plausible. It may be that the Kyrie was still incomplete on 21 December 1791, but Constanze did not give it to Eybler, perhaps simply by oversight, or because she had not yet noticed that the first 'signature', besides the 'Requiem aeternam', contained a movement that was not fully orchestrated. Then Süssmayr later completed this movement as well as the others. This explanation would at least make the layout in bars 50–2 the work of one man, but would require Nowak's theory to be wrong, and also that, when Süssmayr got to the 'Dies irae', he realized his mistake about the accidentals (credible enough) but forgot how high a basset-horn could play (less plausible). (Unless, just conceivably, Süssmayr asked Freystädtler to give him some help with his work.) It also requires Constanze to have acted with apparently uncharacteristic carelessness.

Alternatively, Mozart might, during his last illness when he was physically incapable of writing, have asked Freystädtler and Süssmayr to fill in the orchestral parts in the Kyrie: could such an instruction to Süssmayr have been what Constanze was referring to in her letter to Breitkopf and Härtel of 2 March 1799 (quoted in Chapter 2), when she said that Mozart had told Süssmayr 'how he should finish off where the important ideas were already worked out here and there in the parts'? Possibly Süssmayr and Freystädtler carried out this task more-or-less under Mozart's supervision, but he was too ill to notice their occasional mistakes. This could explain the good orchestral balance in bars 50–2 as being Mozart's idea, even if the parts were written by two different scribes. It is perhaps surprising also that, although Mozart must surely have continued to think about the Requiem during his final illness,[4] there is no other evidence of his having dictated anything to an amanuensis. On the other hand it must be admitted that this hypothesis seems rather far-fetched; it would imply, incidentally, that some of Süssmayr's work actually pre-dates Eybler's.

In preparing the new edition, fortunately, such speculations have few practical implications, since it is reasonably clear that the orchestra should double the chorus, with occasional minor variations as necessary. The new string and woodwind parts are very similar to those in the traditional version, including the layout in bars 50–2. However, all slurs have been omitted since Mozart wrote none in the instrumental bass part, even in such places as bar 33 where there is a slur between two syllables in the tenor part; and Mozart's staccato quavers in the bass in bar 17 have been copied wherever this figure occurs. In bars 14 and 50 Mozart wrote a plain crotchet in the bass even though the chorus have a dotted quaver and semiquaver: this hint has been followed in several places. Other minor alterations have been made in bar 10, basset-horn I and violin I; bar 32, basset-horn I and violin I; bar 38, basset-horn II, bassoon I, and violin II; bars 42–3, woodwind and violins; bar 45, bassoon I and viola; and bar 51, woodwind and strings.

In bars 40–1 and 48–9 the soprano part is too high for basset-horn I; the new version avoids the consecutive octaves in bars 48–9 of the traditional version, and Beyer's bare fifth in the woodwind on the first beat of bar 42. Mozart's standard string layout is used in bars 50–2, with a consequent crossing of violin II and viola in bar 49 (compare bars 45–6 of the 'Requiem aeternam'). The trumpets and drums are perhaps the most problematical, but it seems correct to imitate the very restrained use of these instruments in the 'Requiem aeternam' rather than their more florid parts in, say, the 'Cum sancto spiritu' fugue of K 427. Süssmayr's rather pointless entries in bars 8, 11, and 20 have therefore been eliminated, and trumpets and drums are reserved for the 'recapitulation' in bar 39, the augmented-sixth cadence in bar 43 (analogous to bar 14 of the 'Requiem aeternam', from which the parts have been adapted), and the final bars 49–52. Süssmayr's over-fussy rhythm there has been simplified, and his curious omission on the fourth beat of bar 50 filled in (with the orchestral, not the choral, rhythm).

12

The 'Dies irae'

Before discussing this movement in detail, there is a more general question about the orchestration of the Requiem to consider. Blume (pp. 159 ff.) has argued that the state of Mozart's incomplete autograph makes it impossible to determine whether the instruments specified on the first page of the score represent the complete orchestra for the entire work. Might Mozart have exchanged basset-horns for clarinets, or added, say, flutes, oboes, or horns? Might he have intended extra instruments even at the start, but have put their parts in a separate *particella* since there was no room for them on his twelve-stave paper?

Blume seems to have been unduly pessimistic, for on reflection fairly certain conclusions about the make-up of the orchestra can be established. First, it is very unlikely that Mozart intended to add a *particella* to the score of the 'Requiem aeternam'. Such a practice was common enough in the eighteenth century when composers had insufficient staves on their manuscript-paper for a complete score; but if Mozart had wanted extra instruments he would surely have included them in the main score at the expense of trumpets and drums, which would have been relegated to the *particella*. Thus the inclusion of trumpets and drums in the autograph score appears to rule out additional instruments, at least at the start.

It is also highly unlikely that Mozart had it in mind to add other instruments later. The complete orchestra for the C minor Mass K 427 is heard in the first nine bars, and in both *Die Zauberflöte* and *La clemenza di Tito* the first bar of the overture is played by the entire orchestra, the sole exception being Papageno's glockenspiel in K 620. Certainly clarinets are sometimes exchanged for basset-horns in both operas, and on one occasion a piccolo is used instead of a flute, but these are substitutions, not additions. Except for obvious cases such as the trombones in *Idomeneo* or *Don Giovanni*, the idea of reserving certain instruments for the sake of effect later seems quite foreign to Mozart.

What then of substitutions? Given the orchestra at the start, the only possible one is of clarinets for basset-horns. But if Mozart had wanted this exchange he would have had to allow the players sufficient time to warm up the new instruments and adjust the new mouthpieces and reeds. In *Die Zauberflöte* Mozart allowed ample time—more than half of the long Act I Finale—for the change from clarinets to basset-horns, though admittedly rather less time (about three minutes' worth of spoken dialogue) for the change back to clarinets in Act II. Similarly, in *La clemenza di Tito* Stadler was given three complete arias to get his basset-horn ready for the obbligato in 'Non più di fiori', and had the whole chorus 'Che del ciel, che degli Dei' and part of the succeeding Act II Finale to put it away again and get out his C clarinet. Horns are, on the other hand, sometimes expected to make very rapid changes of crooks, but such a simple operation obviously needs less time than a change of instruments, mouthpieces, and reeds.

It follows, then, that if Mozart had ever wanted clarinets in the Requiem, there would have to have been at least one intervening movement without either basset-horns or clarinets; that is, without any upper woodwind at all. Since basset-horns are specified in the 'Recordare' and 'Confutatis', the only movement in the Sequence where a change to clarinets would have been possible is therefore the 'Tuba mirum'; but only at the expense of doing without either instruments in both the 'Dies irae' and 'Rex tremendae'. It is hard to imagine these movements without any other woodwind than bassoons, so that a change to clarinets for the 'Tuba mirum' cannot be seriously considered. And if basset-horns were to be used throughout the 'Requiem aeternam', Kyrie, and Sequence, a change later in the Requiem, again with the possible disadvantage of at least one movement without upper woodwind, seems extremely unlikely.

In particular, then, Mozart's four empty staves in the 'Dies irae' can be confidently assigned to basset-horns, bassoons, trumpets, and timpani—as indeed Eybler and Süssmayr assumed. Thus the instrumentation for this movement is determined, apart from the question of whether the trombones should continue to double the chorus. It might perhaps be felt that at least the tenor trombone needs a rest after the rather strenuous Kyrie, before the important solo in the 'Tuba mirum'; but experience suggests that it is not unduly fatiguing to play in the 'Dies irae' as well. In any case, it would be a departure from normal Austrian eighteenth-century ecclesiastical practice to omit trombones; moreover the 'Dies irae' is similar in many ways to the final scene between the Commendatore and Don Giovanni in K 527, in which trombones play a prominent part. So trombones should continue to double the chorus in this movement, except in a few obvious places such as bars 41–9.

The most appropriate models for the orchestration of the 'Dies irae' are:

[A] The first twenty bars of 'Der Hölle Rache kocht in meinem Herzen' in K 620. The words express much the same sentiments as in the 'Dies irae'; the key, time-signature, and tempo-marking are all the same; and there is a similar modulation to F major, straight from the dominant of D minor, with a new theme based on an F major arpeggio. Moreover there is much use of repeated semiquavers in the accompaniment.

[B] Bars 34–95 of the Act I Finale of K 621. Again the words are similar, and although the key this time is C minor, the style of the accompaniment is so like that of [A] (compare for example bars 35–6 of [B] with the first two bars of [A]) that the different key does not matter.

Other useful sources are:

[C] The opening of 'Zu Hilfe! zu Hilfe!' in K 620, particularly the wind parts. Mozart originally wrote trumpet and drum parts here,[1] but later cancelled them so as to be able to use E flat trumpets at the entry of the Three Ladies.

[D] Bars 24–33 of the Gloria of K 257, in which all the string rhythms in the first few bars of the 'Dies irae' occur.

[E] The opening tutti of the first movement of the Piano Concerto in D minor K 466, especially the trumpet and drum parts.

Let us now consider the detailed problems as they arise bar by bar.

Bar 1. The string parts are all Mozart's, and the violin I and viola parts closely resemble those in bars 78–9 of [B]. The string pattern strongly suggests that trumpets and drums should have crotchets on the first and third beats (with rests on the second and fourth) as in Mozart's later cancelled parts for [C], and the *f* marking makes woodwind support obligatory. But should the woodwind be sustained, or perhaps follow the chorus rhythm? In bars 78–9 of [B] the woodwind have minims, but marked *fp*; on the other hand, bars 138–40 of 'Non più di fiori' in K 621 show that this string pattern does not necessarily imply detached woodwind chords.

Both [C] and [D] suggest sustained woodwind; [A] does not help. On balance sustained woodwind seems to be preferable, and in any case there would be almost no audible difference between a semibreve and two repeated minims here.

Having decided on the rhythm, what of the actual notes? It seems correct to allow basset-horn I to sustain the top notes of the soprano line in the first four bars, so as to quote the second half of the main Requiem theme at the same time as the basses are quoting the first half. For balance, the basses should therefore be doubled by bassoon II, and hence basset-horn II and bassoon I must double the altos and tenors (this puts the bassoons appropriately high, as in [C]). Trumpet II and timpani ought surely to play the tonic; trumpet I appears to have the choice of tonic or dominant, but, to judge from bars 28–32 of [E], Mozart prefers trumpet I to continue the dominant when the harmony alternates between tonic and dominant.

This solution coincides with Eybler's, except for the trumpet I notes and the woodwind rhythm, where Eybler has ♩ 𝄽 ♩ 𝄽, unlike Mozart in any of the quoted sources. Süssmayr copied Eybler's trumpets and drums, but introduced several consecutives into the woodwind parts (Hess, p. 101). Beyer's bassoons in unison with the instrumental bass are surely contrary to all Mozartian precedents; he also changed the trumpet and drum rhythm to plain minims.

Bar 2. Again the string parts are all Mozart's. As for the woodwind, the rhythm 𝄽 ♩ ♩ is very common as a 'gap-filler' in sources [A]–[D], and fits the chorus rhythm very well. It also occurs prominently in the chorus itself towards the end of the 'Dies irae', at the words 'cuncta stricte'. But the rhythm needs pointing by trumpets and drums, and the third beat needs marking as well so as not to confuse the basic metre. This implies crotchets on all four beats, with the second emphasised by being broken up as ♫ or ♪. ♪. The former occurs, though without the string cross-rhythm, in bars 59 and 62 of the Act II Finale of K 621, but the latter is much more common in [A] and [E], and indeed in Mozart generally. Moreover the dotted rhythm seems almost obligatory in bar 5 against the violins' semiquaver arpeggio, so that even on grounds of consistency alone it is to be preferred in bar 2. It must be admitted that these choices produce quite complicated cross-rhythms in this very early bar, although the combination of woodwind with strings is implied by the chorus anyway, and there is a precedent in, for example, bar 27 of [C]. The suggested trumpet and drum rhythm is no more than an elaboration of the woodwind rhythm, and the combination with strings can be found in the last few bars of K 621 and (almost the same) in bar 67 of [A].

The choice of notes is relatively straightforward: woodwind continue to follow the chorus, and the trumpets should obviously have the dominant (Hess, p. 101), with both in unison as in bar 5, and hence well above the suspended bass.

The result is a more sustained version of Eybler's solution, though without his fussy (and inconsistent) drum rhythm. Süssmayr's version is unconvincing, especially its uncharacteristic rhythm, partially copied by Beyer.

Bars 3–4 are very similar to bars 1–2. Basset-horn I drops a third on the second beat of bar 4 (in unison with the sopranos, and analogous to bar 7 of [C]) to get into position for bar 5; similarly for bassoon II at the end of the bar.

Bars 5–6. Violin II and viola now have to be filled in as well as wind and timpani. The violin I semiquaver arpeggios are surely intended to illustrate the 'flames of Hell' idea in the words, and are strictly analogous to those in bar 109 of the 'Recordare'. So here, too, violin I should be doubled at the lower octave by violin II (compare also bars 8–13 of [C]). This layout also has the advantage of avoiding Eybler's and Süssmayr's 'muddy' § on the second beat of bar 5. Since the bass has now changed to the chorus rhythm (slightly simplified), it seems appropriate for the viola to follow suit, with double stopping to reinforce the rhythm and to complete the harmony on the first beats of the bars, particularly bar 5.

The violin semiquaver arpeggios, especially when doubled in octaves, strongly suggest the same dotted rhythm as in bars 2 and 4 for trumpets and drums, but now without first and hence fourth beats, since they have no available notes for the first beat of bar 5. The low trumpet unison seems appropriate to the words (compare [B]), and keeps well out of the way of violin I. Finally, the woodwind can do little but continue to double the chorus, though still with the rhythm of bars 2 and 4.

Eybler's wind parts are similar in effect, though as before are less sustained. Both Süssmayr and Beyer weaken the trumpet rhythm on the second beats to ♫, though Beyer has ♪♬ in bar 4.

Bar 7. This is a standard progression for violins: compare bar 28 of the 'Requiem aeternam', which shows how to fill in the violin II part. The violas continue to complete the harmony, with the same rhythm as the bass; the woodwind still double the chorus; and the trumpets and drums play only on the fourth beat: the first is silent as in bars 5 and 6, and the third because no suitable note is available (despite Süssmayr's attempt).

Bars 8–9. The strings should certainly be in unison to the fifth quaver of bar 9; for the last three quavers Eybler's harmony is as obviously correct as Süssmayr's is obviously wrong (especially his augmented fifth chord). In particular, the $\frac{6}{3}$ on the last quaver is identical to the harmony on the last beat of bar 14 of the 'Requiem aeternam' and on the last beat of bar 10 of [A]. The latter strongly suggests that the woodwind should also play the last three quavers, and both sources appear to imply that the bassoons should double the basset-horns at the lower octave. However, in the 'Requiem aeternam' these octaves continue for a few bars, and in [A] all the strings are in unison, so that neither is a strict analogue; it seems better, therefore, to follow bar 20 of the Benedictus of K 427 and put the bassoons in unison with the bass.

Hess (p. 101) is surely correct in suggesting that the trumpets and drums should be silent after the second beat of bar 8.

Bars 10–15. The words certainly imply repeated semiquavers in the upper strings, and it is reasonable to use something like the pattern in bar 1, while taking account of the bass arpeggios in bars 12 and 15. It is a matter of placing the accents, which seem to fall naturally on the first beat of bar 10 and the first and third beats of bar 12, the pattern being repeated in the next three bars. This more-or-less settles the violin parts, for all Mozartian precedents suggest that Eybler was right, and Süssmayr and Beyer wrong, not to follow the soprano and alto pattern in bar 11. On the other hand, Eybler should have prepared his *c″* in violin II, bar 13. The viola must now go in contrary motion with violin I as in bar 1, so that the harmony is always complete.

As for the wind, these bars are sufficiently close to bars 35–42 of [B] (note particularly the bass arpeggios in bars 40 and 42) that the wind parts there can be copied, hence with full wind chords including trumpets in bars 12 and 15 only. The available trumpet notes, together with Mozart's rule that the bass of a diminished seventh chord should not be doubled, determine the layout of these chords.

Bars 16–18. The rhythm ♩. ♪ in the tenor in bar 16 usually becomes ♪♩ ♪ in accompanying string parts: see for example bar 38 of the 'Requiem aeternam', soprano and violin I. It is therefore appropriate in bars 16–17 to give the upper strings a modified version of the pattern in bar 2, and thus continue to alternate, though in longer stretches, the 'repeated semiquaver' and 'syncopated crotchet' patterns. This also gives a welcome rest from the endless repeated semiquavers that Eybler, Süssmayr, and Beyer filled in throughout this movement, whether or not they suited the words. Mozart's care and ingenuity in varying the patterns in each of the quoted sources are worth very careful study and imitation.

On the first beat of bar 19 the chorus have a bare fifth, as the last chord of a standard vocal cadence. It does not follow, though, that the orchestra should also have a bare fifth or octave, for Mozart always accompanied this cadence with full chords in the orchestra: see for example the end of the 'Cum sancto spiritu' fugue in K 427. Thus the viola should have a *c'* on the first beat of bar 19, which implies a *d'* on the preceding quaver, in apparent contradiction to the figuring. There is a precedent for such a passing seventh, however, in bar 28 of the 'Requiem aeternam'.

The woodwind should obviously play at the cadence, and the bass pattern implies that they should be sustained in bars 16–17 as well. It would perhaps be tempting to follow Süssmayr and Beyer in using the trumpets in the second half of bar 18, but their only available note is (sounding) *e''*, which would be much higher than the chorus or woodwind, and hence too obtrusive. In any case, there is a feeling of slight relaxation about this cadence after the climax in the phrase a bar or so earlier.

Bars 19–21. A somewhat similar passage, including the use of imitation, occurs in bars 429–30 of the Act I Finale of K 620. This, together with the full figuring, suggests that the strings should be in four parts throughout. In the analogous bar 65 the bass enters two quavers earlier, which makes clear that the sense of bar 19 is of a (fake) modulation to E minor via the Neapolitan sixth (F♮). Two similar quavers have therefore been included in the violin II part in bar 19, which also helps the illusion of imitation at a distance of two quavers. In bar 20, Eybler's layout with the violins in octaves for the scale in §s is perfectly plausible, but produces too bland a rhythm, particularly when compared with bar 66. There should surely be many cross-rhythms in these bars.

Eybler is certainly correct in not giving semiquavers to the violas, and in adding the seventh on the last quaver of bar 21 (compare bar 18) so that the violas can play the third of the chord in bar 22. He must also be right to have omitted the woodwind in these bars, for the harmonic movement is too rapid to allow sustained parts. Süssmayr's and Beyer's bassoons in unison with the bass are plausible at first sight but are not characteristic of Mozart, for it is very striking that he never used the characteristic 'baroque' sound of four-part (as opposed to unison) strings with the bass line doubled by basses and bassoons, in his additional orchestration for Handel's *Messiah*.[2]

Bars 22–9. These bars are similar to bars 1–8, though they are not an exact transposition: for example Mozart's violin I part now has octave leaps instead of smaller intervals (both Eybler and Süssmayr saw fit to alter Mozart's part in bar 22). In bar 22 the pattern of bars 78–83 of [B], with violin II moving at the same time as violin I, fits best. Moreover the harmony in bar 28 is different from that in bar 7, so Eybler's violins in octaves will not work because they make consecutive fifths with the altos. The best arrangement seems to be to take account of the octave leaps in violin I and bass and alternate octaves and fourths between the violins.

The wind parts are a straightforward adaptation of those in bars 1–8, except that trumpets and drums are silent at the cadence in bars 28–9 since a trumpet (sounding) *e″* would be too high.

Bars 29–30. The violin I part seems expressly designed to follow Mozart's rule about 'false relations', that is, to avoid either G♯ or G♮ on the fourth quaver of bar 29, and then to place the G♮ in a different part—violin II is suitable—on the third beat. This procedure also avoids Eybler's and Süssmayr's clumsy violin II progression G♯–G♮–A♭. The violin I figure in bar 30 occurs several times in bars 48–88 of [B], accompanied by (usually dovetailed) sustained double stopping; but the bass there is sustained as well, instead of having repeated quavers with changes of harmony. A better model is bar 72 of 'O zittre nicht' in K 620, where the inner parts have the syncopated rhythm of bar 2. This fits well with violin I in bar 29, though the viola must continue the repeated quavers that are unavoidable at the start of bar 29, to avoid an awkward change of rhythm in the middle of the bar as in Eybler's version.

Woodwind are wanted in bar 30, which is harmonically

equivalent to bars 12 and 15, although trumpets must be omitted because they cannot play on the first beat of bar 31. On the other hand it is best to keep the woodwind silent in the second half of bar 29 so as not to violate Mozart's rule about false relations, and to emphasise the resemblance to bars 12 and 15.

As before, the result is quite close to Eybler, although some details are different. Süssmayr did not continue the syncopated rhythm into bar 30; Beyer did not use it at all, and added independent trombone parts in bar 30, which Mozart very rarely did with a chorus.

Bars 31–6. These bars are analogous to bars 10–15, though again they are by no means an exact repeat. The violin chord on the first beat of bar 31, and the different bass pattern, show that the accompaniment must also be changed to some extent. Mozart was never so inconsiderate as to write a violin chord of only a semiquaver's length in an Allegro assai, so violin I cannot play repeated semiquavers here, and there is another welcome opportunity to vary the accompaniment texture. Bars 11–12 of [A] are an excellent model, and show also how to continue the repeated semiquavers that are essential to the words here in the inner parts (compare also bar 18 of [E]). The same source shows also how to adapt the wind parts to the changes of harmony in bars 33 and 36 (use the rhythm of bar 2), while bar 27 of [C] suggests using violin I to point the rhythm in the absence of trumpets, which would have to be too high in bar 33 and could not play on the first beat of bar 37.

Bars 37–40 are similar, but not identical, to bars 16–18. The 'syncopated' pattern is once again indicated, and confirmed by the alto rhythm in bar 37; but for variety it appears this time only in violin I, while violin II and viola continue the repeated semiquavers: thus the rhythmic combination of bar 30 is inverted. Woodwind double the chorus, though in plain minims to avoid doubling the bass of the diminished seventh chord in the second half of bar 37. Trumpets and drums in bars 39–40 are modelled on bars 45–6 of the 'Requiem aeternam'.

Bars 40–2. Strings should obviously be in unison; wind, including trombones, are unnecessary. (Süssmayr's and Beyer's bassoons are as incorrect here as in bars 19–21.)

Bars 42–4. Eybler's and Süssmayr's attempts to double the sopranos and altos by violin II and viola make too many consecutives in the strings, so it seems best to have only two-part strings. It is a little more difficult to decide whether woodwind doubling is correct, but Mozart's normal practice of doubling cellos by bassoons in the absence of basses, together with a very similar passage in bars 50–1 of the Act II Finale of K 620, suggest that sopranos and altos should be doubled by basset-horns, and the tenors by both bassoons. Whether the woodwind should follow the chorus rhythm or have a smoother version makes very little difference in practice; the former has—somewhat arbitrarily—been chosen.

Bars 44–9 are almost identical to the previous four bars, except that the soprano and alto parts are exchanged and violin I is altered to suit. Beyer's idea of giving violin II the violin I part of four bars earlier appears ingenious at first sight, but makes too many fourths and unisons between the violins. It is therefore better to follow Eybler and keep the violins in unison as before.

Bars 50–2. These bars form a bridge between the thin texture of the previous ten bars and the full tutti of the next thirteen. Since violin I doubles the sopranos in bar 51 it appears that Mozart intended the strings to double the chorus exactly here, so they must get into position in bar 50. This in turn suggests octaves between the violins in bar 50, which are appropriate anyway because of the octaves in bars 52–9.

On the other hand the woodwind should not double the chorus exactly (*pace* Beyer), since $c\sharp'''$ and d''' are rather feeble notes on the eighteenth-century basset-horn. These notes are avoided by Mozart in, for example, 'Non più di fiori' in K 621, and the two obbligato parts in *Al desio di chi t'adora* K 577. Eybler's woodwind layout is better than Süssmayr's because it avoids the consecutive octaves between basset-horn II and bassoon II into bar 52.

Bars 52–6. As in bars 5–6 and 26–7, the violin I semiquaver arpeggios imply octave doubling by violin II, and the dotted rhythm on trumpets and drums. The viola part is adapted from bars 7 and 28, now in double stopping to complete the string harmony and to achieve the maximum sonority.

Mozart's standard layout for woodwind, trumpets, and drums in such a passage of alternating tonic and dominant harmony is to have the trumpets in unison on the dominant throughout, with woodwind pairs playing thirds doubled at the octave: see for example bars 28–31 of [E]. Eybler, Süssmayr, Beyer, and Hess (p. 101) all seem to have overlooked this point.

Bars 56–64. The violins should obviously still be in octaves (Eybler) rather than in unison (Süssmayr), except of course in bars 60 and 64. Violas go in octaves with the bass, in plain quavers (Eybler, Süssmayr) rather than repeated semiquavers (Beyer). It is surely desirable to keep the violins high in the second half of bar 63 so as to avoid a slight anticlimax at the start of bar 64.

The volume of sound here makes any attempt by the woodwind to duplicate the chorus rhythm inaudible, so it is better for them to be sustained, as high as possible, and still in octaves (these octaves are particularly appropriate in bars 60 and 64, where basset-horn II is an octave above the tenors: compare the octave doubling in bars 40–4 of 'Bei Männern, welche Liebe fühlen' in K 620). Trumpets and drums mark the beginning of each bar (except the impossible bar 63) with octaves, as in Mozart's original version of [C], or bars 201–6 of the overture to *Così fan tutte*; they seem to need a more elaborate rhythm than they had in bar 60 at the 'final' cadence in bar 64.

Bars 65–8 correspond to bars 19–21, and likewise need a four-part string layout. It is rare indeed for Mozart to finish a movement with less than the full orchestra, except for trombones when doubling the chorus exactly (see the end of the Act I Finale of K 620, for example), so wind and drums should play in the final cadence; but not before, or else the balance with bars 19–21 would be spoiled. The woodwind pairs have been in octaves since bar 52, so should continue in this way right to the end.

13

The 'Tuba mirum'

The first seventeen bars of this movement are so similar to Sarastro's music in *Die Zauberflöte* that the following models for the orchestration immediately suggest themselves.

[A] K 620, Act I Finale, bars 395–440. The use of basset-horns makes the orchestral sound very similar to that of the Requiem. There are even some thematic resemblances: compare for example Sarastro's phrase in bar 417 with the trombone's in bar 8 of the 'Tuba mirum', or the cadence in bars 423–5 with bars 16–18 of the 'Tuba mirum'.

[B] K 620, 'O Isis und Osiris'. The orchestration is almost identical, and the cadence in bars 45–8 resembles bars 16–18 of the 'Tuba mirum' even more closely than do bars 423–5 of [A].

It might, perhaps, seem rather incongruous that Mozart should write such similar music for a priest of Isis and Osiris as for a setting of the mass. But his views on the subject, expressed in the opening recitative of K 619, appear perfectly plain:

> Die ihr des unermesslichen Weltalls Schöpfer ehrt,
> Jehovah nennt ihn, oder Gott, nennt Fu ihn, oder Brama,
> Hört! Hört Worte aus der Posaune des Allherschers!

The words are of course Ziegenhagen's, not Mozart's; but there can be no doubting the sincerity with which Mozart set them. It is reassuring also, in view of the rubbish that has sometimes been written about the solo trombone part, to learn that Mozart was not alone in his opinion of which instrument most appropriately represented the Almighty.[1]

From bar 18 onwards [A] continues to be an excellent model, as also does

[C] K 620, Act II Finale, bars 29–94. This has the same time-signature and tempo-marking, and nearly the same instrumentation; moreover the three-part construction (bars 1–29, bars 29–94, final 'allegro') is quite similar to that of the 'Tuba mirum' (bars 1–18, 18–50, 51–62).

There are many useful hints also in

[D] K 620, Act II Finale, bars 277–361 (solo voices with a final vocal quartet), and

[E] the 'andante' sections of *Alcandro, lo confesso* K 512 (same time-signature and tempo-marking).

At the start of the autograph of the 'Tuba mirum' Mozart uses an eight-stave score, of which six are labelled for strings, solo voice, and trombone; the score is extended to ten staves for the entry of the quartet in bar 51. Since there can be no question of exchanging clarinets for basset-horns (see Chapter 12), the two unlabelled staves can only be for basset-horns and bassoons; trumpets and drums are therefore omitted. The lowest stave is labelled merely 'Bassi', without the normal 'Organo', and there is no figuring anywhere; so Mozart wanted the organ continuo to be silent throughout this movement.

Bars 1–4. The first two bars should obviously remain un-accompanied, but the bare fifth between bass and trombone in the second half of bar 3 shows that one should beware of jumping to the same conclusion about bars 3–4. Since Mozart wrote rests in the instrumental bass part here, any filling-in must be done by woodwind: but what could be a more fitting accompaniment to Sarastro-in-disguise than sustained chords on (dovetailed) basset-horns and bassoons? It is as well, too, to introduce this character-istic sound as soon as possible, in preparation for what is wanted in bars 10–18.

Bars 5–7. There can be no doubt that the upper strings are meant to play on the second and fourth beats, as in the first few bars of [A]. The same source shows that the violas should go with the violins, and need not double the bass notes. Süssmayr is surely correct to avoid an A♮ on the last beat of bar 6, for Mozart is deliberately keeping the tonality ambiguous in these bars, and does not himself write A♮ until bar 9. There are good precedents for the use of the dominant seventh with missing third over a tonic pedal, in for example K 621, 'Come ti piace, imponi', bar 8, or K 621, 'S'altro che lacrime', bar 2. On the other hand Süssmayr was wrong to anticipate the A♭ on the second beat of bar 5, and ought not to have kept violin I above the trombone.

Because of the 'false relation' G♮ —G♭ in bar 6, and the consequent need, according to Mozart's usual practice, to avoid either version of the note on the second quaver, it is impossible to continue the sustained woodwind into bar 6, and they must therefore finish on the first beat of bar 5.

Bars 8–10. The strings should clearly continue as in bars 5–6, but must avoid an A on the last beat of bar 10 so as not to clash with the trombone appoggiatura (compare the last beat of bar 6 again). It is appropriate to bring back the woodwind at the bass entry in bar 9 so as to be ready for bars 11–14.

Bars 11–13. The instrumental bass rhythm has now changed, and follows the voice. It seems best for the upper strings to go with the bass (Süssmayr), rather than to play on the 'missing' second and third beats (Eybler), which would get in the way of the trombone. The new violin I part is a little higher than Süssmayr's so as to reach the top note on the word 'omnes' in bar 14 instead of a bar later.

It is clear from the trombone part that the harmony changes in the middle of each bar, and this must be made explicit in the accompaniment, by continuing the Sarastro-like woodwind. They are laid out in three parts as in [B] so as not to exceed the range of the trombone arpeggios.

The new version is fairly close to Süssmayr's, but with added woodwind. Eybler's fails to mark the change of bass on the third beat of bar 11, and Beyer's imitative string parts seem rather forced.

Bars 14–15. The word 'omnes' implies a full chord on the first beat of bar 14, and hence (unlike bars 45, 51, and 57) nothing on the second and fourth beats (compare also bars 3–4 of 'Come ti piace, imponi', or bars 50–2 of 'Parto, parto', both in K 621). The new string layout avoids Eybler's consecutive fifths between violin II and viola II, Süssmayr's seventh leap in the viola, and Beyer's crossing of violin II and viola. Eybler was surely correct, by analogy with bar 14 of the 'Requiem aeternam' (or bar 10 of 'Der Hölle Rache kocht in meinem Herzen' in K 620), to put a full dominant seventh chord on the first beat of bar 15.

Bars 15–17. The words call for as full a setting as possible, and the harmony, one of Mozart's favourite chromatic approaches to a $\frac{6}{4}\frac{5}{3}$ cadence, must certainly be filled in (Hess, p. 101). Eybler just left these bars blank, no doubt intending to work out the woodwind parts later; but Süssmayr seems to have concluded that no accompaniment was necessary and wrote in rests in all the parts, in flat contradiction to 'omnes'. No wonder his trombone solo had to continue rather apologetically trying to wake the dead, before itself quietly expiring in bar 34.

Since Mozart himself put rests in the instrumental bass part in bar 16, the filling-in must, quite properly, be done by woodwind again (Hess's and Beyer's upper strings are too feeble—and harmonically incomplete—to do justice to this most solemn of moments). It would be rather tempting to take the words literally, and to follow bars 45–7 of [B] to the extent of bringing back the other two trombones as well, with bass trombone doubling the voice; but there is no room in Mozart's eight-stave score for their parts (and no necessity for a separate *particella*), so it looks as if Mozart did not intend to use them here. In any case, it is difficult to see how the alto trombone could be placed in relation to the solo tenor trombone; moreover Sarastro has no trombone support at similar cadences in bars 423–5 of [A], and just before the final 'presto' of the Act I Finale of K 620.

Thus the correct layout is four-part woodwind, at least in bars 16–17, with upper strings playing as well on the second and fourth beats of bar 17 so as to achieve the fullest sound on 'thronum'. But how should the parts be arranged, and what is the correct harmony?

It is striking that in bars 45–7 of [B] (and also in bars 21–3) the voice is doubled only by bass trombone, with cellos an octave higher, and not by bassoons. Indeed, the bassoons have two bars' rest and then sustain the harmony only in the cadence bar. This suggests that here, too, the bassoons should sustain the harmony in bar 17, and not double the voice; but then the only instrument left to play the bass part is basset-horn II. In fact this unusual arrangement, with basset-horn II below both bassoons, was used by Mozart almost throughout *Al desio di chi t'adora* K 577: notice particularly the cadence in bars 47–8; this 'sandwiched' layout produces a very homogeneous woodwind sound. It must be admitted that Mozart was not completely averse to doubling a bass voice by a bassoon, for he did so in bar 30 of *Per questa bella mano* K 612; but one is left with the impression that he preferred to avoid this combination if something better was available. In any case, the bass part in bars 16–18 fits the low register of the basset-horn very well indeed, especially since it ends on the bottom note of the instrument (note that written *e♭*, though not available on the eight-key basset-horn, had been used by Mozart as early as K 361: see bars 87 and 89 of the second movement).

Since the trombone's $e\natural$ ' on the second quaver of bar 16 is clearly an inessential note, the same is probably true on the sixth quaver (compare violin I in bar 54). The alternative would be to harmonize the sixth quaver as a $^6_{3b}$ on $E\natural$; but this would need at least two more parts moving in quavers, which would in turn suggest some sort of imitative treatment as in bars 60–1 of the first movement of the String Quintet in G minor K 516. However, it would be almost impossible to make such counterpoint fit here without consecutives. Bar 108^2 of the first movement of the Piano Concerto in B flat major K 595 confirms the interpretation of the sixth quaver as an inessential note.

Having settled the harmony, all that remains is to fill in the parts, taking account of the need in bar 17 to sustain the fourth on the first beat so as to prepare the trombone's dissonance on the fourth beat, but also to avoid anticipating or doubling its resolution. The alto in bars 37–8 of the 'Confutatis' shows how to do this. It is also desirable to avoid an F on the third beat of bar 16 in the same octave as the trombone's inessential $e\natural$ '.

Bars 18–22. Repeated quavers in the strings seem entirely appropriate in bars 18–19, but it is all too easy to become boring by continuing them mechanically bar after bar (Blume, p. 163). Mozart's notation makes it quite clear that in bar 20, unlike bars 35 and 38, the appoggiaturas are full crotchets. There is thus a dominant ninth on the third beat (not a $^9_4$ as in Beyer, since the fourth cannot be prepared). It is better in four parts to omit the fifth rather than the seventh, since Mozart's rule about not doubling the bass of a diminished seventh chord prevents a G in the upper parts on the first two beats. 'Dieser Gottheit Allmacht ruhet' in K 623 (especially bar 22) provides a good model for the string pattern in bar 20.

Sustained bassoons are wanted from the middle of bar 19, to bridge the gap in the tenor part, and to fill out the harmony on the first and third beats of bar 20—especially to emphasize the minor ninth. They provide, moreover, a 'dark' colouring very suitable to the words, as in bars 18–20 of 'Se a volto mai ti senti' in K 621, or bars 286–93 of [D]. Beyer attempts something similar, but brings in the bassoons too soon, continues them for too long, and omits them from the ninth chord.

For bars 21–2, the style of the accompaniment in 'Dieser Gottheit Allmacht ruhet' in K 623 gives a welcome relief from repeated quavers, and prepares the way for more legato accompaniment in bars 24–8. As in bars 16–17 of the 'Dies irae', the syncopated rhythm also fits well with the dotted crotchets and quavers in the voice. A more sustained viola part compensates for the lack of bassoon support.

Bar 23. Eybler, Süssmayr, and Beyer merely double the bass arpeggio; but the minim rest in the solo part, and the *f* marking, call for fairly full treatment as in bar 67 of 'Der Hölle Rache kocht in meinem Herzen' or bar 27 of 'Zu Hilfe! zu Hilfe!', both in K 620. In the new version, the sustained syncopated violins, the viola with the bass, and the woodwind rhythm, are copied from these models, the former showing, incidentally, that it is permissible to double the B♮ in the strings on the third beat.

Bars 24–7. The rather legato style of the last few bars, and the bass on the first beats only, suggest legato, not detached, quavers here, rather in the manner of bars 6–9 of *Rivolgete a lui lo sguardo* K 584, or the start of 'Ah guarda sorella' in K 588. Since the first quaver of each bar must be omitted by the violins to avoid a clash with the tenor's appoggiatura on the first beat of bar 25, it is appropriate to use sustained bassoons again as in bars 28–33 of 'Zu Hilfe! zu Hilfe!' in K 620 (where there is for once a similar 'textbook' treatment of the false relation B♮–B♭). The viola takes over again in bar 26, where the bass pattern changes.

Bar 28. Violins have the 'trill' pattern of half close as in bar 8 of the 'Dies irae', leaving the minim rest to be filled by bassoons, viola, and bass, who have the same rhythm as in bar 23 except that there is one moving part to mark the third beat.

Bars 29–33. Once again the change of bass rhythm gives an opportunity to vary the accompaniment texture, but the standard 'offbeat quaver' pattern provided here by Eybler, Süssmayr, and Beyer is wrong (in contrast to bars 34 ff.), since Mozart uses it only with a more static bass. There are several other patterns that normally go with a bass in detached arpeggios, for example repeated quavers with no rests ([D] from bar 286, start of the C major String Quintet K 515, 'adagio' introduction to the last movement of the G minor String Quintet K 516), legato quavers with a sustained part (Piano Concerto in B flat major K 595, bars 66–72 of the Larghetto), or syncopated crotchets (Clarinet Quintet K 581, bars 49–56 of the first movement; see also [E], and the end of the first section of *Vado, ma dove?* K 583). Repeated quavers would quickly become tiresome at this speed, and legato quavers would be very difficult to fit: so the 'syncopated crotchets' pattern is best, at least for the violins. It also fits well with bars 21–3, and is a more sustained version of the rhythm to be used from bar 34; compare bars 19–20 of the 'Requiem aeternam'. Most of the quoted sources have sustained woodwind as well, and it is therefore reasonable to continue the bassoons, without basset-horns, but now to add the viola that has previously alternated with them; the viola thus takes the place of the horns in [D] and [E]. The texture can conveniently be rounded off by joining bassoons and viola to the bass in bar 33, where it would be difficult to continue sustained notes. It would be most uncharacteristic to leave the first half of bar 33 unharmonized as Süssmayr and Beyer did: Eybler certainly got the harmony right, but it is better to use Mozart's standard viola part in a $\frac{6}{4}$ $\frac{5}{3}$ cadence. The resulting diminished third (C♯ —F♮) occurs in just this way in bar 12 of the Menuetto of the G minor String Quintet K 516.

Bars 34–5. The 'offbeat quaver' accompaniment pattern is now correct since the bass is static. A good model is [C], in which bars 72–5 show that it is not necessary in a delicate accompaniment to double the cellos by bassoons in the absence of basses, provided the violas play the bass notes on the offbeats. This model also suggests that it is best not to take violin I above the soloist, as Eybler, Süssmayr, and Beyer did.

Bar 36. There should certainly be an A♭ somewhere in this bar to prepare for the key of C minor in bar 37, but Eybler's minor ninth chord, copied by Süssmayr, is too harsh. The violas ought to be in unison with the cellos, and the violins kept fairly low. Süssmayr's *rf* on the sixth quaver is his own invention, and has nothing to do with Mozart.

Bars 37–9 continue as in bars 34–5, but the alto rhythm on the first two quavers of bar 39 suggests that the upper strings should play on the first beat of this bar as well, and hence also in bar 37. Exactly this rhythm occurs in bars 32, 34, and 36 of [C]. The main beats in bar 39 need marking a little more than in previous bars, which provides an opportunity to bring in the basset-horns here, ready for their sustained parts from bar 40.

Bars 40–3. If the bass in bars 1–18 was Sarastro, and the tenor in bars 18–34 perhaps Tamino, the soprano here is just as recognizable as Pamina.[3] It would be rather tempting, therefore, to use her characteristic accompaniment pattern as in bars 403–5 of [A] or bars 67–8 of [C], where the violins have ♫ on the 'offbeat quavers'. But it would be difficult once having started this rhythm to stop it again in bar 43 or 44: so it is better after all to continue the pattern of the last few bars (it is in fact used often enough to accompany Pamina: see for example bars 72–4 and 89–92 of [C]). Since the basses are playing again, the violas can have an independent part.

There is a precedent in bar 35 of [C] for the clash between the soprano *bb'* and the violin I *a'* in bar 41, as in Eybler's version; Süssmayr's and Beyer's violin I is too high. Violin II and viola cross to avoid fourths and fifths between the violins. On the last beat of bar 43 the D♭ in the German sixth chord has to be dropped to avoid consecutive fifths with the bass: the layout with doubled *bb* and violin II and viola parts crossed on the first beat of bar 44 is copied from bars 29–30 of 'Ach ich fühl's' in K 620; see also bars 45–6 of the Act I Finale of K 621.

By analogy with [D] it is appropriate, having used sustained bassoons to accompany 'Tamino', now to use basset-horns with 'Pamina'. A rest is needed on the first beat of bar 42 to avoid clashing with the soprano appoggiatura, and bassoon I plays the *gb* in bar 43 because (written) *db'* would be a very bad note on the eighteenth-century bassett-horn (written *bb*, as in bar 39, was not so bad, and was used by Mozart in, for example, bars 61–3 of K 577).

Bars 44–50. Bar 7 of 'Come ti piace, imponi' in K 621 shows that Eybler and Süssmayr were wrong to add a viola part to Mozart's violin I and violin II in bar 44.

Bars 45–8 are quite similar to bars 122–7 of the Act I Finale of K 621, and call for the same sort of simple string accompaniment. Eybler's violin II part (copied by Süssmayr and Beyer) has an awkward ninth leap in bar 45, which can be replaced by a more convincing octave in bar 46 provided violin II and viola continue to cross in bars 45–6, and provided also that there is a plain (diminished) triad rather than a full dominant seventh on the second beat of bar 46 (compare bars 117–8 of the Act I Finale of K 621). Hess (p. 102) takes exception to Eybler's $\frac{6}{4}$ on the third beat of bar 48; indeed, Beyer asserts that 'Mozart would have chosen the less compromising (*sic*) sixth chord'. Fortunately, though, an almost identical passage in bars 16–18 of 'Dieser Gottheit Allmacht ruhet' in K 623 settles the question, and shows unequivocally that a full dominant seventh is correct here. On the other hand the same source shows that there should be no seventh on the last beat of bar 49 (the logic of these bars seems to be that a dominant seventh chord is necessary in bar 48 to confirm the modulation back to B flat major, but once the key is re-established a plain dominant triad is sufficient for the cadence in bars 49–50).

On the fourth beat of bar 46 bassoons must be added to support the cellos. It is then appropriate for bassoon I to switch to the violin I part in bar 48, and hence for bassoon II to join violin II when the basses return in bar 49.

Bars 51–3. Mozart obviously wants the strings to alternate with the voices in bar 51, and (*pace* Eybler and Süssmayr) the strings must double the voices exactly to avoid consecutives or wrong notes. Bars 40–1 of 'Bei Männern, welche Liebe fühlen' in K 620 strongly suggest that the wind should go with the voices, not with the strings, in this bar. In bars 52 and 53 Hess (p. 102) is surely correct to suggest the addition of violin II and viola, so as not to leave violin I unharmonized when the harmony nevertheless obviously changes. Bars 15–16 of the Andante of the String Quintet in E flat major K 614 confirm that Hess's suggested parts are correct.

Bars 54–6. Eybler's harmony in bar 54, copied also by Süssmayr and Beyer, is wrong, because the bb'' at the top of the violin I phrase makes no sense against a C minor chord. Presumably Eybler was attempting to adapt bar 26 of the Priests' March in K 620, but without taking account of this contradiction and of the awkward augmented fifth on the fourth quaver (in false relation with the violin I bb''). The only harmony that fits in bar 54 is a plain $\frac{5}{3}$, changing to a $\frac{6}{3}$ on the fourth beat (compare also the prominent E flat major triad at the start of bar 59).

Legato quavers in violin II and viola, similar to those in bars 61 and 24–6, together with full wind support, make a suitably sonorous effect for the *sfp* at the start of bar 54, and lead naturally to Mozart's standard violin II part for the $\frac{6}{4}\frac{5}{3}$ cadence in bar 55. The resulting consecutive octaves between violins I and II on the last beat of bar 54 are as unobjectionable as those, for example, between the soloist and violin I in bars 5–6 of the Adagio of the Clarinet Concerto K 622.

Bars 57–62. Since Mozart does not normally write viola chords in orchestral music, Eybler's layout (copied by Süssmayr) for the first beat of bar 57 is wrong. Beyer's layout is better, but he does not dovetail violin II and viola, and doubles the seventh at the top of both the violin I and violin II chords. A plain c' for viola fits best, because it leads naturally to the sustained part required in the next bar; it also allows Mozart's layout in bar 125 of 'Non più di fiori' in K 621 to be copied exactly.

Octaves for the violins in bar 58 are obviously correct, and can conveniently be continued with the sustained viola part, avoiding Eybler's and Süssmayr's clash between violin II and tenor on the last beat of bar 59, until the first beat of bar 60, where the strings switch to Mozart's standard layout for the cadence, as in bar 33. Eybler's divided violas work well—with one minor alteration—in bars 61–2, since they keep the texture full.

The wind should go with the voices again in bar 57 to preserve the balance, as in bar 51. Since the soprano g'' in bar 59 would be too high for basset-horn I to sustain comfortably for a whole bar, it is best for the wind not to double the voices exactly until bar 60. They must obviously continue to play in the last two bars, though not, as in Süssmayr's version, above the strings.

14

The 'Rex tremendae'

This movement has the same time-signature as the 'Requiem aeternam', and also the 'Gratias' of K 427, both of which make considerable use of dotted semiquaver figuration. These movements are marked 'adagio', so the same tempo-marking seems correct for the 'Rex tremendae' as well. Comparison with the 'Requiem aeternam' also makes it almost certain that the four empty staves in Mozart's autograph are for basset-horns, bassoons, trumpets, and drums.

Apart from the 'Requiem aeternam' (particular bars 26–32) and the 'Gratias' of K 427, it is not easy to find models for the orchestration in the 'Rex tremendae'. Indeed, having just written two movements that might almost have come from *Die Zauberflöte* or *La clemenza di Tito*, Mozart is now beginning to move away from those operas towards a style that, although it has roots in the baroque and is sometimes reminiscent of K 427, is nevertheless quite new and original. This makes the completion of the orchestration more difficult than before, since it is not always clear what Mozart had in mind, and in the absence of exact models one has to fall back on general principles.

Bars 1–2. Obviously the strings should be in octaves, with violins I and II in unison, and the violas mostly with the bass. It would be tempting to add the bassoons to the bass line: for although Mozart does not normally add bassoons to the bass of four-part strings unless the double basses are silent (see Chapter 12), he does sometimes do so when the strings are in unison. There are examples of this texture in the opening of the Piano Concerto in C minor K 491, or at the start of 'Notte e giorno faticar' in K 527. However, the chorus need full wind support in bars 3–5, and sustained woodwind seems correct in bars 7–10 and 12–15, so that the bassoons could not continue to double the bass after the first two bars, and it would therefore be inconsistent to do so in bars 1–2. Bars 744 ff. of the Act II Finale of K 620 show that unison strings do not necessarily imply bassoon support.

Süssmayr's full chord on the second beat of bar 1 robs the chorus entry in bar 3 of its impact, and so should be omitted. Compare 'Che del ciel, che degli Dei' in K 621, where the chorus enter similarly on the second beat of bar 12, although the corresponding place in bar 1 is clearly a weak beat. Bar 2 is so similar to bar 7 of the 'Requiem aeternam' that trombones are certainly wanted, and they should again play full crotchets rather than Süssmayr's and Beyer's detached quavers. Since it is difficult to contrive a complete chord on the trombones on the second beat of bar 2, and since the words suggest the fullest possible sound, woodwind should be added as well this time. Trumpets and drums must be omitted, however, because they could play only the dominant on the first beat of bar 3.

Bars 3–5. Strings continue as before, but go into two parts in bar 5. A small alteration to Eybler's otherwise good parts on the last demisemiquaver of bar 5 allows a full chord on the first beat of bar 6. Woodwind support the chorus, and double them exactly to keep the parts high for maximum volume.

Bar 6. Since Mozart wrote rests in the instrumental bass part, he obviously intended this bar to be accompanied by wind (and drums) only. Trumpets and drums can play the dominant, and bassoons must play the bass, so for well-balanced chords the basset-horns should have Mozart's standard parts for alternating tonic and dominant harmony as in bars 53–6 of the 'Dies irae' (there is little point in Süssmayr's unison between basset-horn I and trumpet I).

An important question that arises in this bar is the correct interpretation of the dotted rhythm: did Mozart expect the baroque 'double-dotting' convention to be applied here? At first sight the question seems absurd, for it is well known that Leopold Mozart was one of the first to advocate the double-dot notation, which was freely used by his son. Can there be any doubt, then, that when Mozart writes ♩. ♪ he means precisely that, and not ♩.. ♪ ?

Further consideration shows, however, that the problem is not quite so simple. For although Mozart uses double-dotted crotchets often enough in *instrumental* parts, it is rare indeed to find them in a solo voice part (they occur in bars 748–9 of the Act II Finale of K 527, but Mozart would have been present to explain their meaning to the singers). And ordinary *chorus* singers, even in Leopold Mozart's Salzburg, were clearly not expected to understand the new notation,[1] for it does not occur at all in K 427.

Indeed, when Mozart needs to specify a double-dotted rhythm, as for example in bars 6–7 of the Kyrie, he has to go to the trouble of writing ♩ ♪. ♪. This is not say that the double-dotting convention had become obsolete, for Leporello was obviously expected to double-dot his dotted crotchets in unison with the bassoon in bars 102–4 of 'Madamina, il catalogo è questo' in K 527, as also were the chorus in bars 28 and 32 of 'Che del ciel, che degli Dei' in K 621. Moreover, although Mozart writes double-dotted crotchets in instrumental parts, he very rarely uses the double-dotted *quavers* explicitly explained by his father.[2] It appears, then, that at least for dotted quavers the convention was still that an exact 3:1 division was not necessarily expected, but rather the effect simply of a crotchet divided into a 'long' note and a quick upbeat. Should there perhaps be double-dotting in the first two bars of 'Dies Bildnis ist bezaubernd schön' in K 620?

As far as the 'Rex tremendae' is concerned, there can be no doubt that double-dotted quavers fit better with the strings' dotted semiquavers in bars 7–10 and 12–15. For the sake of consistency alone, then, there should also be double-dotting in bars 6 and 11; though probably not at the *p* marking in bars 18 and 19. Mozart's simple notation has been retained in the chorus, but the (editorial) instrumental parts are written with double dots.

Bars 7–10. Hess (p. 102) and Beyer have objected to Eybler's *Austerzungen* (copied by Süssmayr), on the rather vague grounds that they produce 'various accidental dissonances' and 'blur essential outlines'. The 'accidental dissonances' do not seem, however, to be much worse than those in bar 128 of the 'Recordare' or bar 102 of 'Parto, parto' in K 621. Certainly Mozart pokes fun at such chains of thirds in K 522, but the moral is surely not that such things are always undesirable, because Mozart writes them himself in bars 26–31 of the 'Requiem aeternam' and bars 67–70 of the 'Domine Jesu', but rather that they must not be overdone, and they must be made to fit properly.

The real objection to the *Austerzungen* in bars 7–10 is that, since violin I and bass are in thirds anyway on the first and third beats of each bar, they automatically make consecutive octaves between violin I and viola, and between violin II and bass. It should be noted, though, that this objection does not apply to bars 12–15, where the parts could very well be arranged differently.

So what should violin II and viola do here? There are already three simultaneous strict canons (soprano and alto, tenor and bass, violin I and instrumental bass), so free 'filling-in' parts seem out of the question. It would be very difficult to contrive yet another canon, say between violin II and viola, and the contrapuntal texture is dense enough anyway. There is therefore no alternative but to put violin II in unison with violin I and the violas in octaves (for otherwise their part would be too low) with the bass, except at the end of bar 10 in preparation for a full chord on the first beat of bar 11. The resulting two-part 'contrapuntal' string texture is similar to that in bars 8–14 of the 'Requiem aeternam' or in most of the 'Gratias' of K 427.

Against such contrapuntal complexity, the woodwind must be kept as simple as possible, and have nothing but long sustained notes to keep the harmony complete and bind together the whole texture, as at the start of the 'Gratias' of K 427 or (without the counterpoint) in bars 4–10 of 'Vengo . . . aspettate' in K 621.

Bar 11 is like bar 6, and calls for wind accompaniment only. Since trumpets are not available this time, basset-horn I can be higher than before, in unison with the sopranos as in the corresponding bar 7 of the 'Dies irae'.

Bars 12–15. These correspond to bars 7–10, but the string parts are not identical, for the octave leaps in the bass produce a bare fifth on the second quavers of bars 13, 14, and 15. Moreover the ninth chord on the first beat of bar 15 (approached by an octave leap in the soprano) is new.

The bare fifths can be filled out by putting violin II in canon at the octave with violin I at a distance of one quaver, and the harmony further completed by a viola part in a sort of composite 'canon' with the bass, partly at the fifth and partly at the unison, again at a distance of one quaver. The overall effect is not unlike Eybler's *Austerzungen*, but is slightly smoother in sound, especially on the fourth quaver of each bar. As observed above, chains of thirds or sixths are not objectionable in themselves, and their combination with the dotted semiquaver rhythm occurs similarly in bars 26–31 of the 'Requiem aeternam'.

The woodwind parts, too, must have a few changes from bars 7–10. On the first beat of bar 15 basset-horn I needs to be in unison with the sopranos on the ninth of the chord, and this note is best approached by the sopranos' octave leap. To make this leap convincing basset-horn I must move on the second and fourth beat of each bar, more-or-less in unison with the sopranos. Otherwise, the woodwind are sustained as in bars 7–10.

Bars 15–17. Mozart's violin I part shows that the chorus must be accompanied by wind, not strings, as in bars 6 and 11. The correct layout seems to be that of bars 20–1 of the Gloria of K 427, where the wind (and drums) go with the chorus and bass, leaving the offbeats to be filled by the upper strings. Süssmayr's compromise weakens the effect because it places too much emphasis on the dotted rhythm on the second and sixth quavers of bar 16. The choice of woodwind notes here is determined by the trumpets' standard sustained dominant (as in bars 52–6 of the 'Dies irae') and the need not to go above the sopranos, who are more-or-less quoting the main Requiem theme again as in bars 4–6 of the 'Dies irae'.

The upper strings can conveniently go in unison (or octaves) throughout, as they must obviously do in bar 17, and as they did in bars 1–5.

Bars 18–19. Süssmayr's wind doubling of the chorus, apparently disliked by Beyer, is very similar in effect to bars 241–5 of the quintet 'Hm! hm! hm!' in K 620, and is therefore perfectly acceptable. But Eybler's string parts (copied by Süssmayr and Beyer) are not quite right, because the harmony is wrong on the fourth quaver of each bar: it is clear from the chorus parts that there is no change of harmony until the sixth quaver. The easiest way to correct Eybler's version is simply to omit his fourth and fifth quavers, and instead bring in violin II and viola only with the bass.

Bars 20–2. Blume (pp. 163 f.) argues that bars 20–1 should be 'a capella', and he even claims to see a rest sign in the violin I part in Mozart's autograph. But if Mozart had wanted the chorus to be unaccompanied here he would not have written repeated quavers for cellos and basses: for as bar 27 of the Kyrie of K 317 shows he was perfectly capable of writing for genuinely unaccompanied chorus if he so wished. It is, surely, much more likely that he wanted a simple string accompaniment, as in bars 46–7 of the 'Requiem aeternam' (Hess's (p. 102) suggested woodwind, with basset-horn I up to written d'''' would be too loud). Eybler's added seventh on the fourth beat of bar 21 should be omitted.

Beyer maintains that in bar 22 'the first crotchet . . . should unquestionably remain without a third, as is the case in the choral parts', and so gives the strings a bare fifth on the second quaver (though he adds the third on the fourth quaver). But almost every piece of Mozart's church music shows that, on the contrary, his normal practice was to accompany such a standard vocal cadence with complete chords in the orchestra: see for example the end of the 'Cum sancto spiritu' fugue in K 427. In any case, the bare fifth in the chorus has time to make its effect because the first quaver of bar 22 is silent in the upper strings. It is easy, not having added the seventh at the end of bar 21, to provide complete chords here.

15

The 'Recordare'

There are several models that throw some light on the formidable problems in orchestrating this movement, the most important of which are:

[A] K 620, Act II Finale, bars 46–63 and 95–190;

[B] K 620, Act II Finale, bars 277–361 (same key and time-signature);

[C] K 427, 'Domine Deus' (relative minor, same time-signature);

[D] K 192, Gloria (same key and time-signature).

Of the three sources in the same key (or the relative minor) and with the same time-signature, [B] is marked 'andante', [C] is 'allegro moderato', and [D] is 'allegro'. Of these, the most appropriate for the 'Recordare' seems to be 'andante', though as [C] and [D] help to confirm Mozart did not take this marking as implying a particularly slow tempo.

Mozart's twelve-stave score uses eight staves for the four soloists and the strings, and another two for basset-horns. The remaining two can therefore only be for two bassoons, so that trumpets and drums are silent throughout the movement.

Bars 1–13 are apparently complete in Mozart's autograph. It is conceivable that he might have added bassoons to the important viola part, as in bars 409–12 of the Act I Finale of K 620, or bars 11–15 of 'In diesen heil'gen Hallen'. But it is not clear whether they would have continued beyond the first beat of bar 12, and in any case Mozart's string parts are complete in themselves. Given this doubt, a modern editor should clearly resist the temptation of such a hypothetical, and perhaps impertinent, addition.

Bars 14–25. Some of the most difficult problems in the whole Requiem have now to be tackled. Which instruments (if any) should double the voices, and should anything be added to Mozart's three-part counterpoint (two solo voices and instrumental bass)?

In K 620 and K 621, numbers that use solo woodwind instruments prominently in the orchestral introduction appear to fall into three main types.

1. One or more wind instruments have what will afterwards be the vocal part(s), but have rests when the voice enters. Normally violin I doubles both the wind instrument and the voice. Example: K 621, 'Non più di fiori'.

2. The orchestral introduction is in 'wind serenade' style, but when the voices enter the wind usually play only in the interludes. Examples: K 620, Act II Finale, bars 1–18, or K 621, 'Ah grazie si rendano'.

3. Apparently similar to 1., but normally without string doubling in the introduction; woodwind continue to play when the voices enter, and usually double them. Example: K 620, 'Hm! hm! hm!', bars 214–47.

Since the basset-horns are not doubled by strings in bars 1–7 of the 'Recordare', it looks as if 1. is not the right model here. In any case Mozart wrote a crotchet in each of the upper string parts on the first beat of bar 14: although he might have changed his mind later, this strongly suggests, despite Beyer's ingenious solution, that he did not intend the violins to double the voices in bars 14–19. Model 2. is also inappropriate, since bars 1–7 certainly do not sound like a 'wind serenade', which would be quite out of place in a requiem mass anyway. Hence 3. must be the correct model. But which wind instruments should double which voices, and at what pitches?

It is clear from the overlap in bar 20 that if all four voices are to be supported (and the effect would be unbalanced otherwise), then four woodwind instruments are necessary. The soprano part in bars 20–5 is too high to be doubled in unison by a basset-horn, and would lie too much in the throat register an octave down, so the only possibility is to double soprano by bassoon I at the lower octave. This means that bassoon I has a top *a'* in bar 23, but there are precedents, for example in bars 144–5 of 'Ah guarda sorella' in K 588—not to mention the 'Quoniam' of Bach's B minor Mass. It would be absurd simultaneously to double the tenor an octave higher by a basset-horn, so bassoon II must go in unison with him. But now the only possibility that remains for bars 14–19 is to put basset-horn I in unison with the alto, and basset-horn II an octave above the bass. They consequently have essentially the same parts as in bars 1–7, which of course fit their range very well.[1]

So parts for basset-horns in bars 14–20 and for bassoons in bars 20–6 can be filled in. What are the strings to do meanwhile? There is a clue in the wind doubling layout that has just been deduced: for it is Mozart's habit when doubling a high and a low voice by equal wind instruments (one in unison and one at the octave) also to double the voices at the other octave as well, by other wind instruments if available, but otherwise by strings. A good example is bars 40–4 of 'Bei Männern, welche Liebe fühlen' in K 620. In addition, the high *a*'s that occur from time to time in the bassoon I part of K 588 are almost always 'covered' by violin I an octave higher. These facts strongly suggest that the voices should be doubled at the higher octave by violins in bars 20–5. For balance, therefore, alto and bass should be doubled at the lower octave, hence by divided violas, in bars 14–19 (compare bars 21–3 of the Kyrie of K 427, where wind are similarly doubled an octave lower by violas). But there is still a difficulty: Mozart's crotchet in bar 14, and the more-or-less self-evident need to put violins I and II in octaves with violas I and II in bars 19–20, mean that the string doubling cannot be exact, at least in bars 14 and 20. One gets the impression from the 'Requiem aeternam', though (see particularly bars 26–31), that Mozart went to a good deal of trouble to write contrapuntally independent string parts whenever possible, while at the same time giving the voices full support. It is possible to maintain this principle to some extent, and also to circumvent the difficulty in bars 14 and 20, by altering the layout in the strings so that in bars 14–19, for example, viola II has all the suspensions and viola I all the upper notes.

It now remains to fill in violins I and II in bars 14–20 and the violas in bars 20–6. Notice that the harmony is not quite the same both times: there is a $\frac{6}{5}$ on the first beat of bar 18 but a $\frac{9}{3}$ in bar 24, and the resolutions of the ninths in bars 17 and 23 are onto different inversions of the corresponding chords. Much of the harmony would be pretty thin if nothing were added to Mozart's three parts, for the $\frac{6}{5}$s would have no thirds and the $\frac{9}{3}$s no sevenths or fifths, so it looks as if a certain amount of harmonic filling-in by strings is necessary. Eybler attempted this with a viola part in free imitation of the bass, but his part is unconvincing because the imitation is not strict enough and the general effect is fussy and contrived. Moreover he made a few mistakes, such as the wrong note (*c'*) on the second beat of bar 19 and the anticipated resolution on the first beat of bar 22. Süssmayr omitted Eybler's extra part in bars 14–19 and altered it in bars 20–5—disastrously, as Hess (p. 103) points out, since he has consecutive octaves with the resolution of each suspension. Beyer omitted all the extra parts.

In the new version the harmony is filled out in as simple a style as possible. It seems appropriate to make the harmony slightly richer in bars 20–5, and in any case a seventh cannot be added on the first beat of bar 16 because its normal resolution would make consecutive octaves with the bass. The viola part in bars 21–5, which cannot double the cellos because they go too low, calls for some comments. First, there can be no third (a') on the first beat of bar 21 because it would have to move either in octaves with the cellos or to a doubled B♮ on the second beat. Secondly, the sevenths are unconventionally resolved a fifth downwards because otherwise the violas would be in consecutive fifths with violin I; but there are Mozartian precedents for such unconventional resolutions (particularly with a 'correctly' resolving ninth) on the third beat of bar 27 of the 'Domine Jesu', or in bars 36 and 38 of 'S'altro che lacrime' in K 621. (The alternating octaves and fifths that result between violin I and viola are similar to the soprano and bass in bars 46–9 of the 'Recordare'.) Finally, the violin parts in bar 25 are not doubled by divided violas this time because they could not prepare the suspensions on the second beat (it does not matter anyway, for the bassoons have taken over the role played by the violas in bar 19).

Bars 26–34. The approach to the cadence in bars 32–4 is quite similar to bars 346–8 of [B]. That model does not have the repeated quavers in the bass, but they do occur quite extensively in [C], with a variety of patterns in the upper strings, both detached and sustained. Perhaps the closest parallel elsewhere to the combination of repeated quavers in the bass with striking chromatic harmony is the opening of the C major String Quartet K 465, which suggests fairly sustained upper strings and a viola part in the low register (here modelled also on the tenor in bars 111–12). Since the lead in bar 27 is taken by soprano and tenor, it is appropriate to continue the layout of bars 20–5, with violins doubling at the upper octave and bassoons at the lower, except that it is now the violins that double exactly while the bassoons are slightly more sustained so as to complete the harmony on the first beats of bars 29 and 31, and generally to bridge the large gap between violins and lower strings. On the second beat of bar 31, however, the basset-horns enter so as to emphasize the approach to the cadence, and then the four woodwind instruments double the four voices. In any case, bassoon I could not continue to double the soprano in bar 33 for it would be in consecutive fifths with the alto. Violin II and viola cross in bars 33–4 to avoid fourths between the violins.

The new string parts are quite similar to Eybler's, except for the additional viola part. But Eybler's harmony is wrong on the first beat of bar 33, for when Mozart uses IV7 to approach a $\begin{smallmatrix}6\\4\end{smallmatrix}\begin{smallmatrix}5\\3\end{smallmatrix}$ cadence he omits the fifth (and sometimes adds the ninth) and resolves the seventh before the bass changes: see for example bar 42 of 'S'altro che lacrime' in K 621, or bar 23 of the Adagio of the Clarinet Concerto K 622.

Süssmayr's version of these bars has too many repeated quavers, and his doubling of soprano and tenor by violins and basset-horns in bars 27–9 is unbalanced because the soprano is doubled twice in unison and the tenor once in unison and once at the octave. Beyer's doubling is also unbalanced, and like Süssmayr he has a bare augmented second on the first beat of bar 29.

Bars 34–8. These bars obviously correspond to bars 7–13; moreover a slightly different version was written out almost in full by Mozart in bars 126–9. Eybler's solution is better than Süssmayr's (copied by Beyer) because it retains something of the characteristic viola part of bars 7–12, but his *a* on the second beat of bar 35 lies below the cellos and produces an odd second inversion. It is better to use the model of bars 126–9, with the viola an octave higher than in Eybler's version so as not to cross the cello part. Eybler and Süssmayr (again copied by Beyer) both went wrong in the violin II part in bar 36, since they doubled the fourth on the third beat. Moreover Eybler's added seventh on the last quaver of bar 37 is inconsistent with bar 13.

Bars 38–45. The key sequence in these bars is similar to that in bars 72–83, while the tenor and bass parts are very reminiscent of bars 128–30 of the 'Quoniam' of K 427, and should therefore be doubled by bassoons in exactly the same way. For balance, the soprano and alto must also be doubled, by basset-horns

The string parts present more of a problem. Eybler's, Süssmayr's, and Beyer's repeated quavers are boring, and something better is wanted, perhaps along the lines of bars 19–23 of [C]. On the other hand these bars must not be too elaborate, for the austere solo parts (and the words!) in bars 46–9 demand a complex contrapuntal accompaniment. Fairly simple imitative parts prepare for bars 46–9, and a sustained viola part somewhat in the manner of 'O zittre nicht' in K 620 stops the texture from falling apart. The bare octave on the first beat of bar 38 is in accordance with Mozart's normal treatment of the 'false relation' E♮ —E♭ .

Bars 46–52. Both Eybler and Süssmayr attempted some imitation in bars 46–9, though as Hess (p. 103) points out Süssmayr's F♯ on the second quaver of bar 46 is obviously wrong. Eybler, at least, realized that there are implied suspensions on the first beats of bars 47, 48, and 49, rather as in bars 1–6. These suspensions need careful handling so as not to create consecutives with the instrumental bass; but this difficulty can be overcome by giving violin II and viola a canon at the ninth based on a slight alteration of the bass motif, while violin I has an inversion of the figure used in bars 38–9 and 42–3, in partial canon at the fourth with the bass. Basset-horn I and bassoon I complete the harmony, bassoon I having delayed resolutions of the suspensions (more-or-less in unison with the tenor) to avoid consecutives with the string parts.

Bars 50–2 are more straightforward. The woodwind double the soloists, though with a more sustained rhythm to bring out the hemiola. The strings do likewise, but with the inner parts interchanged to fit with bars 46–9 and Mozart's viola part in bar 52.

Bars 52–3. Eybler's violin II (copied by Süssmayr and Beyer) will not do, for it is in consecutive octaves with the viola; but it is easy to correct. Since these bars are based on bars 7–11 and 34–6, and since it seems best to have only a light string accompaniment in bars 54–60, it would be wrong to add woodwind here.

Bars 54–60. Observe that the tenor part goes below the cellos in bar 55, so that it must be regarded as if it sounded an octave higher than its actual pitch. This means that the part cannot be doubled by a bassoon as in bars 20–5; for similar reasons the soprano part cannot be doubled at the lower octave by a bassoon, nor can it be doubled in unison by a basset-horn because the part would be uncomfortably high. Hence there can be no wind doubling at all in these bars. The high cello part, considerably altered from that in bars 1–6 or 20–5, suggests anyway that a thinner texture is wanted here. Doubling of the voices by violins, though with the parts modified as in bars 20–5, together with 'standard' support of cellos by violas, fits well and makes a suitably light texture, reminiscent of bars 1–6 and in good contrast with bars 14–25 and 93–104.

Bars 60–71 are an exact transposition in Mozart's autograph of bars 26–37, and there is no good reason why the additional parts should not follow suit.

Bars 72–83. As observed above, the key sequence is similar to that in bars 38–45. The 'offbeat quaver' accompaniment specified by Mozart's violin I part in bars 72–9 is very reminiscent of bars 74–

7 and 87–90 of [D] and most of [A], and is of course used in several places in the Requiem itself, notably in bars 1–7 of the 'Requiem aeternam'.

Eybler's violin II and viola parts, copied by Süssmayr and Beyer, are obviously correct, except for his use of the dominant seventh on the third beats of bars 75 and 79 and the consequent missing fifths and doubled thirds on the first beats of bars 76 and 80: it is surely better to have plain dominant triads and complete tonic chords there. The woodwind can have dominant sevenths in these places, however, since the string chords are complete; but it seems best to use them only to bridge the gaps (marked *f*) in the vocal parts.

Bars 83–7. As Hess (p. 103) observes, Süssmayr got the harmony wrong on the first beats of bars 85 and 87, where plain triads are much more plausible than minor ninths, or even Beyer's sevenths (perhaps Süssmayr was trying to adapt bars 60–3 of [A], but without taking account of the change of bass). Hess's simplification of Eybler's slightly over-fussy version works well, and is suitably reminiscent of bars 294–7 of [B].

Bars 87–92. As in the previous seven bars, it is clearly correct to accompany the soloists by strings only up to *f* marking in bar 91. Since the instrumental bass doubles the bass voice in bars 89–90 it is best for the upper strings to follow suit, but with the usual alteration of the rhythm in the violin I part in bar 89.

The *f* on 'spem' in bar 91 calls for maximum sonority, with added woodwind and violins in (dovetailed) double stopping: compare bar 9 of 'Dies Bildnis ist bezaubernd schön' in K 620. Eybler burgeons into semiquavers here, while Süssmayr and Beyer revert to their usual repeated quavers.

On the first beat of bar 92 Eybler adds the seventh to the $^9_4$ chord (and Süssmayr ignores the suspensions altogether in his accompaniment (Hess, p. 103)). Eybler's harmony is perfectly possible, but bars 75, 79, and 83 suggest on the contrary that there should be no seventh here.

For the second half of bar 92 Eybler's version works well, and is in fact identical to bar 60 of 'Lange sollen diese Mauern' in K 623. Each of Hess's (pp. 103 f.) suggested improvements on Süssmayr is slightly wrong because the viola must obviously have an *f* at the start of bar 93.

Bars 93–104. This is an exact recapitulation by the soloists of bars 14–15, except for the altered cadence in bars 103–4. But the instrumental bass is inverted in bars 93 and 99, decorated in bar 97, and slightly modified in a few other places. These changes of detail do not seem to imply more than minimal alterations to the previous orchestration, such as to violin II in bars 94 and 97 to avoid consecutive octaves with the bass.

Bar 104 has been adapted from bar 2 of 'Che del ciel, che degli Dei' in K 621, which also shows that Eybler was correct to add the sixth on the first beat. Basset-horns are added for a fuller sound at this 'structural' cadence—which is not to say that they should play forte, for the continuing absence of double basses and the obvious contrast with bar 105 show that this cadence is still piano.

Bars 105–9. Mozart's octaves in bar 109 obviously imply that the upper strings should be in octaves with the bass in bars 105–8. As in bars 5–6 of the 'Dies irae' (see Chapter 12), these octaves seem intended to illustrate 'igne'. Woodwind support the voices, but with a smoother rhythm, and an interchange of parts in bars 108–9 since otherwise basset-horn I would be too high.

Bars 110–18 recapitulate bars 26–34 and 60–8, but are not an exact repeat because the alto and tenor parts have been exchanged and the new tenor part starts two bars earlier than the alto did before. The previous viola part will still fit, but is now in a less telling part of the register and so needs bassoon support. Doubling of soprano and alto by basset-horns as well as violins compensates for the consequent lack of bassoons to fill out the harmony.

Bars 118–26. Notice that bars 122–6 are not exactly the same as bars 118–22, since the alto and tenor parts are to some extent exchanged; so there is no need for both statements to be accompanied in exactly the same way. Indeed, the resemblance to bars 330–48 of [B] (in which there is a similar exchange of parts), and the alternation of woodwind and strings at the beginning of the 'Recordare', suggest quite strongly that the voices should be accompanied by strings only the first time, and by woodwind as well at the repeat. Mozart's instrumental bass part shows that the strings are expected to double the voice parts, and indicates also how to arrange the bowing so as to bring out the hemiola cadences.

Süssmayr's and Beyer's use of the 'flames' motif from bars 105–9 to fill the gaps in bars 118 and 122 is quite inappropriate to the new words, as well as being rhythmically wrong because the ♪♫ figure is on the first instead of the second beat of the bar. Eybler's attempt to extend the canon between soprano and tenor backwards by two beats, though ingenious, fails because he cannot contrive a sufficiently exact canon. What is wanted here is surely a 'neutral' arpeggio such as Mozart used in bar 45 of the Act II Finale of K 621.

Bars 126–30. The string parts are almost complete in Mozart's autograph, and bar 129 should obviously be like bar 13, that is, without Eybler's and Süssmayr's added seventh on the last quaver. Bar 130 has been adapted from bar 100 of 'Lange sollen diese Mauern' in K 623, which also confirms that it is correct, as in the 'Dies irae', to bring back the woodwind for the final cadence.

16

The 'Confutatis', 'Lacrymosa', and 'Amen'

The 'Confutatis' is reminiscent of parts of K 620, for example bars 744 ff. of the Act II Finale, and bars 143–5 and 149–51 of the Act I Finale. It is also not unlike the 'Qui tollis' of K 427, the penultimate scene of *Don Giovanni*, and (in its use of unison strings) the 'Rex tremendae'. There are no very exact models, but most of the time, fortunately, it is clear enough what the orchestra should do.

Mozart's twelve-stave score uses eight staves as usual for the chorus and strings, and two more staves for basset-horns and bassoons in bars 26–9. Although both Eybler and Süssmayr contrived trumpet and drum parts in bars 1–6 and 11–15, they are not very convincing because of the very limited range of notes available on D trumpets in the key of A minor. On the other hand the use of independent trombones in the 'Qui tollis' and Sanctus of K 427 (unusually, with the chorus), and also in K 620 and K 527, suggests that perhaps Mozart intended the remaining two staves for trombones instead. It must be admitted that Mozart normally used three staves and clefs for three trombone parts,[1] but in the 'Qui tollis' of K 427 he used only two, with the alto and tenor trombones sharing one stave and the alto clef.[2] At any event, independent trombones seem more probable than trumpets and drums in this movement.

Bars 1–5. Mozart's violin I part in bars 10–12 shows that the upper strings are intended to be in octaves with the bass here, and there is no need for Eybler's pointless and inconsistent change of octave by the violas in bar 4, which was copied by Süssmayr and delayed two beats by Beyer.

Since it appears that the basset-horns should support the sopranos and altos in bars 7–10 and 17–25, for maximum contrast they should remain silent in bars 1–5 and 11–15. Hence Eybler's sustained woodwind is wrong, and the bassoons may (if they play at all) either double the voices as in Süssmayr's and Beyer's versions, or go with the unison strings (see the discussion in

Chapter 14 of bars 1–2 of the 'Rex tremendae'). The choice depends on what the trombones play, for as noted in Chapter 13 Mozart did not care much for the sound of men's voices doubled only by bassoons; though as bars 18–21 of 'Bewahret euch vor Weibertücken' in K 620 show doubling by *both* bassoons and trombones is acceptable (in which case the correct layout, *pace* Beyer, is bassoon I, alto trombone, and tenor trombone with the tenors, and bassoon II and bass trombone with the basses).

Should the trombones double the voices or have independent parts? As Hess (p. 104) observes, Süssmayr is unable to make up his mind. Eybler did not specify what he wanted the trombones to do here, but it is interesting that, unlike Süssmayr, he put his trumpet and drum chords on the second and fourth beats rather than the first and third, so as to emphasize the voice entries. They therefore have (if the idea is not too far-fetched) a slowed-up version of the characteristic 'offbeat' accompaniment pattern used first in bars 1–7 of the 'Requiem aeternam', and to be reused in modified form in bars 25–39 of the 'Confutatis' and at the start of the 'Lacrymosa'. It is a pity that the restricted range of available notes prevented Eybler from continuing this pattern beyond bar 4. But if the idea is transferred to trombones it can continue right through bars 1–5 and (in modified form) bars 10–15; moreover the pattern leads naturally to the full chords that seem necessary in bars 5–6. There are Mozartian precedents for such offbeat trombone chords in bars 16–18 of the Act I Finale of K 620, and especially at the entry of the Commendatore in the penultimate scene of K 527.

Given that the trombones are to have independent parts, the choice for bassoons now reduces to silence or doubling the strings. For maximum contrast in volume with bars 7–10 and 17–25 the latter is obviously to be preferred.

Bar 6. There are two slightly different possibilities for the harmony on the third beat: either the model of bar 10 of 'Der Hölle Rache kocht im meinem Herzen' in K 620 can be followed, with a diminished triad and Eybler's, Süssmayr's, and Beyer's unison strings, or alternatively there can be a $\frac{6}{3\sharp}$, as in bar 91 of 'Die ihr des unermesslichen Weltalls' K 619. Both these models confirm that the fourth (G) should be added on the fourth beat, as in bar 14 of the 'Requiem aeternam' and bar 9 of the 'Dies irae' (Beyer is surely wrong to retain the G♯ on the second beat, and his doubled upwards-resolving diminished seventh on the third beat is most unconvincing). The more appropriate model to follow is K 619, since it is at the same pitch and occurs in a more nearly similar context. Because the fourth should be added on the fourth beat, the strings must be in four parts, not in unison (despite the unison on the first beat of bar 7, as bars 91–2 of K 619 again show).

Bars 7–10. Hess's (p. 104) suggestion of basset-horn support for the sopranos and altos fits well, and follows on naturally from bar 6. The combination with unison violins copies almost exactly the layout in bars 79–87 of 'Zu Hilfe! zu Hilfe!) in K 620, and is a very characteristic late-Mozart sonority, in good contrast with bars 1–5 and 10–15.

Bars 10–15 obviously correspond to bars 1–5, but the passage is altered in various ways and extended by two beats. The same string layout as before is quite in order, and in particular it is surely better to keep the violas in unison with the violins rather than put them an octave lower as in Eybler's and Süssmayr's versions. The trombones start as in bars 1–5, but the more rapid harmonic movement in bars 11–12 and the sequence of suspensions and resolutions in bars 13–14 imply more sustained parts. For the usual reasons the fifth of the German sixth chord in bar 15 must be avoided.

Bar 16 needs only a small alteration to bar 6 so as to move back to A minor instead of to C major. As in bar 6, the correct harmony on the third beat is a $\begin{smallmatrix}6\\3\end{smallmatrix}$, not Beyer's $\begin{smallmatrix}4\sharp\\3\flat\end{smallmatrix}$ or Süssmayr's incredible $\begin{smallmatrix}6\\4\sharp\\2\sharp\end{smallmatrix}$ with basset-horn II moving in seconds with the bass.

Bars 17–24. As in bars 7–10, basset-horns support the sopranos and altos, and this time also complete the harmony where one or other vocal part has a rest.

Bars 25–40. Eybler's violin II and viola parts, copied with a few minor alterations by Süssmayr and Beyer, can be improved a little in one or two places. There seems no good reason to break the pattern at the start of bars 26, 30, and 34 (and Eybler is not consistent in bar 36); also Eybler's unresolved fourth on the third beat of bar 32, and his doubled root and missing fifth on the first beat of bar 35, are wrong (these two mistakes were corrected by Süssmayr). Eybler's anticipation of the seventh on the second beat of bar 38, however, seems almost unavoidable in view of the way Mozart's violin I part moves, and makes a better viola part than Beyer's (Mozart himself did exactly the same sort of thing in his basset-horn II part in bar 28).

The woodwind parts were written out in full by Mozart in bars

26–9, and can easily be adapted in bars 30–9. Süssmayr has received some well-deserved abuse for altering Mozart's parts here, and especially for bringing in the woodwind a bar too early in bar 25. Compared with bar 29, he also continued them a bar too long at the end (Beyer copied the latter mistake, but Eybler was careful to avoid it).

The trombones should obviously be silent in this section: compare bars 27–9 of the Kyrie of K 427.

The first task in the 'Lacrymosa' is to complete the orchestration in the first eight bars. Since the tonality has returned to D minor there is no longer any reason to keep the trumpets and drums silent, so the four empty staves in Mozart's autograph should be allotted, as in the 'Requiem aeternam' and 'Dies irae', to basset-horns, bassoons, trumpets, and drums. Trombones revert to their usual role of doubling the three lowest chorus parts except in piano passages.

It has already been shown (see Chapter 4) that the 'Lacrymosa' was probably intended to be only a short continuation of the 'Confutatis', leading to the 'Amen' fugue. This conclusion suggests that the 'Lacrymosa' should go at the same speed as the 'Confutatis', in the sense that the new dotted-crotchet beat should be the same length as the old crotchet beat. The last bar of the 'Confutatis' appears to support this hypothesis, as also does the 'Amen' sketch, whose dotted minims seem intended to go at the same speed as the previous dotted crotchets. In other words, the basic metre should remain the same throughout the 'Confutatis'—'Lacrymosa'—'Amen' sequence. For the 'Lacrymosa', therefore, Mozart's tempo-marking 'andante' at the start of the 'Confutatis' still applies.

Bars 1–2. Nothing should be added to Mozart's violins I and II and viola. The return to D minor, together with the fairly slow speed and the close resemblance of the rhythm to that of bars 8–9 of the 'Requiem aeternam', are obviously intended to recall to mind the opening of the Requiem.

It should be noted that Mozart's violin I part allows for the fact that the second of each pair of quavers will probably continue to sound into the succeeding quaver rest, for when this continuation makes a dissonance with the new chord it is resolved properly. See for example the first and third beats of bar 2: the former resolves the possibly still audible bb'' onto a'', and the latter has a decorated resolution of the previous g''.

Bars 3–4. The effect of 'recapitulation' continues, for the harmony is an almost exact transposition back to D minor of bar 32 of the 'Requiem aeternam'; moreover the soprano line, especially in bars 4–5, is clearly derived from the main Requiem theme. The new bassoon parts are therefore also based on the 'Requiem aeternam'.

The string pattern of bars 1–2 should certainly continue (as in Süssmayr's and Beyer's versions), though the violin I part needs careful fitting so as to follow the general shape of the voices, with the emphasis on the third beat of each bar, but to avoid harmonic and contrapuntal mistakes (there is an excellent precedent for what might be objected to as a doubled leading note between violin I and violin II, in bar 474 of the Act II Finale of K 620). Süssmayr's attempt to copy bar 1 is obviously wrong because the sopranos' resolution is anticipated and there is a very nasty clash between the violins on the first beat of bar 4; moreover the ninths on the fourth beats are uncalled-for. Beyer copies this ninth in bar 4, but unlike Süssmayr does not resolve it properly.

On the other hand Beyer is certainly right to reserve the trombones for the climax in bars 7–8. Süssmayr's sustained trombones and woodwind in bars 5–6 create a most extraordinary effect, reminiscent of the ballroom scene in *Don Giovanni* or even the works of Charles Ives, of a distant brass band playing a quite different piece of music.

Bars 5–6. Sussmayr's violin I part (copied by Beyer) 'shadows' the bass on the second of each pair of quavers. He also has bare fifths on the third beat of bar 5 and on the first and third beats of bar 6. The new parts are designed to avoid these errors, so that there are no bare fifths on the main beats and there is a properly balanced chord at each violin I entry; moreover the inner parts are as far as possible contrapuntally independent of the voices.

There is thus no need for woodwind to complete the harmony, and it is best anyway to omit them so as to have plenty in reserve for the crescendo in bars 7–8. As in bars 3–4, bars 471–4 of the Act II finale of K 620 provide a good precedent, not only for the 'doubled' leading notes, but also for the use of this string pattern without any wind support.

Bars 7–8. Süssmayr's violin I part works well enough in bar 7, but must be corrected in bar 8 to avoid doubling the bass of the German sixth chord. Beyer's revised version is perfectly acceptable, but undivided second violins make a more exact continuation of the previous texture.

The crescendo in bar 7 and the *f* in bar 8 obviously call for full wind support, and for maximum sonority (and to make more explicit the resemblance between bar 8 and bars 3–4) the woodwind are kept as sustained as possible. Trumpets and drums are wanted at the climax, though the trumpets are fairly sustained in line with the woodwind and to avoid too much emphasis on the fourth beat of bar 8.

We have now reached the end of Mozart's autograph of the 'Lacrymosa', and have to consider how best to complete the movement. Süssmayr's version is no help because, as shown in Chapter 4, it is entirely his own invention and is not based on any Mozartian material.

Since the most likely chord at the start of bar 9 is D minor, and since the chorus need a short rest after bars 7–8, the most reasonable procedure is to add two orchestral bars akin to bars 1–2, and then to set the remaining three lines of text at roughly the same speed as the first three. Mozart's first eight bars thus become the first half of a short binary movement. However, although bar 9 must start in D minor, bars 1–2 cannot simply be repeated, for that would create a very strong expectation of a repeat of at least bars 3–4 as well; but the music of bars 3–4 would not fit the new words, 'huic ergo parce Deus'. The only way to avoid this unwanted repeat is to use bar 10 to modulate to a different key, which can conveniently be done by grafting a version of bars 19–20 of the 'Requiem aeternam' onto a repeat of the orchestral parts in bar 3 of the 'Lacrymosa' (which were anyway modelled on the 'Requiem aeternam'), so as to modulate to F major.

Having now arrived at the key of F major, 'huic ergo parce Deus' should clearly be set to a new theme in that key.[3] The idea that the 'Lacrymosa' recapitulates the 'Requiem aeternam' suggests quite strongly that bars 27–9 of that movement should be reused, though now transposed into F major and with the rhythm of the lower parts simplified. Thus transposed, the theme closely resembles the first half of the subject of the coming 'Amen' fugue; that is, it is more-or-less an inversion of the main Requiem theme, which has already been quoted by the soprano in bars 4–5. Moreover the characteristic diminished fourth leap in the bass in bar 11, copied from bar 27 of the 'Requiem aeternam', also refers back to the tenor in bar 6. Quite apart from its relevance in the 'Lacrymosa' as the inversion of the main Requiem theme, the reuse of the plainsong 'Te decet hymnus' theme in a later movement is an idea that can be traced back to one of Mozart's chief models for the Requiem, for it is what Michael Haydn did in the Benedictus of his Requiem in C minor (see Ex. 8.6).

How should the next line, 'Pie Jesu Domine', be set? It is clear that 'Domine' needs a half close, as for example in bar 14 of the 'Requiem aeternam'; and since the following line, 'dona eis requiem', must finish with a full D minor cadence so as to resolve the tension of the half close in bar 8, it seems appropriate at this point to remind the listener of that half close. Hence the half close on 'Domine' should be in D minor. This is not to say that the whole line 'Pie Jesu Domine' should be in D minor; indeed, the feeling of resolution at the final cadence would be weakened by too much previous use of that key. The solution to the problem appears to be to use bar 13 to modulate to G minor, by an orchestral bar reminiscent of bars 3, 4, and 9, and then to move gradually in bars 14–15 from G minor to D minor in preparation for 'Domine' in bar 16. The words 'Pie Jesu' are repeated so that the length of the phrase approximates that of the previous line. The material in bars 14–16 comes from bar 5 of the 'Lacrymosa', transposed up a fourth, and bars 13–15 of the 'Hostias', transposed up a tone; thus the soprano part recalls that in bars 7–8, while the bass has a retrograde version of the main Requiem theme.

It might be objected that it is inconsistent to quote the first half of the 'Te decet hymnus' theme in bars 11–13, but not to reuse the second half, as in bars 30–2 of the 'Requiem aeternam'. However, there are excellent precedents in Michael Haydn's Requiem in C minor, for in both his 'Requiem aeternam' and his Benedictus Haydn used only the first phrase of the Tonus Peregrinus and then continued with other material. In any case, the second half of the plainsong cannot be made to fit at this point in the 'Lacrymosa' because it ends not with a half close but a full close, and because there are two more lines of text to set.

Bars 17–20 provide the expected resolution of the half close in bar 8, and are intended to balance bars 7–8: hence the crescendo to the *f* marking at the cadence (as bar 8 of the 'Requiem aeternam' shows, the word 'requiem' does not necessarily imply *piano*). Bars 18–20 are adapted from bars 38–40 of the 'Dies irae', while in bar 17 the soprano completes the statement of the Requiem theme begun in bar 16 and repeated in retrograde form in bars 18–20 (thus bar 17 is a transposition of bar 14). At the same time the tenor completes a retrograde statement, and the alto an inversion. The soprano part and the harmony in bars 15–17 are also reminiscent of bars 27–32 of the 'Tuba mirum'.

The binary-form movement is complete by the first beat of bar 20, but a short coda has to be added to lead to the 'Amen' fugue, and to create the necessary feeling of relaxation after the strong cadence. Bars 46–8 of the 'Requiem aeternam', obviously intended for just such purposes, can easily be adapted (after a preliminary bar like bar 9 again) so as to finish in the right position for the start of the 'Amen'.

Not much needs to be said about the orchestration in bars 9–24, which simply continues in the style of bars 1–8. There is a precedent in bar 18 of the 'Requiem aeternam' for both the doubled suspension and resolution in bar 10 (basset-horn II and viola), and for the unprepared fourth in the viola on the first beat of bar 16. As in bars 51–2 of the Kyrie, basset-horn II switches to the tenor part in bars 18–20 so as not to duplicate the only available trumpet note, and so as to finish with an octave rather than a fourth between the basset-horns on the first beat of bar 20. For the combination in bar 19 of sustained trumpets with a more elaborate drum rhythm (see also bar 8), compare 'Che del ciel, che degli Dei' in K 621 or the final chorus of Act I of K 620.

There can be no doubt that Mozart's sixteen-bar 'Amen' fugue sketch was intended to form the final section of the Sequence: for the subject is derived by strict inversion from the main Requiem theme, and in any case this is the only place in the text of the Requiem where the word 'Amen' occurs. Perhaps the completion of this fugue is not quite the same urgent necessity as some sort of completion of the 'Lacrymosa', which could not be omitted in even the most austerely purist of performances since the Sequence would then end most inconclusively—and in the wrong key—on the first beat of bar 40 of the 'Confutatis'; for one could at a pinch use Süssmayr's makeshift plagal cadence instead. But it is quite clear that Mozart intended a much more elaborate treatment that would form, with the 'Lacrymosa', a 'recapitulation' to balance the 'exposition' of the 'Requiem aeternam' and Kyrie, so that a mere

plagal cadence would falsify Mozart's carefully considered pro-
portions for the whole work. In any case, to leave out the 'Amen'
would be to omit sixteen unquestionably genuine bars of Mozart's
setting.

   Models of Mozart's fugal writing in the last year of his life are
rather scarce, but there is much to be learnt from the Kyrie, and
from the Fantasia for Mechanical Organ K 608 (especially the first
fugue, in which much use is made of inversion and stretto). The
'Lacrymosa' of Biber's Requiem is also helpful, for it contains
various combinations in stretto of almost the same subject and
countersubject. There are of course many vocal fugues in Mozart's
earlier church music, and the Fugue in C minor for Two Pianos
K 426 is almost an encyclopaedia of contrapuntal devices. But
Mozart's attitude to the fugue seems to have changed considerably
in the years 1780–90. Earlier examples tend to be fairly long and
rather loosely organized: one gets the impression that Mozart was
much less concerned then with the overall structure, than with
showing off his amazing contrapuntal skill by writing stretto after
stretto of ever-increasing complexity and ingenuity. By 1791,
however, the technical mastery could be taken completely for
granted, and Mozart was writing much shorter, tautly organized,
fugues that succeed in reconciling fugue with sonata form. The
Kyrie fugue, for example, has a clearly recognizable 'development
section' starting in bar 15, which ranges through various keys other
than D minor, and then has a 'recapitulation' beginning at the bass
entry in the original key in bar 39. The first fugue in K 608 has a
similar sonata-like form, though on a smaller scale.

   The first task in the 'Amen' is obviously to finish the exposition.
Mozart's sketch is complete for the first ten bars, and in the next
five all that is missing is the end of the second countersubject in the
soprano.[4] But the sequential nature of the first countersubject
strongly suggests a similar pattern for the second, so there is little
doubt about the soprano in bars 11–12. Then it will be noticed that
the alto in bars 12–13 has a diminution of the answer as given by the
tenor in bars 7–13, and that the first countersubject as in bars 2–5 is
itself a decorated form of the same answer. So Mozart apparently
intended much use of diminution, and therefore also other standard
thematic manipulations such as inversion and retrograde motion, in
an almost completely monothematic fugue. In this spirit, it is
appropriate for the soprano, having had a'–$g\sharp'$ in bar 12, to

continue with $a'–b\natural'–c''$ in bar 13, so as to form an inversion in diminution of the first half of the subject (this inversion being, of course, the original Requiem theme transposed up a fifth). The soprano in bar 13 and bars 14–15 continues in imitation of the alto (compare also the soprano in bar 7), adapts the eighth bar of Biber's 'Lacrymosa' (see Ex. 8.20), and then drops out for three bars' rest before re-entering with the answer in bar 19. Such a rest was regarded as almost obligatory by Fux:[5] compare for example the alto in bars 5–7 of the Kyrie.

Although Mozart's sketch stops at bar 15, except for another bar in the alto, there is no difficulty in filling in bars 16–18. In bar 18 the tenor follows the model of bar 6 rather than that of bar 12 since the bass has the subject, not the answer. By analogy with the completely regular exposition (with no 'codetta') of the Kyrie, there is no reason to delay the soprano entry with the answer in bar 19. Thus the soprano, and by implication also the bass, can be continued to the first beat of bar 25, which marks the end of the exposition. However, the tenor cannot have the expected second countersubject because the resulting fourths on the third beats of bars 21 and 23 would be incorrectly approached by leap. The suspensions and resolutions of the second countersubject can be preserved, though, by giving the tenor a retrograde inversion of the first half of the subject (that is, a retrograde version of the main Requiem theme); and the rising fourths of the second counter-subject can be given to the alto instead, which in bar 22 helps to make clear that the $f\sharp$ in the bass is an inessential note.

The exposition is now complete, and the form of the rest of the fugue must next be settled. It seems virtually a rule in 'sonata-form' fugues such as the Kyrie or K 608 that middle entries should be in keys other than the tonic or dominant, and that the 'recapitulation' should start with the original subject in the bass. For the middle section here the better model is the 'development' of K 608 because it is brief and sticks to the subject (and leads to a recapitulation involving the inverted subject), whereas that of the Kyrie has six recognizable subject entries and a four-part stretto of the counter-subject as well. If the middle section of K 608 is copied, including its key scheme, the following plan emerges:

1. middle entries (either or both in stretto) in G minor, then F minor, followed by
2. 'false entries' in the bass, in B flat minor and then C minor,

leading to a complete bass entry in D minor to start the recapitulation.

(Some of the corresponding entries in K 608 are in the major, but the semitone steps of the 'Amen' subject obviously cannot be altered.)

On further consideration, both complete middle entries should be accompanied by a second entry in stretto at a distance of two bars. For, having already occurred twice in the exposition, a three-part passage consisting of, say, the subject with both counter-subjects would be otiose; but if one tries to add a fourth part to such a three-part passage it quickly becomes apparent that the subject, at a distance of two bars, is the only thing that will fit. Moreover only one layout of these two stretti will work satisfactorily: for since the bass is to lead the recapitulation it must take part in the first rather than the second stretto; indeed, it must lead the first stretto since otherwise the addition of either countersubject produces incorrect $^6_4$s. The following voice in the first stretto could be soprano or tenor (not alto, because the subject in G minor would be either uncomfortably low or impossibly high). But if it were the tenor the second stretto would have to be taken by soprano and alto, and then whichever of them were the second voice would have to enter on a most undesirable unison with the first voice. Hence the second voice in the first stretto must be the soprano, and the second stretto must be taken by alto and tenor—the alto leading for otherwise the resulting tenths between alto and tenor would make for very awkward spacing of the parts.

To sum up, part 1. of the middle section must be arranged as follows:

1.(*a*) stretto in G minor, at a distance of two bars, bass followed by soprano;

1.(*b*) stretto in F minor at two bars' distance, alto followed by tenor.

It remains, in part 1., to bridge the gap between the end of the exposition and the first stretto, and to fill in the other two parts in both stretti. Both the Kyrie and K 608 suggest a very short, possibly sequential, episode after the exposition. Following Fux's recommendation, the bass entry in bars 28–9 is harmonized as an interrupted cadence (compare also bars 18–19 of the Benedictus of K 337), and this is approached by a retrograde inversion of the subject in the soprano and a straight inversion in the tenor, while the alto imitates the bass at the fourth. During the first stretto the two countersubjects fit perfectly well (with minor modifications), and the layout with the first countersubject in the alto and the second in the tenor produces better spacing than the other way round, and also compensates the tenor for having missed the second countersubject in the exposition. For variety, however, the second stretto is accompanied by a stretto of the first counter-subject, and the necessity for a second episode is avoided by joining the second stretto straight onto the first. In consequence the soprano has an *ab '* instead of the expected *a'* in bar 35, but such a chromatic alteration of the subject is akin to Mozart's treatment of his countersubject in the Kyrie (bars 34 ff.), and has already been hinted at in bar 5, where the soprano has *bb '* in what is otherwise a decorated version of the answer. Tenor and bass cover the join in bars 34–7 with, respectively, a diminution of the subject (at the same pitch as it is about to appear in stretto), and a motif derived from the second countersubject: thus in bars 36–8 the bass has an inversion of the first half of the subject. Soprano crosses alto (ending on a unison) as in bars 32–3 of the Kyrie.

For part 2. of the middle section the model of K 608 has been followed quite closely, with a sequential episode based on the first three notes of the subject. The tenor is derived from both countersubjects, and the soprano now expands the last part of the second countersubject (previously hinted at in the alto in bars 42–3, as it was in the bass in bars 34–6) into a complete inversion of the subject, in preparation for the recapitulation. Meanwhile the alto imitates the tenor, with two chromatically altered statements of the subject.

The recapitulation starts as if it were a continuation of the previous episode, but this time the subject in the bass is complete, and the augmented sixth in bar 53 already marks the change from the sequential pattern. The plan of the recapitulation is suggested by K 608 again, together with the fact that the 'Amen' subject is an inversion of the main Requiem theme: instead of alternating subject and answer as in the exposition, the subject is now alternated with its inversion, so as to make explicit at last the derivation of the subject from the main Requiem theme (of course, this derivation has been hinted at before in various places, but the inverted subject has not previously been heard except in diminution). This scheme seems particularly appropriate in a 'sonata-form' fugue, for although the entries in the recapitulation start alternately on the dominant and tonic as they did in the exposition, no modulation to the dominant *key* is now necessary, and the whole of the recapitulation can stay in the tonic. As recommended by Fux, these four entries are spaced rather more closely than they were in the exposition. The bass lead more-or-less fixes the order tenor—alto—soprano for the subsequent entries.

Minor alterations to the first countersubject allow its use in the soprano in bars 53–8 (continued by a motif from the countersubject of the Kyrie), and in bars 60–1 the bass imitation uses the diminished subject once again. An extra entry of the inverted subject in the bass starts in bar 64, while the alto inverts the first countersubject and the tenor is based on the second countersubject. This bass entry is expanded chromatically by two bars so as to quote the soprano in bars 7–8 of the 'Lacrymosa', and to build up to the main cadence in bars 72-4 which, with the doubled tonic pedal in the succeeding coda, is intended to resolve the long-range tension of the half close in bar 8 of the 'Lacrymosa', which was only partially resolved by the cadence in bars 19–20 there. The tension just before the cadence is further increased by the high soprano part which, having just finished the inverted subject, now continues with the subject itself, overlapping with its retrograde inversion.

The coda in bars 75–9 prepares for the key of G minor in the 'Domine Jesu', by the use of a slightly expanded form of plagal cadence copied from the end of the String Quartet in D minor K 421. Apart from leading to the key of the next movement, the suggestion of G minor here serves also to show that, although the tension set up in the 'Lacrymosa' has now been resolved, we have not yet by any means reached the end of the whole Requiem, so that too great a feeling of repose would be inappropriate. At the same time, though, G minor is not totally unexpected, for it has already been hinted at in bars 60–1 and 69–70.

The tenor in bars 70–7 has a final statement of the answer, but using *b♭* instead of *b♮* as in the first countersubject, or in the soprano in bar 35.

Once the four vocal parts are complete the rest is easy. Since the dotted minims are to go at the same speed as the dotted crotchets in the 'Lacrymosa', 'allegro' is the correct tempo-marking. As for the orchestration, strings and woodwind double their corresponding voices exactly as far as bar 68 (except where the soprano part is too high for basset-horn I in bars 39–42 and 61–8). At the cadence and its approach in bars 68–74, however, a measure of independence is called for, to allow the violins to maintain the rhythmic impulse with their quaver arpeggios, and to give the wind their own characteristic layout. It seems best, as in the Kyrie, to make very sparing use of trumpets and drums, so they mark only the start of the recapitulation, and the final cadence and coda.

17

The 'Domine Jesu' and 'Hostias'

As in the 'Confutatis', it is better to use the two empty staves for trombones, since trumpets and drums could contribute little in the key of G minor. Moreover the trombones seem to need an independent rhythm in bars 3 and 21–8.

The speed of this movement, and hence also the tempo-marking, need careful consideration. The resemblance of bars 1–3 to bars 11–13 of the Credo of K 192, and the extensive use there of the accompaniment pattern to be used in the 'Quam olim Abrahae' fugue, imply that Süssmayr's 'andante', even with Beyer's addition of 'con moto', is too slow (in the traditional version, the 'busy' semiquavers in bars 1–2 and similar places are all Süssmayr's, not Mozart's). Thus something like 'allegro moderato' would be more appropriate. However, Mozart writes merely 'allegro' in the Credo of K 192, and also in the quick section of the Adagio and Allegro for Mechanical Organ K 594 (which seems to go at exactly the right speed for the 'Domine Jesu'), so these precedents have been followed, with the qualification 'moderato' left to be understood.

Bars 1–3. The contrast in words and dynamics between bars 1–2 and bar 3 suggests the maximum contrast in the orchestration as well, so that bars 1–2 should be accompanied by strings only, but bar 3 should be full. The same principle of contrast is another reason why Süssmayr (copied by Beyer) was wrong in bars 1–2 to anticipate the semiquaver movement of bar 3. In addition, his semiquaver arpeggio figure is irrelevant to the various rhythmic patterns used by Mozart throughout the 'Domine Jesu', and he is unable to continue the figure in bars 32–40.

In bars 1–2 the choice for the upper strings' rhythm appears to lie between , ♩♩♩ and the same rhythm as the chorus. The former corresponds closely to what happens in the 'Quam olim Abrahae', and is analogous to bars 26–31 of the 'Requiem aeternam'; the latter corresponds to bars 17 and 20 and various other places in the 'Domine Jesu', and is used in diminution in bars 21–7 and throughout the 'Quam olim Abrahae'. Since the 'Domine Jesu' relies for many of its effects on the gradual development of rhythmic patterns, it seems better not to anticipate them, but to choose the latter for its simplicity at the start. The same principle of increasing rhythmic complexity can be found, for example, in bars 1–2, 22–3, and 128–9 of the 'Quoniam' of K 427.

Once this rhythm has been chosen, there is little alternative in bars 1–2 but for the strings to double the chorus exactly. There is a precedent in the first bar of 'Der Hölle Rache kocht in meinem Herzen' in K 620 for the missing bass of the chord on the first quaver of bar 1.

In bar 3 Süssmayr's version has consecutive octaves between violin II and bass from the second to the third beats. This is bound to happen if the tenors are doubled by strings, so that it is preferable to put the strings in unison, as they must obviously be anyway in other places were the bass has semiquavers, such as bars 17, 20, and 21–30. The wind can conveniently have the rhythm of bar 1 (again as in bars 17 and 20), with trombones in unison with their corresponding voices but with woodwind in doubled thirds to go with the tenths between soprano and tenor (compare the discussion in Chapter 15 of bars 14–25 of the 'Recordare').

Bars 4–6. Since strings and tutti were alternated in bars 1–3, these bars should be accompanied by strings only. It would be tempting, in view of the resemblance to bars 26–9 of the 'Recordare', to adapt the (new) viola part there by doubling the altos at the lower octave; but this would be wrong since it would invert into fifths Mozart's fourths between the inner parts into bars 5 and 6, and would produce poor spacing on the first beat of bar 7. Hence the strings must double the voices in unison, though as usual with their own version of the rhythm.

Bars 7–10. Süssmayr's absurd syncopations in the upper strings are best forgotten; and Beyer's repeated staccato semiquavers are more suggestive of fairy glades than the torments of hell. Süssmayr's violin I part, however, is otherwise perfectly acceptable, and breaks up the sopranos' semibreve in one of Mozart's standard ways—it is used by Mozart himself in bars 75–6. The start of bar 7 is reminiscent of bar 10 of 'Der Hölle Rache kocht in meinem Herzen' in K 620 and of bar 9 of the 'Dies irae', and obviously needs full woodwind support (Hess, p. 106); similarly for bar 9. The unison strings on the second and third quavers of these bars are modelled on bar 10 of 'Der Hölle Rache kocht in meinem Herzen', and correspond also to the layout that appears necessary in the first half of bar 32. In bars 8 and 10 the altos and tenors have the same rhythm as in bar 1, and can conveniently be doubled by violin II, viola, and the two bassoons.

Bars 11–14. These are sufficiently like bars 26–39 of the 'Confutatis' to call for the same sort of sustained woodwind support; and the basset-horn parts in the throat register are quite consistent with the effect of a sudden piano in bar 11.

Süssmayr's and Beyer's repeated quavers in the upper strings have been avoided (except in bar 13) lest they become tedious; instead, the syncopated rhythm of bars 8 and 10 is continued. A sustained viola part holds the texture together and fits well with the tenor part in bar 13: compare bar 43 of 'Dieser Gottheit Allmacht ruhet' in K 623.

Bar 14 has been kept as simple and 'neutral' as posible, so as not to anticipate the rather more complex rhythms of the next few bars.

Bars 15–20. Bars 15–16 and 18–19 are very similar to bars 1–2, but the suggestion of imitation between the sopranos and the other parts implies a corresponding elaboration of the string parts, though something must be kept in reserve for the fugal exposition in bars 32–40. The violins seem to fit best if violin I alternates with violin II and bass.

The missing bass notes on the first beats of bars 15 and 18, the horn-like fifth between tenors and basses in bar 16, and the almost Schubertian harmony in bars 18–19, all strongly suggest sustained (divided) violas, doubling tenors and basses. They can be balanced by basset-horns doubling sopranos and altos, whose parts then closely resemble those in bars 7–10 of the 'Confutatis'.

In bars 17 and 20 the orchestra should obviously reinforce the chorus in unison and octaves. Bars 22 and 24 of the 'Dies irae', and bars 78–9 and 82–3 of the Act I Finale of K 621, both confirm that Süssmayr's violins in contrary motion with the bass are correct. It is less clear, however, that the violas should follow the violin pattern; indeed, bars 810–17 of the Act II Finale of K 620 suggest, on the contrary, that the violas should go with the bass here. Trombones and bassoons double their corresponding voices in bar 17, but for maximum volume continue the same layout in bar 20 even though the tenors are now in the lower octave. Similarly, both basset-horns double the sopranos in unison. The resulting top notes for basset-horns and bassoon I on the first beat of bar 20 are appropriate to the words and were within the range of eighteenth-century instruments, for *ab'* occurs several times in the bassoon parts of K 620 and Mozart takes the clarinet up to (written) *e'''* in K 581.

Bars 21–30. It is almost self-evident that the strings should be in unison, as in bars 1–5 and 10–15 of the 'Confutatis'—and in any case the rapidly moving bass needs doubling at the upper octave for the sake of clarity.

On the other hand the wind parts are quite difficult to fit. Süssmayr's sustained woodwind (except for his pointless single bassoon with the strings), though surely correct in principle, is almost inaudible in practice (Hess, p. 106); and Beyer's parts lie even lower in the first four bars. Moreover Beyer has consecutive fifths between basset-horns and tenors from the third to the fourth beats of bar 22. The new woodwind parts are similar to those in bars 7–10 and 12–15 of the 'Rex tremendae', but with the basset-horns in octaves to make a more penetrating and slightly exotic sound, appropriate to the words: compare bars 121–2 of the last movement of K 361. These octaves also mollify the effect of the consecutive fifths in bar 22: for basset-horn I moves in fourths with the tenors, so that the fifths occur merely because basset-horn I is doubled at the lower octave. Perhaps they may therefore be as excusable as those between violin II and bassoon I in bar 20 of the 'Requiem aeternam', or those between oboe I, trumpet I, and the altos, in bars 12–13 of 'Che del ciel, che degli Dei' in K 621.

In bar 25 the C♯ on the fourth beat specified by Mozart's figuring is best put in the top part, so as to avoid a perfect fifth followed by a diminished fifth with the altos. The natural movement of the resulting basset-horn I part makes a quotation of the main Requiem theme almost inevitable, but this allusion is quite in order because the instrumental bass outlines a retrograde version of the theme at the same time (this outline has been made more explicit in bassoon II). Having now introduced a quicker movement into the woodwind parts, it is best to keep it going in bars 27–8. This makes it possible for basset-horn II to resolve the sevenths without making consecutive octaves with the bass, and also leads naturally to the more rapid change of harmony on the third beat of bar 28.

As usual the trombones double the voices, though with a slightly smoother rhythm in bars 26–8, where it is the words that force repeated notes in the vocal parts. Beyer's staccato crotchets, too, serve to point the rhythm of each entry (except that of the sopranos, but the more rapid movement of the bass compensates), and make obviously better parts than Süssmayr's. A similar combination of rapid strings, sustained woodwind, and detached trombones occurs, though more slowly, in bars 190 ff. of the Act II Finale of K 620.

Bar 31 is sufficiently similar to bars 8, 10, and 11–13 to call for the same style of accompaniment.

Bars 32–40. Süssmayr's semiquavers in the first half of bar 32 are, of course, copied from Mozart's in bar 43, but are inappropriate here because there is no *f* marking. The correct layout is surely that of bar 26 of the Kyrie of K 427.

The fugal exposition in these bars develops bars 1–2 in a way that was hinted at in bars 15–16 and 18–19. Thus a corresponding development in the accompaniment texture is in order, and anyway leads naturally to the string pattern indicated by Mozart in the 'Quam olim Abrahae' fugue. The layout of the accompaniment there, bars 21–31 of the 'Requiem aeternam', and a certain resemblance to bars 190 ff. of the Act II Finale of K 620, all suggest that as far as possible the string parts should be contrapuntally independent of the voices, in contrast to bars 15–16 and 18–19 where the more homophonic vocal writing perhaps allowed a violin I part that more-or-less doubled the sopranos. It would at first sight be an attractive idea to combine the alternation of violin and bass rhythms with a sustained viola part as in bars 15–16 and 18–19; but it would be difficult in practice to make such a part fit, partly because of the irregular harmonic movement in bars 37 and 39, but mainly because the texture of the violin and bass parts would make it almost impossible to keep the harmony reasonably complete. So the viola part has to move as well, and, as bars 26–31 of the 'Requiem aeternam' show, it is best for it to go with the bass so as to avoid bare second and fourth beats.

Though the rhythm of each string part is now fixed, it is still quite difficult to decide on the actual notes, and a few pitfalls must be avoided. For example, in the first half of bar 35 the combination of the soprano line and the A♭ in the bass strongly suggests a German sixth, but this harmony would be wrong because the consequent progression from F♯ to G would clash oddly with the alto part. Again, the correct harmony on the fourth quaver of bar

37 is $^6_{3\flat}$, since Mozart's *f'* in the alto and doubled A♭ rule out a properly spaced $^6_{4\natural\,3\flat}$. On the last quavers of bars 35, 37, and 39 the passing notes in the voices would clash badly with the third of the chord in the same octave, and so the third must be omitted (similarly on the sixth quavers of these bars, except in bar 35 where the *b♮* in violin II is in the lower octave). To prevent a bare fifth in the strings in such places, the seventh has to be added in the viola, except on the sixth quavers of bars 37 and 39 where there is a plain octave instead. On the other hand, a bare fifth between the violins is acceptable on the first quaver of bar 36 because it completes the chord and is approached by oblique motion; similarly for the fourth on the first quaver of bar 38.

Finally, is woodwind support wanted in these bars? Should the voices be doubled, as in bars 196–204 of the Act II Finale of K 588, or bars 190 ff. of the Act II Finale of K 620? (Beyer's interjections are unconvincing, because in bar 38 the bass trombone is in consecutive fifths with the soprano, a mistake Mozart's instrumental bass part is carefully designed to avoid.) The difficulty with such woodwind doubling, however, is that it could not be stopped convincingly in bar 40, and so bars 40–3 could not have the plain string accompaniment as in bars 4–6 that seems to suit these bars so well. In any case, the vocal parts are sufficiently sustained here to hold the texture together without additional woodwind parts: compare 'Soll ich dich Teurer nicht mehr sehn?' in K 620.

Bars 40–3. These are an exact repeat of bars 4–6, except for the use of solo voices, and the augmented sixth chord in bar 43. The slight intensification of the harmony in this final bar before the fugue suggests woodwind support for the cadence itself.

Bars 44–64. As Hess (p. 106) remarks, it is not as easy as one might think to continue Mozart's string parts throughout the fugue. Süssmayr cannot quite decide at the start whether the violins should be in unison or not; and his viola part in thirds with the bass has to be fudged slightly in bar 55, and produces several consequential mistakes, such as the oddly doubled diminished seventh in bar 44 and the anticipation of the tenors' resolution in bar 47. But even his violin I part is by no means faultless, for there are unresolved sevenths in bars 46 and 47, and there is an unpleasant clash with the tenors on the last quaver of bar 48. Beyer's version also has unresolved sevenths, for example in bar 47, and he inexplicably abandons the pattern in bar 53; moreover his violin II and viola parts are rather unconvincing because they merely fill in the harmony and are without contrapuntal significance (there is also a doubled diminished seventh in bar 44 and an unresolved seventh in bar 46).

The very regular pattern in Mozart's violin I part in bars 44–6 is akin to that in bars 8–14 of the 'Requiem aeternam', which was used similarly to provide an extra contrapuntal part during a fugal exposition. It is pretty clear that here, too, violin I was meant to be contrapuntally independent, as indeed is the instrumental bass. Since it would be almost impossible to contrive yet more independent parts for violin II and viola, there is no alternative but to follow bars 8–14 of the 'Requiem aeternam' (and also bars 7–10 of the 'Rex tremendae'), and put the violins in unison, and the violas as far as possible with the bass: the first quaver of many groups lies too low, so for consistency it is best to omit them all from the viola part, except in bars 61–4 where the cellos and basses diverge.

There are various detailed points that arise in the completion of the violin part.

1. There are no descending leaps of a single octave in Mozart's violin I part in bars 44–6, although there are several in bars 71–3 where the choral texture becomes more homophonic. This hint has been followed elsewhere, so that single octave leaps are avoided except in bars 58–61. On the other hand double octave leaps have been used wherever convenient, following Mozart's example in bar 46.

2. Mozart's part in bars 44–6 shows that the second quaver of each pair may well double the bass note, but does not necessarily have to; a bare perfect fifth with the bass should be avoided, however. On the other hand bare fifths are sometimes needed on strong beats, especially with a suspended fourth: see the third beat of bar 45, and observe how Mozart avoids any suggestion of consecutive fifths when two such fifths follow on successive strong beats.

3. The pair of semiquavers will normally fall a fifth when the bass has the third of the chord, but in other places it may fall a third (for example in bar 48) or even a second (bar 54), the unresolved sevenths here and in bar 57 occurring, unlike Süssmayr's and Beyer's, only on the last semiquaver, where they seem to be unavoidable. Occasionally the fifth may be diminished, as in bars

59 and 60, where Mozart's thirds in bars 71–3 cannot be copied because of the rule that forbids the doubling of the bass of a diminished seventh chord.

Having filled in the string parts, what of the wind? The trombones should certainly double the chorus exactly in a fugue, though it is best to drop the alto trombone in bars 51–2. But should the woodwind do likewise, as in Süssmayr's version (though he changes his mind about the bassoons in bar 51), or should they perhaps just sustain the harmony in some way, as in Beyer's? There are certainly places where the harmony is incomplete, particularly on those strong beats where the strings have a bare fifth, such as in bar 45. In these places, however, the third is missing in the chorus only because the relevant part has a quaver rest following a crotchet instead of a tied note; but in a sufficiently resonant building the third would continue to be audible into the next beat, and would to some extent fill out the bare fifth. This effect can be made more certain by giving the woodwind a more sustained version of the suspensions and resolutions, though it seems best not to double the vocal parts otherwise. The overall woodwind sound is as a result rather similar to that in bars 21–8: compare also Mozart's oboe parts in bars 29–30 of the Benedictus of K 337.

From bar 58, however, the woodwind parts can be a little more elaborate. The basset-horns are in unison in bars 58–9 because the sevenths on the first and third beats do not occur in any other part, and the 'German sixth' cadence in bar 60 is copied (as is the chorus) from bars 42–3. In bars 61–4 the antiphonal exchange between the sopranos and the rest of the chorus corresponds almost exactly to what happens in bars 43–4 of the 'Requiem aeternam', and for good balance needs the same maximum woodwind support for the sopranos.

Bars 65–70. The violin I part in bars 65–6 is modelled on Mozart's in bars 75–8. Otherwise, these bars recall bars 11–13. Trombones should obviously be silent here.

In bars 67–70 the only part to be filled in is the viola, but Süssmayr's consecutive octaves with violin II in bars 68 and 70 are to be avoided, as also are Beyer's near-consecutive octaves with the sopranos in bars 67–9 and his consecutive fifths with the tenors into bar 70.

Bars 71–8. The string parts are easy: the two-part layout of bars 44–64 is resumed in bars 71–3, where the violin I part is Mozart's anyway. In bar 74, too, Mozart's violin II part in bar 70 can be copied, though with a small alteration to avoid consecutive octaves with the bass. Trombones double the voices again, and the woodwind return to the style of the corresponding bars 58–60, from which, as in Süssmayr's version, the suspended sevenths on the first beats of bars 72 and 73 are copied: see also the soprano part at the start of bar 74. To give the basset-horns a chance to breathe in bar 75 (at the same time as the sopranos), they have the same rhythm as in the previous few bars and many other places: compare also bar 119 of the Act II Finale of K 621.

The trombones should surely be omitted from the 'Hostias', so that the remaining four staves in Mozart's twelve-stave score are for basset-horns and bassoons only. Bars 23–34 resemble bars 72–83 of the 'Recordare' quite closely, and therefore suggest the same speed and tempo-marking ('andante'). As for the dynamics, Mozart's first marking is the *p* in bar 24; but the fact that the *f* in bar 39 must be intended to continue to the *p* in bar 46 presumably implies that bars 44–5 are still forte. Hence bars 1–2 should be forte as well, and there is no good reason for dropping below this level in the first twenty-four bars, except in bars 13–15 by analogy with bars 36–8.

Bars 1–2 are complete in Mozart's autograph. It is pretty clear from these two bars and from Mozart's violin I part in bars 46–52 (and also from the resemblance of bars 23–34 to bars 72–83 of the 'Recordare') that, *pace* Hess (p. 106), the syncopated rhythm of the inner parts in the first two bars should continue throughout the movement, though not necessarily in the same parts. Indeed, the change from violin II to violin I at bar 46 strongly suggests that violin I should always have this rhythm while the chorus are singing. There are hints on how to handle this type of accompaniment in bars 83–8 of the Act II Finale of K 620, and also in a few bars of the Sanctus of K 192 and the Agnus Dei of K 220.

Bars 3–21. Given that violin I has the syncopated rhythm, what should violin II and viola do? Süssmayr puts them with violin I, though not completely consistently; Beyer takes them with the instrumental bass. But the unison between violin II and viola in bars 1–2, and the general 'feel' of the movement, particularly in such places as bars 7–8, suggest that the strings should remain in three parts. Thus the violins should be in unison from bar 3, at least as far as the cadence in bar 20. For the viola part, violin I in bars 1–2 suggests something more sustained, and this impression is supported by those places in the Sanctus of K 192 and the Agnus Dei of K 220 where the same syncopated rhythm is used (compare also bars 29–33 of the 'Tuba mirum').

Having decided on this layout for the strings, the violin part almost writes itself, given that the shape of bars 1–2 (and 46–52) is to be preserved as far as possible, because in places where a note is held over a change of harmony the pitch of that note is nearly always uniquely determined. And, once the violin part is filled in, there is usually little doubt about the viola. There is a rest on the second beat of bar 4 to avoid a clash with the tenors' passing note, and for consistency there is a similar rest in bar 3 (it is filled by the instrumental bass anyway). Süssmayr's dominant seventh in bar 4 is wrong, despite Mozart's use of the same harmony in bar 2, because the normal resolution of the Ab would produce the undesirable progression of a diminished fifth followed by a perfect fifth, with the bass. In bars 6 and 10 the new violin part has the ninth of the chord as part of an arpeggio but does not resolve it by stepwise descent; however, there is a precedent in bars 19 and 21 of the Credo of K 317. There has to be a break in the pattern in bar 14 since the chords on the second and third beats have no note in common, but a slight increase of movement suits the cadence in bars 14–15, and leads naturally to the greater animation (now in the bass as well) in bar 20, where the parts are modelled on those in bar 28 of the 'Requiem aeternam'.

What should the woodwind do in these bars? Süssmayr's compromise between the chorus and the instrumental bass parts is as unconvincing here as it was in the 'Dies irae', and Beyer's only partial support does not feel right either. There seems no good reason why the woodwind should not double the chorus throughout, and hence keep the harmony complete in the orchestra; though they should be as sustained as possible to compensate for the violins' syncopated rhythm, and should have their own slightly different layout in bars 11 and 18–21.

Bars 21–2 are a transposition up a fifth of bars 1–2 (and bars 44–5). There is therefore no point in Süssmayr's and Beyer's substitution of too-obtrusive octaves for Mozart's unison between violin II and viola.

Bars 23–34. As in bars 72–83 of the 'Recordare', it is best to follow the shape of the vocal parts, and so keep the violins high in the *f* bars and low in the *p* bars (large gaps between violins and violas can be bridged by the basset-horns). For maximum contrast in dynamics the woodwind should play only in bars 23–4, 27–8, and 31–2 (as happens also in Süssmayr's and Beyer's versions, though Beyer's upbeats in bars 26 and 30 are inconsistent with his bar 22). For balance, and to complete the harmony, the chorus are supported by divided violas in bars 24–6, 28–30, and 32–4. There is a precedent for divided violas with unison violins in bars 21–3 of the Kyrie of K 427.

Bars 34–44 are a recapitulation, though not an exact repeat, of bars 11–21, and obviously call for the same accompaniment layout. The augmented sixth in the violins in bar 37 does not resolve up a semitone, but this unorthodox treatment is unavoidable in three parts if there is to be a complete chord on the first beat of bar 38.

Bars 44–54. The violas should be in unison with violin II again in bars 44–5; and it is not too difficult to fit them with Mozart's violin and bass parts in bars 46–52. As before, the woodwind support the chorus and keep the harmony complete.

As Hess (p. 107) remarks, Mozart's violin I part in bars 53–4 implies changes of harmony, which must therefore be made explicit (compare bars 52 and 53 of the 'Tuba mirum'). This must be done by violin II and viola, without bass (*pace* Hess), since Mozart writes rests in that part. Hess's suggested parts are not quite right anyway because his violin II makes the $c\sharp''$ on the second quaver of bar 53 sound like an essential note; but such an interpretation is wrong because the D major chord in the chorus and bass is still sounding. Beyer correctly treats the $c\sharp''$ as inessential, but doubles the diminished seventh on the third beat.

18

The Agnus Dei, 'Lux aeterna', and 'Cum sanctis'

It has been shown in Chapter 7 that the chorus parts in the Agnus Dei, except in bars 19 to 21 or 22, were very probably sketched by Mozart, as also were the outer string parts in bar 1. The task of reconstruction is therefore very similar to that in the earlier movements.

In considering the speed of this movement, little help is given by the models cited in Chapter 7, for their tempo-markings range from the 'allegro con spirito' of the Gloria of K 317 to the 'adagio' of the Agnus Dei of K 192. But the traditional 'larghetto' seems quite suitable, for it was a favourite tempo-marking of Mozart's in his later years, especially for a movement in triple time: see for example the second movement of K 581, or 'Non più di fiori' in K 621. Moreover 'larghetto' appropriately suggests a slightly slower speed than the 'andante' that seemed right for the 'Recordare'.

Trumpets and drums are not wanted here, despite their inclusion in Süssmayr's version. His *ff* in bars 8–9 betrays his usual insensitivity, and in any case he forgot the trumpets and drums completely for the rest of the movement. As for the trombones, the dynamics for the 'Agnus Dei' sections must first be fixed; for the 'dona eis requiem' sections are obviously piano and hence should have no trombones. Models such as the Agnus Dei of K 192, or that of K 275, suggest that the long crescendos provided by Süssmayr in (his) bars 48–50 and by Beyer in bars 5–8 (though, oddly, not in his bars 37–40) are out of place here, and a straightforward alternation of *f* and *p* would be more appropriate. Hence the 'Agnus Dei' sections should be forte, with the chorus doubled by trombones in the usual way.

Bar 1. Given that violin I is almost certainly genuine, it is impossible to put violin II below violin I on the first beat, and so Süssmayr's unison violins are correct. Repeated quavers for viola as well as bass are perfectly plausible, being similar in effect to those in the Agnus Dei of K 275 or at the start of the last movement of the

String Quintet in G minor K 516 (or, of course, those in bars 26–33 of the 'Recordare'). But it is less clear that Süssmayr was right to divide the violas in this bar, for the resulting clash between the *a* in viola I and the *g♯'* and *b♭'* in the violins is a little harsh. The opening bars of the Symphony in G minor K 550 confirm that such a clash is best avoided.

Bars 2–9. Süssmayr's violin part can be improved a little, so as to follow more closely the pattern of bar 1 and to relate better to the soprano part (Beyer abandons the pattern of bar 1 in bars 6 and 7, but retains it in bar 5 where the odd progression *c♯"–b♭'–e♮"* results). It must be admitted that, as in Süssmayr's and Beyer's versions, the bass of the diminished seventh is doubled on the second beat of bar 5; but in the new version the strings have only a first inversion of a diminished triad on C♯ there, not a complete diminished seventh: compare the incomplete chord and doubled bass note in Mozart's chorus parts in bars 5 of the 'Dies irae'.

The viola quavers continue, sometimes divided to fill out the harmony, but still avoiding unpleasant clashes as far as is practicable. Beyer's violas are divided into no less than four parts by bar 8, a texture that seems more characteristic of Villa-Lobos than of Mozart.

Woodwind double the chorus, though with a quicker rhythm in bars 7–8 where there is a suggestion of increasing animation in the vocal phrase. This also gives the players a chance to breathe before their more sustained parts in the next few bars.

Bars 9–14. The repeat by the woodwind of the last three bars of this section was Süssmayr's idea, and is best omitted. The woodwind may therefore be used to accompany bars 9–14, which makes the maximum contrast with bars 1–9. Such a layout also allows Süssmayr's awkward gap in bars 9–10 to be filled by a copy of Mozart's modulation in bars 14–15 of the 'Requiem aeternam', complete with the omission of C♯ or C♮ for as long as possible. It seems best to keep the woodwind sustained here; but then something has to be added to prevent the rhythm disintegrating, especially in bars 10 and 13. Mozart not infrequently added cellos (without basses) to what would otherwise be a passage for wind alone: see for example bars 190 ff. of the Act II Finale of K 620, or the 'wind' band at Don Giovanni's supper-table. A cello part mostly in plain crotchets marks the main beats while avoiding the tedium of continuous repeated quavers.

Bars 14–22. (Note that the bar-numbering is now different from Süssmayr's.) Süssmayr's superfluous repeat has been replaced by a single bar corresponding to bar 1; thus the 'dona eis requiem' section is effectively six bars long.

At the end of bar 17, and for the next few bars, Süssmayr's mistakes in the chorus parts have to be corrected. It is easy enough in bars 17–19 to substitute a modulation to A minor for Süssmayr's premature C major, while at the same time sticking very closely to his reading of the soprano part and also maintaining the harmonic rhythm of bars 1–9 (one change of chord per bar). A Neapolitan sixth in bar 20 plausibly recalls bar 28 of the 'Dies irae' and leads naturally to the $g\sharp'$ in the soprano part in bar 22: since the $g\natural'$ in bar 23 is part of a dominant chord instead of a tonic chord like the corresponding c'' in bar 11, it seems for once best to keep the chromatically altered note in the same part, contrary to Mozart's usual treatment of 'false relations'.

Once the chorus parts are fixed there is no difficulty in filling in the orchestra in the manner of bars 1–9.

Bars 22–9. Like bars 9–14, these bars are accompanied by woodwind and cellos only. The rising minor third in the woodwind in bars 22–3 is intended to recall the basset-horn I part in bars 10–11, which is used again in bars 37–8.

Bars 29–37. As before, Süssmayr's orchestral 'repeat' (which is particularly illogical here) is replaced by a single bar like bar 1. The rest of this section needs only minor revision of Süssmayr's orchestral parts.

Bars 37–47. Bars 37–41 obviously call for the same accompaniment as in bars 9–14 and 22–9; a small alteration to the bassoon I part in bars 40–1 allows a complete chord on the last beat of bar 40. As shown in Chapter 7, the bass note in bar 41 should be G♭, not G♮.

From bar 42 to the end it is appropriate to double the voices by strings as well as woodwind, so as to integrate the two previous accompaniment textures. Bars 46–8 of the 'Requiem aeternam' suggest that Süssmayr's and Beyer's syncopations in the upper strings should be replaced by plain held notes. Although the trombones remain silent in bars 42–5 because of the continued *p* marking, it would be wrong to omit them from the final chord; a suitable model for their parts there is provided by the end of the 'Qui tollis' of K 427.

For the 'Lux aeterna', Süssmayr, possibly acting on Mozart's instructions (see Chapter 7), reused bars 19–48 of the 'Requiem aeternam'. This is clearly the best possible solution in the circumstances, for it leads naturally to the repeat of the Kyrie fugue, and convincingly continues the 'recapitulation' in the overall sonata-like form of the whole Requiem. Moreover the words, 'Requiem aeternam dona eis Domine: et lux perpetua luceat eis', themselves recapitulated in the text, are consequently set to the same music as in the 'Requiem aeternam'—a procedure adopted also by Michael Haydn in his Requiem in C minor. It does not matter that the plainsong theme from bars 21–6 of the 'Requiem aeternam' is now used with different words, for Mozart himself used it there to set two different lines of text, which itself implied consequential alterations to the rhythm. In any case, the only conceivable alternative to the reuse of part of the 'Requiem aeternam' would be to omit the 'Lux aeterna' altogether.

Süssmayr's sole contribution here is the alteration to the rhythm in bars 3–14 necessary to fit the new words. There are a few places where his underlay can be improved, especially in bar 8 where he brings in the altos, tenors, and basses one quaver earlier than in Mozart's original. In bars 11–12, in the same three parts, Süssmayr divides Mozart's crotchet into two quavers but for no good reason alters the pitch of the first of each pair. The bass part in bar 26 of the 'Requiem aeternam' shows that Mozart had no objection in this context to repeated quavers at the same pitch. These faults can easily be corrected; and in addition the tenor and bass in bar 12 have been given a closer approximation to Mozart's original rhythm, so that Süssmayr's awkward reversal of the stress on 'tuis' in the bass is avoided.

Finally, Süssmayr used the Kyrie fugue again for the 'Cum sanctis', which according to Constanze was at Mozart's express request. Perhaps, if he had lived to finish the Requiem, Mozart would have written an even more elaborate final fugue incorporating the main Requiem theme, its inversion as in the 'Amen', and also the themes of the Kyrie (although the inverted Requiem theme already appears in diminution in the Kyrie: see the alto in bar 3). But it is not out of the question that Mozart might after all have decided simply to repeat the Kyrie fugue as the final section of the 'recapitulation'. Certainly Constanze thought such a repeat to be the normal procedure in a Requiem setting;[1] and Michael Haydn's 'Cum sanctis' has a subject very similar to that of Mozart's Kyrie (see Ex. 8.15). There can in any case be no alternative for a modern editor but to carry out what was probably Mozart's specific instruction.

Süssmayr's fitting of the new words to the music of the Kyrie leaves much to be desired, however. In particular, his underlay for the countersubject is very clumsy in putting four successive syllables to pairs of semiquavers; and he got into such a muddle in bar 33 that he had to continue Mozart's soprano part for an extra two beats. There are many occasions, too, where Süssmayr unnecessarily altered Mozart's placing of consonants and lengths of phrases allotted to single vowels.

There seems no way of improving Süssmayr's underlay for the first four bars of the subject of the fugue, though it is a pity that the prominent ♩. ♪ rhythm at the start has to be changed to a plain minim, carrying a mere preposition in a strongly stressed position. It would be tempting to replace this minim by a crotchet rest followed by a crotchet, so as to put 'cum' on an unaccented beat; but such a change would alter the musical sense of the fugue too much. There is in any case a precedent in Michael Haydn's 'Cum sanctis' subject for setting 'cum' to a long stressed note. In the second half of the second bar of the subject Mozart's quaver rest has to be replaced by a quaver to accomodate 'in ae-' on a pair of quavers; but this alteration gives a clue as to how the underlay for the countersubject may be improved. For if the first of the three repeated quavers at the start is omitted, the remaining two can carry 'in ae-', and then the whole of the succeeding semiquaver passage can take the single syllable '-ter-'. There is thus an effect of imitation between the settings of 'in ae-' in both subject and countersubject; moreover in both places the original 'e-lei-son' can be replaced by 'ae-ter-num' with almost no change in the vowel sounds, and with a similar voiced nasal consonant at the end of the phrase. It might at first seem that the omission of the first quaver at each entry of the countersubject would spoil the harmony and rhythm, but in fact the harmony is never left too incomplete because the countersubject almost always enters on the root or fifth of the chord, so that there is never a bare fifth where the quaver has been omitted. As for the rhythm, in the few places such as bar 5 where no voice now moves on the second half of the beat the rhythmic impetus can be restored by substituting an octave leap in quavers for the plain crotchet in the instrumental bass part, as Mozart himself did on the first beat of bar 6.

The straightforward replacement of 'eleison' by 'aeternum' in both subject and countersubject can also be made in other places, so as to preserve the distribution of vowels and consonants in Mozart's Kyrie. An example occurs in the bass part in bar 5, where Süssmayr continued the syllable '-ter-' through the first two beats, although in the Kyrie Mozart repeated 'eleison', starting on the second quaver. Similarly, the new underlay in the bass part in bars 6–8 sticks more closely to the pattern of Mozart's original; and in numerous other places where Süssmayr has attempted to fit 'cum sanctis' where Mozart had 'eleison', 'aeternum' has been substituted without further comment. It is after all the most suitable word in the text of the 'Cum sanctis' for long-drawn-out treatment.

Finally, a few consequential amendments have been made to the orchestral parts in the Kyrie, for example in the first bar of the subject, where the chorus rhythm has been altered.

19
Performance

So far, this book has been mostly concerned with establishing a text for Mozart's Requiem that comes as close as possible to what the composer had probably already worked out in his mind, and would have written down in full if he had lived to do so. But he must have had a clear mental picture, not merely of the appearance of his music on paper, but also of its actual sound; so it would be inconsistent to try to reconstruct the musical text but to give no thought to its performance.

It is obviously impossible to reproduce exactly what Mozart heard in his imagination. Indeed, perhaps it is fortunate that we have no gramophone records of Mozart playing his own music, for nothing can be more lifeless than slavish and unimaginative reproductions of composers' performances. On the other hand, there is a clear obligation to transmit the composer's message to his audience with the least possible distortion. This is the ultimate justification for the current 'authentic performance' movement; which is not to say that one should necessarily try to reproduce all the conditions of one particular eighteenth-century performance, for that performance may well have been different from what the composer imagined. But it is only through careful study of the instruments of the time, and the corresponding vocal and playing techniques, that one can reconstruct as accurately as possible the framework within which the composer's imagination moved, and hence the limits we must set ourselves in trying to bring his music to life. Modern scholarship can fix these limits with some precision; and in particular Mozart could never have imagined the sound of twentieth-century orchestral instruments. No one knew better than Mozart, himself a supreme performer, exactly what the instruments of his time could do, or had a more profound understanding of how to write for them in combination, so that his music will always be a little out of focus if it is performed on their modern equivalents. Of course, it would be unrealistic and over-dogmatic to demand that Mozart should always be played on 'period' instruments; but we ought at least to take account of how orchestral sounds and capabilities have changed over two hundred years, and not make the mistake of equating 'change' with 'improvement'. The instruments of Mozart's day were neither worse, nor better, than ours: they were simply different.

It is sometimes argued that our ears have been irrevocably altered by the music of the last two centuries, and therefore that 'authentic' performances are misconceived because our perception of them is necessarily different from that of Mozart's contemporaries. But this argument misses the point that the aim of 'authenticity' is not to reproduce for ourselves the experience of the eighteenth-century listener, but rather to try to recreate the composer's own mental image of his work. Of course it must be agreed that we do not listen to Mozart in quite the same way as his contemporaries did, and so one link in the chain of communication from composer to audience has become distorted; but it certainly does not follow that we will come closer to the spirit of his music by altering other links as well, for such distortions tend to be cumulative. To take an example: Mozart's mature keyboard music is conceived specifically for the Viennese fortepiano of *c.* 1785; but that instrument no longer sounds to us, as it did to the composer, like a 'normal' piano. This 'normality' can be translated into our terms by playing the music on the modern piano instead, though only at the price of several other distortions of Mozart's intentions, for Mozart's piano differed from the modern instrument in other ways than merely tone-colour. For example, the less sharp dampers of the modern piano, and modern pedalling technique, prevent Mozart's meticulously detailed articulation markings from being observed literally; moreover the modern gain in power of the bass is inseparable from a corresponding loss in clarity, the balance between the piano and other instruments has altered radically, and so on. The cumulative effect of these factors is such that, while a performance of a Mozart piano concerto on modern instruments may be more easily related to our familiar aural experience, it is bound to differ in very many details from the composer's original conception.

Enough has been written on historical performance practice, and the result of such scholarship can be heard nowadays on many excellent recordings, that it is unnecessary here to repeat the general principles as they apply to Mozart's Requiem. But the 1801 reviewer in the *Allgemeine Musikalische Zeitung* (7 October) has an interesting specific suggestion to make concerning speeds: 'The reviewer believes, and from experiment in several performances regards it as virtually certain, that at the repeat of the Quam olim a somewhat faster speed—though it should not be overdone—makes a good effect and is quite appropriate.'[1]

There are, however, two problems that arise which are not adequately treated in the literature: what balance of forces did Mozart expect, and how should the Latin text be pronounced?

The first of these questions can obviously have no definite answer, since if Mozart did not know the identity of the man who commissioned the Requiem he can have had no idea of the size of his musical establishment, or even whether a fully liturgical or a 'concert' performance was intended. However, the latter point has in practice little bearing on the balance of forces expected, for the normal resources for either sort of performance in Vienna at the end of the eighteenth century seem to have been very similar.

There can be no doubt that, until well into the twentieth century, and in all parts of Europe whether Catholic or Protestant, church choirs consisted invariably of men and boys, with no women.[2] On the other hand it was obviously acceptable in Mozart's time to use women's voices for solo parts: for example Constanze sang the soprano solos in the first performance of K 427, and Josefa Duschek took part in a Requiem by Rössler sung at a memorial service for Mozart in Prague on 14 December 1791[3] (Count Walsegg used a castrato and a female contralto in his own performance of K 626: see Chapter 2). Clearly, operatic-style solo parts were considered to be beyond the capabilities of choirboys; possibly eighteenth-century purists would have insisted on castrati, but in practice female soloists were often employed.

Quite how many performers Mozart imagined for the Requiem must remain a matter of conjecture, though a reasonable guess is that he had in mind forces similar to those used in his arrangement of Handel's *Messiah* for Gottfried van Swieten on 6 March 1789. (It was van Swieten who arranged the first performance of K 626 for Constanze's benefit on 2 January 1793, though unfortunately no details are recorded; probably some such performance would still have taken place if Mozart had lived.) A copy of the printed text for Mozart's *Messiah* has a handwritten note that the soloists on that occasion were Aloysia Lange (soprano I), Katharina Altomonte (soprano II), Valentin Adamberger (tenor), and Ignaz Saal (bass), and the choir numbered only twelve.[4] Moreover the complete set of performing material survives:[5] it confirms the identity of the soloists and the size of the choir, and shows in addition that the twelve choristers were divided into three to a part, and that the orchestra had three desks each of first and second violins and 'bassi', with two desks of violas, and full wind and timpani including three trombones. Each soloist had a part-book including all the choruses as well as their own arias, so presumably the soloists joined the choir throughout. According to Abert (ii: 617) the choir came from the Hofkapelle.

If Mozart had used similar forces for the Requiem, then, he would have had two female and two male soloists, a choir of twelve men and boys (but including also the stronger voices of the soloists throughout), and an orchestra of probably 6, 6, 4, 4, 2 strings plus wind and timpani. There would in practice be little difference in sound between, say, a top line sung by three trebles plus an experienced professional soprano, and the same line sung by four women; so it is possible to approximate Mozart's balance quite closely even with a modern mixed choir, provided it is kept fairly small in relation to the orchestra.

To turn to the question of the pronunciation of the Latin text: it is important first to realize that the 'Italian' style nowadays almost universal has become the standard pronunciation of ecclesiastical Latin only in the present century, after Pope Pius X's recommendation in 1912 that it be adopted throughout the Catholic Church (Brittain, pp. 39 f. and *passim*). (This followed a move towards standardization initiated at the Vatican Council of 1870.) From the fall of the Roman Empire to the end of the nineteenth century, however, Latin was pronounced in each European country on the same principles as the vernacular; indeed, there seem to have been regional variations even in Classical times. Erasmus noted many peculiarly national styles of pronunciation in his *De recta Latini Graecique sermonis pronuntiatione* of 1528, the local accents being then so strong that, at a meeting of the Emperor Maximilian and various ambassadors, everyone made the mistake of thinking that the others were talking their own native languages instead of Latin.[6] Attempts were made to introduce the 'classical' style of pronunciation recommended by Erasmus in England and France, but with little success, for it was said later in the sixteenth century that, in France, 'Requiescant in pace' was indistinguishable from 'Hé, qui est-ce? Quentin. Passez!' (Marouzeau, p. 6). In England, too, the standard sixteenth-century pronunciation used the consonants and vowels of contemporary spoken English (in particular C before E or I was pronounced 'S'), and for the next three centuries all that happened was that the sounds of the vowels altered with those of English. The 'Italian' style (with the characteristic 'TSH' pronunciation of C before E or I, and 'Continental' vowels) was deliberately adopted by the Oxford Movement in the middle of the nineteenth centry, but was ridiculed as 'chees and chaws' by older-established English Catholics, who continued to use the tiaditional English pronunciation for at least another fifty years; indeed, Brittain (p. 70) noted in 1955 that, even then, the Jesuits 'still used the old liturgical pronunciation, combining current English consonants with old-fashioned English vowels'.

In German-speaking countries the German-style pronunciation described by Erasmus in 1528 and still to be heard on German and Austrian recordings of Latin church music appears to have survived as an unbroken tradition to the present day, though there are signs that it is beginning to give way to the standardized Italian style.[7] The continuity of this tradition is confirmed by the large number of Latin loan-words in German, which are invariably pronounced with hard Gs (even before E or I), and with C before E or I pronounced as a German Z (i.e. 'TS')—indeed, most such loan words are nowadays spelt with a Z instead of a C (Zentrum, Dezember, Zentner, . . .). This observation also helps to show that Mozart himself used this pronunciation, and did not adopt the Italian style with which he must have become familiar during his youthful visits to Italy: for although he normally followed eighteenth-century practice in spelling such loan words with a C (December, Concept, produciren, . . .), it is clear from his lack of consistency that he himself pronounced these Cs as German Zs. This is neatly demonstrated by his alternative spellings of Concert/ konzert (for example he entered K 449 in his *Verzeichnüß* on 9 February 1784 as 'Ein klavierkonzert', but described it in a letter of 15 May 1784 to Leopold as 'das Concert ex E♭ '), and by his use of no less than five different spellings of his own wife's name (konstanze, Constanz, Costance, Constance, Costanza). The division of the Latin text into syllables in Mozart's autograph of the Requiem also confirms that he would have taken the Austro-German style of pronunciation for granted, for he always divided

GN in the middle of a word ('dig-nae', 'benig-nae'), which shows that the Gs are still hard here.

In any performance with serious pretensions to 'authenticity', therefore, it is just as important for the singers to use the correct pronunciation as it is for the orchestral parts to be played on 'period' instruments. This is not simply a matter of pedantic historical accuracy, for the difference between German and Italian sounds, especially consonants at the start of syllables, can have a very marked effect on the articulation of the music, closely similar to that of different styles of tonguing on wind instruments. Consider, for example, bar 5 of the 'Lacrymosa': there is a big difference between the clean staccato attack of the German hard G in '-get' on the fourth beat, and the more fuzzy Italian 'DZH' sound. Similarly, the German 'TS' pronunciation of C before E or I nearly always gives a sharper attack than the Italian 'TSH'

The principles of the German-style pronunciation of Latin may be summarized as follows.[8] G is always hard (note especially 'Ag-nus', not 'A-nius'), and C before E, I, AE, or OE is pronounced 'TS', as also is TI before all vowels. Initial H is aspirated, and initial and intervocalic S is voiced. QU is approximately 'KV', though strictly speaking the V is a bilabial fricative, not a labio-dental fricative. AE, OE, and Y are pronounced as German Ä, Ö, and Ü respectively. Experience suggests that it is relatively easy to persuade an English-speaking choir to use the correct consonants (though the Italian C can be rather persistent), but more difficult to get them to give up their familiar English vowels.

ENDNOTES

Books and articles are referred to by the author's name only, with the date of publication added in brackets where necessary. The abbreviations AMZ, MBA, and NMA stand respectively for the *Allgemeine Musikalische Zeitung*, the collection of letters of Mozart and his family published as *Mozart: Briefe und Aufzeichnungen*, and the Neue Mozart Ausgabe complete edition of Mozart's works. For full details, see the Bibliography.

Chapter 1 (Introduction)

1. 'Die Kontroverse über die echten und unechten Teile des Requiems wäre unnötig gewesen, wenn man die . . . Erklärung hätte wahr haben wollen, die Süßmayr . . . über seinen Anteil an dem Werk . . . abgegeben hatte. Süßmayrs Wahrheitsliebe und Redlichkeit anzu-zweifeln, liegt kaum ein Grund vor; er hätte Konstanze einen großen Dienst geleistet, wenn er diesen Anteil als möglichst gering hätte hinstellen können. Der vielfach beliebten Feststellung seiner absoluten Minderwertigkeit, die zum Schluß geführt hat, auch das ganze Lacrimosa, das Benedictus, das Agnus Dei könne nur von Mozart selbst herrühren, müßte eine genauere Untersuchung der Kirchen-werke Süßmayrs zugrunde liegen, als sie bisher angestellt worden ist.'
2. 'nur unterwerfen die bereits bekannten Kunstprodukte des Herrn Süssmayer die Behauptung eines wesentlichern Antheils an diesem grossen Werke einer ziemlich strengen Kritik'. The reviewer was clearly familiar with the content of Süssmayr's letter of 1800.
3. Published by Oxford University Press.
4. 'Süßmayr war ein guter Musiker, aber ich habe keinen Respekt vor seiner Orchestrierung.'
5. *Wolfgang Amadeus Mozart: Requiem K.626. Instrumentation Franz Beyer* (Edition Eulenburg, Zürich, 1971.)
6. See NMA I:1/2/i, and also Plath.

Chapter 2 (The Genesis of the Requiem)

1. 'in der Blüthe ihres Lebens'. (Herzog, *Wahre und ausführliche Geschichte des Requiems von W. A. Mozart*, 1839, reprinted in Deutsch (*Addenda*), pp. 101 ff.)
2. 'wollte ihr ein doppeltes Denkmahl, und zwar auf eine ausgezeichnete

Art, gründen. Er ließ durch seinen Geschäftsträger, Herrn Dr. Johann Sortschan, Hof- und Gerichts-Advokaten, in Wien, bey einem der vorzüglichsten Bildhauer Wiens, ein Epitaphium, und bey Mozart ein Requiem bestellen, von welchem er sich wieder, wie gewöhnlich das alleinige Eigenthumsrecht vorbehielt.

Ersteres, welches um 3000 fr kostete . . .

Das Requiem aber, das jährlich am Sterbetage der Frau Gräfin aufgeführt werden sollte, blieb länger aus; denn der Tod überraschte Mozart in der Mitte dieser ruhmvollen Arbeit . . .

Nachdem also Hr. Graf von Walsegg die Partitur des Requiems erhalten hatte, schrieb er dieselbe sogleich, nach seiner gewöhnlichen Weise, mit eigener Hand von Note zu Note ganz rein ab, und übergab solche stückweise seinem Violinspieler Benard, damit er die Auflage-stimmen ausschreibe.

Unter dieser Arbeit saß ich oft stundenlang an Benards Seite, und verfolgte den Gang dieses ausgezeichneten Werkes mit steigendem Interesse; denn zu jener Zeit war mir der ganze Vorgang mit dem Requiem durch den Hr. Oberbeamten Leitgeb, der die Abtragung des Honorars dafür, aus der Gypsniederlage in Wien, zu besorgen hatte, durchaus bekannt.

Da nun alle Auflagestimmen ausgeschrieben waren, so wurde sogleich die Einleitung zur Aufführung des Requiems getroffen. Weil sich aber in der Umgegend von Stuppach, nicht alle dazu geeigneten Musiker auf bringen ließen, so wurde veranstaltet, daß die erste Aufführung des Requiems in Wiener Neustadt geschehen sollte. Man traf die Auswahl unter den Musikern so, daß die Solo- und wichtigsten Parte von den besten, wo man sie fand besetzt wurden; daher geschah es, daß der Sopranist Ferenz von Neustadt, die Altistin Kernbeiß von Schottwein, der Tenorist Klein von Neustadt und der Bahsist Thurner von Gloggnitz zu den Soloparten verwendet wurden. Am 12. Dezember 1793 wurde Abends auf dem Chore in der Cisterzienser-Stifts-pfarrkirche zu Wiener-Neustadt die Probe, und am 14. Dezember um 10 Uhr ein Seelenamt in der nähmlichen Kirche abgehalten, wobey dieses berühmte Requiem zum ersten Mahle, zu seinem bestimmten Zweck, aufgeführt wurde.

Herr Graf von Walsegg dirigirte selbst das Ganze.' (Ibid.; for the correction Benaro ➜ Benard, see NMA I:1/2/ii, p. IX, n. 14.)

3. 'stand . . . mit vielen Compositoren, aber immer ohne seinen Nahmen zu nennen, in Verbindung, die ihm Werke lieferten, von denen er sich ausschließlich den Alleinbesitz vorbehielt, und sie daher gut honorierte. Nahmentlich hat Hr. Hoffmeister viele Flöten-Quartette geliefert, in welchen die Flötenstimme ganz practikabel, die drey übrigen Stimmen aber ungemein schwer gesetzt waren, damit sich die Spieler recht ausarbeiten mußten, wozu Hr. Graf lachte.

. . . Die auf geheimen Wege erhaltenen Partituren, schrieb er gewöhnlich mit eigener Hand ab, und legte sie dann zum Ausschreiben der Auflagestimmen vor. Eine Original Partitur haben wir nie zu sehen bekommen. Die Quartetten wurden dann gespielt, und nun mußsten wir den Auctor errathen. Gewöhnlich riethen wir auf den Hr. Graf selbst, weil er wirklich zuweilen einige Kleinigkeiten komponierte; er lächelte dazu, und freuete sich, daß er uns, nach seiner Meinung, mystifizierte; wir aber lachten, daß er uns für so leichtgläubig hielt.

Wir waren alle junge Leute, und hielten das für ein unschuldiges Vergnügen, was wir unserm Herrn machte. Und auf solche Weise ging das Mystifizieren unter einander einige Jahre fort.' (Ibid.)

4. 'Der edle Anonymus, welche dem sel. Mozart wenige Monate vor seinem Tode den Auftrag gab, ein Requiem zu componieren.' (Constanze to Breitkopf and Härtel, 18 Oct. 1799.)

5. 'bevor noch Mozart den Auftrag erhielt nach Prag zu reisen, wurde ihm ein Brief ohne Unterschrift von einem unbekannten Bothen übergeben, der . . . die Anfrage enthielt, ob Mozart eine Seelenmesse zu schreiben übernehmen wollte? . . .

Mozart der ohne Mitwissen seiner Gattin nicht den geringsten Schritt zu thun pflegte, erzählte ihr den sonderbaren Auftrag . . .' Niemetschek also said (p. 52) that he 'sah eines der Billette, die der unbekannte Besteller an Mozart schrieb'.

6. Deutsch, p. 346.

7. 'mir ist ganz lieb wenn ich nach und nach meine Messen bekomme' (Mozart to Leopold, 27 June 1781); 'haben sie die güte und legen das Rondeaux . . . wieder hinein nebst . . . etwelche sparten von meinen Messen' (Mozart to Leopold, 23 Mar. 1782); 'mit dieser gelegenheit könnten sie mir wohl noch was mitschicken,—zum beyspiell; meine Messen in Partitur' (Mozart to Leopold, 12 Mar. 1783). In the last letter, Mozart goes on to explain that he is arranging a performance for Baron van Swieten.

8. 'Morgen wird in Baaden ein Amt von mir aufgeführt.' (Mozart to Puchberg, on or before 12 June 1790). It is likely that this mass was K 317, since Mozart wrote to Stoll, choirmaster at Baden, in May 1791, to ask him to return the score of this work.

9. 'Ich habe eine bitte an Sie, und die ist, Sie möchten die güte haben mir gleich mit dem ersten Wagen morgen die Messe von mir exB, welche wir verflossenen Sonntag gemacht haben . . . herein schicken— versteht sich, nicht die Partitur, sondern die Stimmen—weil ich gebeten worden bin in eine kirche eine Messe zu dirigiren.' (Mozart to Stoll, 12 July 1791).

10. Deutsch, p. 345; see also Volek, Moberly and Raeburn, and Tyson (1975).

11. Deutsch, p. 355.
12. 'Mozart entschuldigte sich mit der Nothwendigkeit der Reise [nach Prag] und der Unmöglichkeit . . . davon Nachricht geben zu können: übrigens würde es seine erste Arbeit bey der Zurückkunft seyn . . . Bey seiner Zurückkunft nach Wien nahm er sogleich seine Seelenmesse vor, und arbeitete mit viel Anstrengung und einem lebhaften Interesse daran.'
13. Mozart entered K 622 in his *Verzeichnüß* on 28 September, but in a letter to Constanze of 7 Oct. 1791, describing what he had done that day, he said, 'dann Instrumentirte ich fast das ganze Rondó vom Stadler' [i.e. the last movement of K 622].
14. 'heute früh habe ich so fleissig geschrieben daß ich mich bis ½2 uhr verspätet habe . . . Gleich nach Tisch gieng ich wieder nach Hause und schrieb [bis] zur Oper zeit.'
15. Niemetschek (p. 51) said 'in wenig Tagen' after the performance of K 623 (say 21 or 22 Nov.); a report in the *Wiener Zeitung* of 25 January 1792 (quoted in Deutsch, p. 386) said, 'dessen Ausführung [K 623] er zwey Tage vor seiner letzten Krankheit . . . dirigirt hat'. Nissen (p. 572) said, 'Seine Todeskrankheit, wo er bettlägerig war, währte 15 Tage' (so started on 20 Nov.).
16. Reprinted in facsimile in NMA I:1/2/i.
17. The paper with the printed vertical lines (Paper I in NMA I:1/2/i) is used from the start of the Requiem until bar 45 of the Kyrie, and from the 'Dies irae' to bar 10 of the 'Recordare'; Paper II is used for the end of the Kyrie and for everything after bar 10 of the 'Recordare'. Apart from the Requiem, Paper I is used only for those parts of K 620 written after Mozart's return from Prague, for part of K 623, and for the Requiem sketch sheet; Paper II, apparently used in the Requiem only to *supplement* Paper I, had been used by Mozart from March 1791 (K 612). (A. Tyson, private communication.)
18. Deutsch, p. 361.
19. 'Als sie eines Tages mit ihm in der Prater fuhr, um ihm Zerstreuung und Aufmunterung zu verschaffen, und sie da beyde einsam saßen, fing Mozart an vom Tode zu sprechen, und behauptete, daß er das Requiem für sich setze . . . 'Ich fühle mich zu sehr, sagte er weiter, mit mir dauert es nicht mehr lange: gewiß, man hat mir Gift gegeben! Ich kann mich von diesem Gedanken nicht los winden.— '

      Zentnerschwer fiel diese Rede auf das Herz seiner Gattin; sie war kaum im Stande ihn zu trösten, und das Grundlose seiner schwermüthigen Vorstellungen zu beweisen. Da sie der Meynung war, daß wohl eine Krankheit im Anzuge wäre, und das Requiem seine empfindlichen Nerven zu sehr angreife, so rufte sie den Arzt, und nahm die Partitur der Komposition weg.

      Wirklich besserte sich sein Zustand etwas, und er war während desselben fähig eine kleine Kantate, die von einer Gesellschaft für ein Fest bestellt wurde, zu verfertigen. Die gute Ausführung derselben und der große Beyfall, mit dem sie aufgenommen ward, gab seinem Geiste neue Schnellkraft. Er wurde nun etwas munterer und verlangte wiederholt sein Requiem fortzusetzen und zu vollenden. Seine Frau fand nun keinen Anstand ihm seine Noten wieder zu geben.'

20. 'die Oper ist, obwohl sammstag allzeit ein schlechter Tag ist, mit ganz vollem Theater mit dem gewöhnlichen beifall und repetitionen aufgeführt worden . . .—izt habe ich eben ein kostbares Stück Hausen zu leib genommen, welches mir D: Primus (welcher mein getreuer kammerdiener ist) gebracht hat—und da mein Apetit heute etwas Stark ist, so schickte ich ihn wieder fort mir noch etwas zu bringen . . .—nur gieng ich auf das theater bey der Arie des Papageno mit dem GlockenSpiel, weil ich heute so einen trieb fühlte es selbst zu Spielen.—da machte ich nun den Spass, wie Schickaneder einmal eine haltung hat, so machte ich eine Arpegio—der erschrak—schauete in die Scene und sah mich—als es das 2:^te mal kamm—machte ich es nicht—nun hielt er und wollte gar nicht mehr weiter—ich errieth seinen Gedanken und machte wieder einen Accord—dann schlug er auf das Glöckchenspiel und sagte halts Maul—alles lachte dann . . . —künftigen Sonntag komme ich ganz gewis hinaus—dann gehen wir alle zusammen auf das Casino und dann Monntag zusammen nach Hause . . .

NB Du must vermuthlich die 2 paar gelbe WinterHosen zu den Stiefeln in die Wäsch geschickt haben, weil ich und Joseph Sie vergebens suchten.'

21. 'Gestern . . . ist Hofer mit mir hinaus zum Carl, wir speisten daraus, dann fuhren wir herein, um 6 Uhr hohlte ich Salieri und den (sic) Cavalieri mit den Wagen ab, und führte sie in die Loge—dann gieng ich geschwind die Mama und den Carl abzuhohlen, welche unterdessen bey Hofer gelassen habe. Du kannst nicht glauben, wie artig beide [Salieri und Cavalieri] waren,—wie sehr ihnen nicht nur meine Musick, sondern das Buch und alles zusammen gefiel.—Sie sagten beide ein Opera,—würdig bey der größten festivität vor dem größten Monarchen aufzuführen . . . Nach dem Theater ließ ich sie nach Hause führen, und ich supirte mit Carl bei Hofer.—Dan fuhr ich mit ihm nach Hause, allwo wir beyde herrlich schliefen. Dem Carl hab ich keine geringe Freude gemacht, daß ich ihn in die Oper abgehohlt habe. . . . Morgen Sonntag komme ich mit ihm hinaus zu dier—dan kannst du ihn behalten, oder ich führe ihn Sonntag nach Tisch wieder zu Hecker.'

22. 'Nun als Moz: Erkrankte machten wir beyde jhm die Nacht Leibel, welche Er Vorwärts anzihen könte weil er sich vermög geschwulst nicht trehen könte, und weil wir nicht wusten wie Schwer Kranck er

seie, machten wir jhm auch einen Watirten Schlaf Rock (wozu uns zwar zu allem das Zeig seine gute Frau meine Liebste Schwester gab) daß wen Er auf stehete er gut Versorgt sein mögte. und so Besuchten wir jhn fleisig er zeigte auch eine Herzliche freude an den Schlafrok zu haben. ich ging alle Täge in die Stadt jhn zu besuchen. und als ich ein mahl an einem Sonnabend herein kam, sagte M: zu mir Nun Liebe Sophie sagen Sie der Mama daß es mir recht gut gehet, und daß ich jhr noch in der Octave zu jhrem Namens feste komen werde, ihr zu Craduliren, wer hatte eine größere Freude als ich meine Mutter eine so frohe Nachricht bringen zu können, nach deme Selbe die Nachricht immer kaum erwarten könte, ich Eillte dahero nach Hauße sie zu Beruhigen, nach deme er mir wircklich auch selbsten sehr heiter und gut zu sein schin.'

23. 'Gott Lob Liebe Sophie dass du da bist, heute Nacht ist er so schlecht geweßen, daß ich schon dachte er erlebt diesen Tag nicht mehr, bleibe doch nur heute bey mir den wen er heute wieder so wird so Stirbt er auch diese Nacht, gehe doch einwenig zu jhm, waß er macht, ich suchte mir zu faßen, und ging an sein bette, wo Er mir gleich zu rüffte, ach gut Liebe Sophie daß Sie da sind, Sie müßen heute Nacht da bleiben, Sie müßen mich Sterben sehen, ich suchte mich stark zu machen, und jhm es aus zu reden allein er erwiederte mir auf alles, ich habe ia schon den Todten scheschmak auf der Zunge, und wer wird den meiner Liebsten Constance beystehen wen Sie nicht hier bleiben, ia Lieber M: ich muß nur noch zu unserer Mutter gehen, und jhr sagen, dass Sie mich heute gerne bey sich hätten sonst gedenkt sie es seie ein Unglück geschehen . . . die arme Schwester ging mir nach und bat mich um Gottes willen zu denen geistlichen bey St. Peter zu gehen, und Geistlichen zu bitten . . . Nun lief ich zu der mich ängstVoll erwardenden Mutter es war schon finster . . . ich Lief wieder was ich Konte zu meine Trost Loßen Schwester, da war der Sissmaier bey M: am Bette dan Lag auf der Deke das Bekante Requem und M: Explicirte jhm wie seine Meinung seie daß er es Nach seinem Todte Vollenden sollte.'

24. 'Selbst an dem Vorabende seines Todes liess er sich die Partitur des *Requiem* noch zum Bette hinbringen und sang (es war um zwey Uhr Nachmittags) selbst noch die Altstimme; Schack, der Hausfreund, sang, wie er es denn vorher immer pflegte, die Sopranpartie, Hofer, Mozart's Schwager, den Tenor, Gerle, später Bassist beym Mannheimertheater, den Bass. Sie waren bey den ersten Takten des Lacrimosa, als Mozart heftig zu weinen anfing, die Partitur bey Seite legte, und eilf Stunden später um ein Uhr Nachts, verschied.' (AMZ, 25 July 1827.)

25. Deutsch, p. 356.

26. Deutsch, p. 416. See also pp. 417, 418, and 421.

27. 'Endesunterzeichneter bekennet hiemit, daß ihm die verwittwete Frau Konstanzie Mozart das von ihrem seligen Herrn Gemahl angefangene Seelenamt zu vollenden anvertraut; derselbe erkläret sich, es bis auf die Mitte der künftigen Fastenzeit zu enden und versichert zugleich, daß es weder abgeschrieben, noch in andere Hände als die der Frau Witwe gegeben werden soll.' (Deutsch, p. 375.)

28. 'Ich kam . . . nach Wien in desselbe Seminarium, wo früher auch die berühmten Männer, Albrechtsberger, Joseph, Michael Haydn u.a. ihre Ausbildung erhalten hatten. Hier empfing ich nun, neben allgemeinen wissenschaftlichen Vorkenntnissen, auch Unterricht in Gesang, In-strumentenspiel und Generalbass. Jener mein Gönner, meine Fort-schritte wahrnehmend, liess mir dann, in den Jahren 1777, 78, 79, von dem vortrefflichen Albrechtsberger gründlichen Unterricht in der Composition ertheilen . . . Und ich habe das Glück gehabt, seine [Mozarts] Freundschaft bis an seinen Tod unversehrt zu behalten; so dass ich ihn auch in seiner schmerzvollen Todeskrankheit gehoben, gelegt, und warten geholfen habe . . . Den als Mozart die Oper *Così fan tutte* schrieb, und mit dem Instrumentiren noch nicht fertig war, gleichwohl die Zeit drängte: so ersuchte er mich, die Gesangsproben zu halten und besonders die beyden Sängerinnen, Fer[r]arese und Villeneuve, einzustudiren . . . ich bewarb mich im Jahre 1792 um die Stelle des Chordirectors in der Pfarrkirche der P. P. Carmeliten.' (AMZ, 24 May 1826.)

29. See also the letter of Joseph Haydn to Eybler, 22 March 1789: 'Küssen Sie stat meiner die 2 grossen Männer Mozart und Albrechtsberger'. (Deutsch, p. 296.)

30. 'Ich Endesgesezter bescheine hiemit daß ich Vorzeiger dieses Hr: Joseph Eybler als einen würdigen Schüller seines berühmten Meisters Albrechtsberger, als einen gründlichen Komponisten, sowohl in kammer- als in kirchen-styl gleich geschickten, in der Sing-kunst ganz erfahrnen, auch vollkommen Orgel- und klavierSpieller, kurz, als einen Jungen Musiker befunden habe, wo es nur zu bedauern ist, daß seinesgleichen so selten sind.' (Deutsch, p. 322)

31. 'Daß ich's Eybler'n angetragen habe, es fertig zu machen, kam daher, weil ich eben (ich weiß nicht warum) böse auf Süßmayer war, und selbst Mozart viel auf Eybler gehalten hat, und ich mir dachte, daß es ein jeder ausführen könne, indem die Hauptstellen alle ausgesetzt waren. Und so ließ ich den Eybler zu mir kommen, und theilte ihm meinen Wunsch mit; da er mir's aber sogleich mit schönen Worten abschlug, bekam er's nicht in die Hand.'

32. Constanze to Breitkopf and Härtel, 17 Nov. 1799: 'Sie vielleicht nicht übel thäten, Sich mit dem hiesigen Kapellmeister Süssmayer darüber in briefwechsel zu sezen'.

33. 'Ihre gütige Zuschrift vom 24ᵗ Jenner hat mir das größte Vergnügen

gemacht, da ich aus derselben ersehen habe, daß Ihnen an der Achtung des deutschen Publikums zu viel gelegen ist, als daß Sie dasselbe durch Werke irre führen sollten, die nicht ganz auf die Rechnung meines verstorbenen Freundes Mozart gehören. Ich habe den Lehren dieses großen Mannes zu viel zu danken, als daß ich stillschweigend erlauben könnte, daß ein Werk, dessen größter Theil meine Arbeit ist, für das seinige ausgegeben wird, weil ich fest überzeugt bin, daß meine Arbeit dieses großen Namens unwürdig ist. Mozarts Composition ist so einzig, und ich getraue mir zu behaupten, für den größten Theil der lebenden Tonsetzer so unreichbar, daß jeder Nachahmer besonders mit untergeschobener Arbeit noch schlimmer wegkommen würde, als jene Rabe, der sich mit Pfauen-Federn schmückte. Das die Endigung des Requiem-s, welches unseren Brief-Wechsel veranlaßte, mir anvertraut wurde, kam auf folgende Weise. Die Wittwe Mozart konnte wohl voraussehen, daß die hinterlassenen Werke ihres Mannes würden gesucht werden; der Tod überraschte ihn, während er an diesem Requiem arbeitete.

Die Endigung dieses Werkes wurde also mehreren Meistern übertragen; einige davon konnten wegen gehäuften Geschäften sich dieser Arbeit nicht unterziehen, andere aber wollten ihr Talent nicht mit dem Talente Mozarts compromittiren. Endlich kam dieses Geschäft an mich, weil man wußte, daß ich noch bey Lebzeiten Mozarts die schon in Musik gesezten Stücke öfters mit ihm durchgespielt, und gesungen, daß er sich mit mir über die Ausarbeitung dieses Werkes sehr oft besprochen, und mir den Gang und die Gründe seiner Instrumentirung mitgetheilt hatte. Ich kann nur wünschen, daß es mir geglückt haben möge, wenigstens so gearbeitet zu haben, daß Kenner noch hin und wieder einige Spuren seiner unvergeßlichen Lehren darinn finden können.

Zu dem Requiem samt Kyrie—Dies irae—Domine Jesu Christe —hat Mozart die 4 Singstimmen, und den GrundBaß samt der Bezifferung ganz vollendet; zu der Instrumentirung aber nur hin und wieder das Motivum angezeigt. Im Dies irae war sein letzter Vers —qua resurget ex favilla—und seine Arbeit war die nemliche, wie in den ersten Stücken. Von dem Verse an—Judicandus homo reus etc: hab ich das Dies irae ganz geendigt.

Das Sanctus—Benedictus—und Agnus Dei—ist ganz neu von mir verfertigt; nur hab ich mir erlaubt, um dem Werke mehr Einförmigkeit zu geben, die Fuge des Kyrie, bei dem Verse—cum Sanctis etc. zu wiederhohlen.

Es soll mir herzlich lieb seyn, wenn ich Jhnen durch diese Mittheilung einen kleinen Dienst habe leisten können.' (Deutsch (*Addenda*), pp. 89 f.)

34. 'So wie es gedruckt herauskam, ist es von Süssmayer vollendet, u.z.

vom Sanktus angefangen. Und dieß hat Süssmeyer mir selbst gesagt,
da er vor 17 Jahren bey mir wohnte.' (MBA iv. 455 and vi. 725.)

35. 'Als er seinen Tod vorhersahe, sprach er mit dH: Süßmayer . . . bat
ihn, wenn er wirklich stürbe ohne es zu endigen, die erste Fuge, wie
ohnehin gebräuchlich ist, im lezten Stük zu repetiren, und sagte ihm
ferner, wie er das Ende ausführen sollte, wovon aber die hauptsache
hie und da in Stimmen schon ausgeführt war.'

36. See for example Blume, pp. 155 and 162.

37. 'hatte Mozart nur Dies irae, Tuba mirum, Rex tremendae, Recordare
und Confutatis in allen Hauptstimmen gemacht, und in den Mittelstimmen wenig oder gar nichts: diese wurden von einem Andern
gemacht . . . Das Sanctus . . . ist in der Originalhandschrift dessen,
der dieses Stük wie den Rest gemacht hat . . . Also Sanctus ist ganz
vom Ergänzer.'

38. Othmar Wessely, in his article 'Süssmayr' in The New Grove, puts
forward the guess that Mozart and Süssmayr may have met in 1790;
but this seems unlikely, as the following discussion shows. Wesseley's
article contains other speculations that are unsupported by real
evidence, such as '[Süssmayr] was . . . employed by Mozart as a
composer'.

39. MBA iv. 412.

40. 'Gestern speißte ich mit Süßmaiern bey der ungarischen Krone zu
Mittag.'

41. See NMA X:30/1.

42. 'seinem Fr̄ ᴜnde und Schüler'.

43. 'als er sich aber schwach fühlte, mußte Süßmayer öfter mit ihm und
mir das, was geschrieben war, durchsingen, und so bekam Süßmayer
förmlichen Unterricht von Mozart. Und ich höre noch Mozart, wie
oft er zu Süßmayer sagte: "Ey—da stehen die Ochsen wieder am
Berge; das verstehst du noch lange nicht;" nahm die Feder und schrieb
vermuthlich Hauptstellen, die dem Süßmayer zu rund waren.'
(Cassell's *German and English Dictionary* (London, 1957) translates 'Er
steht da wie der Ochse am Berge' as 'He stands there like a duck in a
thunderstorm'.)

44. See also Angermüller.

45. 'dem Süßmayer werde Mündlich antworten—mir ist leid ums Papier.'

46. 'NB. Grüße mir den Snai—ich laß ihn fragen wie's ihm geht?—wie
einem Ochsen halt, er soll fleißig schreiben daß ich meine Sachen
bekomme.'

47. 'Ich bitte dich sage dem Süssmayer dem Dalketen buben, er soll mir
vom ersten Ackt, von der Introduction an bis zum <u>Finale</u>, meine Spart
schicken, damit ich instrumentiren kann. gut wäre es, wenn ers heute
noch zusammen machte, damit es mit dem ersten Wagen morgen früh
abgehet, so bekomme ich es doch gleich zu Mittag.—eben waren ein

paar Engländer da, die nicht Wienn verlassen wollten, ohne mich kennen zu lernen—aber es ist nicht wahr—Sie haben Süssmayer den Großen Mann kennen lernen wollen, und sind nur zu mir gekommen um zu fragen wo er wohnt, weil sie gehört haben daß ich das glück habe etwas bey ihm zu gelten.—ich habe gesagt sie sollen zur Ungarischen Krone gehen; und dort warten bis er von baaden zurück kömmt!—Snai!—Sie wollen ihn Engagiren als lichter Putzer.'

48. 'Süssmayer soll mir doch N:° 4 und 5 von meiner schrift schicken— auch was ich sonst begehrt habe, und soll mich im Arsch lecken.'

49. Mozart's messages to Süssmayr, in his letters to Constanze, cover the periods 24 June–7 July, and 8–14 Oct.

50. Giegling points out that there is no documentary evidence whatever to support the theory that Süssmayr wrote the secco recitatives for K 621.

51. 'Auch waren nur die Arien und Chöre von seiner, die Recitative von einer andern Hand.' (*Musikalisches Wochenblatt*, Berlin, 31(?) Dec. 1791, quoted in Deutsch, p. 380.)

52. 'Die wenigen instrumentirten Rezitative sind von Mozart, die übrigen alle—was sehr zu bedauern ist,—von einer Schülerhand.' According to pp. 134 f. of the facsimile reprint of Niemetschek, this statement was unchanged from the 1798 edition.

53. See for example pp. 554–5, which include almost verbatim the quotations from Niemetschek in nn. 5 and 12.

54. 'er liess auch die dialogisirenden Recitative von seinem Schüler Süssmayr fertigen.'

55. 'Dazu sind . . . die dialogisirenden Recitative von einem seiner Schüler gefertigt.'

56. A. Tyson (private communication). Dr Tyson tells me that he has established that the last movement (K 514) of the Horn Concerto in D major K 412 was written by Süssmayr *c.* 1792. Mozart's and Süssmayr's autographs are both on Paper II (see n. 17).

57. Letter to Stadler, 31 May 1827, quoted in n. 43.

58. 'Die Wittwe sagte mir, es hätten sich auf Mozart's Schreibpulte nach seinem Tode einige wenige Zettelchen mit Musik vorgefunden, die sie Herrn Süßmayr übergeben habe. Was diesselben enthielten, und welchen Gebrauch Süßmayr davon gemacht habe, wußte sie nicht.'

59. 'Was man dem Mozart vorwerfen könnte, ist, daß er nicht sehr ordentlich mit seinem Papier war.' See also Baroness Sonnenburg ('Nannerl') to Breitkopf and Härtel, 4 August 1799: 'Alle Sparten meines Bruders so noch in Händen unsers Vatters waren, übersendete ich alsogleich im Jahre 1787 nach dem Tode unsers Vatters meinem Brudern nach Wienn, bedauere aber selbst daß ich nicht einige von seinen jüngern Compositionen zurück behalten habe, bey mir wären sie doch gut aufgehoben worden, da ich hingegen von sichere Hand,

und von einem Augenzeüg erfahren habe, daß seine Sparten bey ihme nur immer unter dem Clavier herum lagen, und die Copisten davon nehmen konnten was sie nur wollten . . . ich zweifle also nicht daran, daß viele seiner jüngern Werke werden verlohren gegangen seyn.'

60. Blume (p. 150) asserts that their existence was 'constantly repeated by all contemporary and immediately following witnesses'. In support of this assertion, he states only that Constanze had also described them to Vincent Novello, and refers to Medici and Hughes, pp. 119 ff. This part of Medici and Hughes, however, is not taken from the Novellos' diaries, but is (modern) editorial comment; indeed, the sole mention of the 'Zettelchen' occurs in a footnote referring back to Stadler's report (n. 58).

61. Compare also Constanze to Stadler, 31 May 1827: '*Setzen wir den Fall*, daß Süßmayer Trümmer von Mozart gefunden hatte (zum Sanctus etc.)' (my italics).

62. See the NMA volumes. For *Le nozze di Figaro*, for example, there are extant sketches for the overture and eight numbers, plus two separate drafts for an earlier abandoned version of 'Deh vieni non tardar'.

63. Unless, just possibly, the Kyrie had not been completed when Constanze gave the score to Süssmayr: see Ch. 11.

64. It has been suggested by Nowak (NMA I:1/2/ii) that an agreement between Constanze and the Prussian Ambassador on 4 Mar. 1792, containing the additional remark 'für das Requiem 450[f]' shows that Süssmayr must then have been nearly finished. Possibly, though, the money was paid in advance, or the remark may have been added to the agreement later. It is scarcely credible that Eybler should have made his contribution, that Constanze should have approached several other musicians and then Süssmayr, and that Süssmayr should have nearly finished his work, including the additional movements, all within a space of just over two months.

65. Deutsch, p. 409. A written-out organ continuo part by Süssmayr, extending from bar 21 of the 'Requiem aeternam' to the end of the Kyrie, is preserved in the National Széchényi Library, Budapest (Ms.mus. IV. 52).

66. 'alles bis auf der Anfang des Dies irae [ist] von Mozart allein . . . und . . . diese seine Handschrift [ist] im Besitz des anonymen Bestellers, wie ich voriges Jahr selbst gesehen habe. Alles übrige, was Mozart selbst gemacht und daher selbst geschrieben hat, ist in meine Verwahrung und mein Eigenthum. Süßmayr ist so brav gewesen, mir es vor geraumer Zeit unerwartet zu geben; ich hatte nicht daran gedacht daß er es haben müßte. Dieses Manuskript geht bis an das Ende des Confutatis. Ein großer Theil der Mittelstimmen und vielleicht mitunter etwas mehr darin sind nicht von Mozart; aber alles, was nicht von Mozart ist, ist mit einem Bleyfeder eingezirkelt, wie es

überdem für einen guten Handschriftenkenner deutlich wäre . . .
Auch muß ich Ihnen sagen, daß Süßmayer, der offenbar mir <u>nur</u>
Mozarts Arbeit geben wollte und <u>nur</u> diese mir zu geben sich
einigermaßen schuldig glauben konnte, mir auch das Sanctus gegeben
hat, worin keine Note und kein Wort von Mozarts Handschrift ist.'
67. 'Süßmeyers Arbeit ist also das Sanctus, welches auch, so hübsch es ist,
gewaltig gegen den himmlischen ernsten Ton, der anderen ächt
Mozartschen Sätze absticht und vom ächten Kenner des Geistes
Mozarts nicht unbemerkt gelassen wird.' (MBA vi. 725.)
68. 'componirte selbst das Sanctus, Benedictus und Agnus Dei'. Blume (p.
151) was evidently wrong to attribute any doubts to Stadler.
69. 'das, welches nach seiner Handschrift gegeben würde, [ist] von
ihm . . . ob und was von dem Uebrigen von ihm ist, bleibt in
Ewigkeit ungewiß. Wahrscheinlich und natürlich hat Süssmayer
benutzt, was für Ideen M . . . wahrscheinlich so gar mit seinem
ausdrüklichen Auftrag, mitgetheilt hat. S. wünscht in dem . . . briefe
an Breitkopf, <u>Spuren</u> davon gelassen zu haben. Wie weitläufig wäre es
gewesen, sie zu detailliren! und <u>wo</u> hätte es geschehen sollen?'

Chapter 3 (Mozart's Counterpoint)

1. Published in NMA X:30/1.
2. Fux's chapters on counterpoint are translated in Mann (1965), and
those on fugue in Mann (1959).
3. National Széchényi Library, Budapest (Ms.mus.3000); published by
Oxford University Press.
4. Dr Kecskeméti points out that two of the works ascribed to Süssmayr
in Kecskeméti (1959) are now known to be spurious: for an up-to-date
list of works by Süssmayr in Budapest see Kecskeméti (1962, 1966).

Chapter 4 (The 'Lacrymosa' Completion)

1. Attwood Studies (NMA X:30/1), p. 123.
2. This point was, apparently, first noticed by Abert (ii: 874).
3. Except, of course, the 'Amen' sketch, which Süssmayr did not use at
all.
4. It must be admitted that 'segue' there might possibly be in Eybler's,
not Mozart's hand.

Chapter 5 (The Sanctus and 'Osanna')

1. Michael Haydn, Requiem in C minor (Edition Breitkopf No. 6330,
Wiesbaden, 1962).
2. See for example F. Rochlitz's review of a Requiem by Eybler (Rochlitz

makes several comparisons with Mozart's Requiem): 'Das Sanctus und Osanna . . . glaubt E[ybler] in einem Requiem, d.h. eine Messe für einen geliebten Entschlafenen . . . ganz anders fassen zu müssen, als in einer Messe für frohe oder überhaupt andere Kirchenfeste. Wer könnte ihm Unrecht geben? Grossartigkeit und möglichste Würde musste zwar sein Ziel . . . seyn, und war es auch: aber alles Glänzende und auch der freudigen Aufschwung (im Osanna) beiseitigte er, und liess selbst in den letzten Worten der feyerlichen Ernst vorwalten: nur diesen etwas bewegter, nicht im Takt, sondern im Thema und seiner Führung, sich aussprechen. Der Satz, in C moll, . . .' (AMZ, 17 May 1826.)

Chapter 6 (The Benedictus)

1. In 'Requiem but no Peace', and his preface to the Eulenburg miniature score of the Requiem (Edition Eulenburg No. 954).
2. Lach, p. 51. Curiously enough, as noted by Hyatt King (p. 152), the same 1784 exercise book also contains a remarkable anticipation of the theme of the Priests' March in *Die Zauberflöte*: see Lach, p. 52.
3. NMA X:30/1, p. 53.
4. National Széchényi Library, Budapest (Ms. mus. IV. 10).
5. 'ein besonderes Kennzeichen der Sprache Mozarts'.
6. 'so souveräner Vertauschung der Stimmen, wie sie nur der letzte Mozart vornehmen konnte'.

Chapter 7 (The Agnus Dei)

1. See the entry for K 220 in the Köchel catalogue, and the preface to NMA I:1/1/ii, for speculations about the history of the (now lost) autograph of K 220.
2. See for example the sketch for Cherubino's 'Non so più cosa son, cosa faccio' in *Le nozze di Figaro* (NMA II:5/xvi).
3. Compare Plath, p. 187: 'Es ist ein tragikomische Vorstellung, die aber jede Wahrscheinlichkeit für sich hat: Süßmayr in Besitz von Requiem-Skizzen, mit denen er nichts anzufangen weiß, weil er sie weder erkennen noch lesen kann!'
4. The harmonic progression in bars 36–41 is very similar, at its original pitch, to a modulation scheme suggested by C. P. E. Bach in his chapter on improvisation: see Bach, p. 334, third example.
5. This form of interrupted cadence (with a plain augmented sixth, at least) is listed as a standard type by Türk (p. 352 in 1789 edn., pp. 392 f. in 1802 edn.). Türk does not include Süssmayr's form (first inversion of diminished seventh on IV♯) in his list.
6. Attwood Studies (NMA X:30/1), p. 36.

Chapter 8 (Mozart's Models for the Requiem)

1. The first two movements of Gassmann's Requiem are published in *Denkmäler der Tonkunst in Österreich*, vol. 83 (Universal-Edition, Vienna, 1938). A copy of the complete score is in the library of the Gesellschaft der Musikfreunde, Vienna.
2. Published in *Denkmäler der Tonkunst in Österreich*, vol. 59 (Universal-Edition, Vienna, 1923).
3. See the facsimile and transcription in NMA I:1/2/i.

Chapter 9 (Somes Notes on Mozart's Orchestration)

1. See Tyson (1981).
2. See NMA V:14/iv.
3. It must be admitted that Mozart's autograph of the Kyrie contains a very few alterations that might suggest the opposite conclusion. For example in bar 30 he first wrote

in the four voice parts, and then crossed this out and continued with the familiar version instead. But it is difficult to draw any firm conclusions from this mistake, for the alto and tenor parts plainly do not fit the bass. Could it have been a copying error from an earlier draft?

Chapter 11 (The Orchestration of the Kyrie)

1. In the preface to his edition of the Requiem (Eulenburg, Zürich, 1971).
2. Franz Jakob Freystädtler (1761–1841) was a native of Salzburg, and was organist of St Peter's there from 1778 to 1784; he is therefore likely to have taken part in the first performance of K 427 on 26 Oct. 1783. He arrived in Vienna in May 1786, and accompanied Mozart on his

visit to Prague in Jan. 1787 (see Mozart's letter of 15 Jan. 1787 to Gottfried von Jacquin).
3. See NMA I:1/2/i, I:1/2/ii.
4. According to Niemetschek, 'Mozart blieb während seiner Krankheit bey vollkommenem Bewußtsein bis an sein Ende'.

Chapter 12 (The 'Dies irae')

1. See the facsimile in NMA II:5/xix.
2. See NMA X:28/1/ii. The bassoons are always given independent parts, written out separately.

Chapter 13 (The 'Tuba Mirum')

1. It should also be remembered that 'last trumpet' = 'letzte Posaune' in German.
2. Bar 101 in the Eulenburg miniature score (Edition Eulenburg No. 775, ed. F. Blume), in which bars 47–53 inclusive are unaccountably omitted.
3. It is sometimes suggested that the soprano solo part in the Requiem is intended for a boy treble, not a woman. That this view is erroneous is shown, for example, by Mozart's solo parts for Constanze in the C minor Mass K 427; see also Ch. 19.

Chapter 14 (The 'Rex tremendae')

1. In all printed editions of K 317 the chorus is given the rhythm ♩. ♪ in bar 13 of the Sanctus. It is difficult to believe that this is what Mozart wrote, and the rhythm does not occur anywhere else in K 317 (not even in bar 5 of the Sanctus). Unfortunately the autograph of K 317 is now lost, and all current editions are based on the old *Mozart Gesammtausgabe* (I, Leipzig, 1878), which cannot be relied upon to reproduce Mozart's notation exactly: for example in bar 93 of the Act II Finale of K 620 the *Gesammtausgabe* changed Mozart's ♩. ♪ ♪ ♪♪ ♪ to ♩.. ♪♪ ♪♪ ♪.
2. For a rare example, see the Adagio of the Piano Sonata in C minor K 457.

Chapter 15 (The 'Recordare')

1. This suggestion is due to Blume, p. 164.

Chapter 16 (The 'Confutatis', 'Lacrymosa', and 'Amen')

1. See for example the facsimiles in NMA II:5/xix (K 620).
2. See the facsimile of the autograph of K 427, ed. K. -H. Köhler and M. Holl (Kassel, 1983).
3. Gassmann, too, set this line of text to a new theme in the major.
4. Mozart's sketch has what might be interpreted as a ♭ in front of the *e'* in the tenor in bar 15. It seems almost impossible to make sense of an ♭' here, however, so Mozart's sign is more likely to be a ♮, or even simply a slip of the pen.
5. See Mann (1959).

Chapter 18 (The Agnus Dei, 'Lux aeterna', and 'Cum sanctis'

1. See Constanze's letter to Breitkopf and Härtel of 27 Mar. 1799, quoted in Ch. 2, n. 35.

Chapter 19 (Performance)

1. 'Rec. glaubt, und hält sich durch Versuche bey mehrmaligem Aufführen beynahe überzeugt, dass bey der Wiederholung dieses: quam olim etc. eine etwas geschwindere Bewegung—aber ja nicht übertrieben—von guter Würkung und dem Zwecke angemessen sey.'
2. See the article 'Chorus' in The New Grove for a summary of the evidence. In most Cambridge colleges the change to mixed choirs has taken place within the last twenty years.
3. *Wiener Zeitung*, 24 Dec. 1791, quoted in Deutsch, pp. 375 f. See also Niemetschek, pp. 55 f.
4. Deutsch, p. 294.
5. See the Kritische Bericht to NMA X:28/1/ii.
6. Erasmus, *Opera omnia* 1–4, p. 100. Erasmus quotes the German ambassador as saying 'Caesarea maghestas pene caudet fidére fos, et horationem festram lipenter audifit'.
7. A recent (1985) broadcast recording of Bach's B minor Mass, made in Aachen Cathedral, used an orchestra of 'period' instruments but adopted Italian style pronunciation of the Latin text because, the conductor said afterwards, the German style 'would have sounded quaint'.
8. For more details, see Wardale, pp. 33 f.

BIBLIOGRAPHY

References to music by Mozart are to *W. A. Mozart: Neue Ausgabe sämtlicher Werke* (Internationale Stiftung Mozarteum, Kassel, 1955–) [NMA], except for the few works that have not yet appeared in that series, such as the Masses K 275, K 317, and K 337, where the only currently available source is the old *Gesammtausgabe* (Leipzig, 1877–83). Eybler's and Süssmayr's versions of the Requiem are in NMA I:1/2/ii; Beyer's is published as *Wolfgang Amadeus Mozart: Requiem K. 626. Instrumentation Franz Beyer* (Edition Eulenburg, Zürich, 1971).

Quotations from the letters of Mozart and his family are taken from W. A. Bauer, O. E. Deutsch, and J. H. Eibl, eds., *Mozart: Briefe und Aufzeichnungen* (7 vols., Kassel, 1962–75) [MBA]. Mozart's *Verzeichnüß aller meine Werke* has been reprinted in facsimile, ed. O. E. Deutsch (Vienna, 1938).

Abert, H., *W. A. Mozart: neu bearbeitete und erweiterte Ausgabe von Otto Jahns 'Mozart'* (2 vols., Leipzig, 1919-21).

Allgemeine Musikalische Zeitung (Leipzig, 1798–1848) [AMZ].

Angermüller, R., 'Süßmayr, ein Schüler und Freund Salieris', *Mitteilungen der Internationalen Stiftung Mozarteum*, 21 (1978), 19–21.

Bach, C. P. E., *Versuch über die wahre Art das Clavier zu spielen* (Berlin, 1753), facsimile reprint, ed. L. Hoffman-Erbrecht (Leipzig, 1957).

Bär, C., *Mozart: Krankheit, Tod, Begräbnis* (Schriftenreihe der Internationalen Stiftung Mozarteum, i., Kassel, 1966).

Blume, F., 'Requiem but no Peace', *The Musical Quarterly,* 17 (1961), 147–169.

Brittain, F., *Latin in Church* (2nd edn., London, 1955).

Dent, E. J., 'The Forerunners of Mozart's Requiem', *Monthly Musical Record*, 1907, 124–6 and 148–50.

Deutsch, O. E., *Mozart: Die Dokumente seines Lebens* (Kassel, 1961); *Addenda und Corrigenda* (Kassel, 1978).

Einstein, A., *Mozart: his Character, his Work* (London, 1946).

Erasmus, D., *De recta Latini Graecique sermonis pronuntiatione* (Basel, 1528). Reprinted in vol. 1–4 of *Opera omnia Desiderii Erasmi Roterodami* (Amsterdam, 1973).

Fischer, W., 'Das "Lacrimosa dies illa" in Mozarts Requiem', *Mozart-Jahrbuch*, 1951, 9–21.

Giegling, F., 'Zu den Recitativen von Mozarts Oper "Titus" ', *Mozart-Jahrbuch*, 1967, 121–6.

Handke, R., 'Zur Lösung der Benediktusfrage in Mozarts Requiem', *Zeitschrift für Musikwissenschaft*, 1 (1918), 108–30.

Hausner, H. H., 'Süßmayrs Kirchenmusikalisches Werk', *Mitteilungen der Internationalen Stiftung Mozarteum*, 12 (1964), 13–18.

Hess, E., 'Zur Ergänzung des Requiems von Mozart durch F. X. Süßmayr', *Mozart-Jahrbuch*, 1959, 99–108.

Hussey, D., *Wolfgang Amade Mozart* (London, 1928).

Kecskeméti, I., 'Süßmayr-Handschriften der Nationalbibliothek Széchényi in Budapest', *Mozart-Jahrbuch*, 1959, 206–18.

—— 'Süssmayr-Handschriften in der Nationalbibliothek Széchényi, Budapest', *Studia Musicologica Academiae Scientarum Hungaricae* 2(1962), 283–320, and 8(1966), 297–378.

King, A. H., *Mozart in Retrospect: Studies in Criticism and Biography* (London, 1955).

Köchel, Ludwig Ritter von, *Chronologisch-thematisches Verzeichnis sämtlicher Tonwerke Wolfgang Amade Mozarts* (3rd edn., ed. A. Einstein, Leipzig 1937; 6th edn., ed. F. Giegling, A. Weinmann, and G. Sievers, Wiesbaden 1964).

Lach, R., 'W. A. Mozart als Theoretiker', *Denkschriften der Akademie der Wissenschaften in Wien (philosophisch-historische Klasse)*, 61 (1918), 1. Abhandlung.

Mann, A., *The Study of Fugue* (London, 1959).

—— *The Study of Counterpoint* (London, 1965).

Marguerre, K., 'Mozart und Süßmayer', *Mozart-Jahrbuch*, 1962–3, 172–7.

Marouzeau, J., *La pronunciation du latin* (Paris, 1931).

Medici di Marignano, N., and Hughes, R., *A Mozart Pilgrimage: Being the Travel Diaries of Vincent and Mary Novello in the year 1829* (London, 1955).

Moberly, R., and Raeburn, C., 'The Mozart Version of La Clemenza di Tito', *The Music Review*, 31 (1970), 285–94.

Niemetschek, F. X., *Lebensbeschreibung des k. k. Kapellmeisters Wolfgang Amadeus Mozart* (Prague, 1808); facsimile reprint, ed. P. Krause (Leipzig, 1981). (First edition of Niemetschek, as *Leben des k. k. Kapellmeisters Wolfgang Gottlieb Mozart*, Prague, 1798.)

Nissen, G. N., *Biographie W. A. Mozarts nach Originalbriefen* (Leipzig, 1828); facsimile reprint (Hildesheim, 1964 and 1972).

Nowak, L., Preface to *Mozart: Requiem-Fragment* (NMA I:1/2/i, 1965).

—— 'Wer hat die Instrumentalstimmen in der Kyriefuge des Requiems von W. A. Mozart geschrieben?', *Mozart-Jahrbuch*, 1973–4, 191–201.

Plath, W., 'Über Skizzen zu Mozarts Requiem', *Bericht über den Internationalen Musikwissenschaftlichen Kongress Kassel 1962* (Kassel, 1963), 184–7.

Rosen, C., *The Classical Style: Haydn, Mozart, Beethoven* (London, 1971 and 1976).

Schnerich, A., ed., *Mozarts Requiem, Nachbildung der Originalhandschrift Cod. 17561 der k. k. Hofbibliothek in Wien in Lichtdruck* (Vienna, 1913).

Stadler, M., *Vertheidigung der Echtheit des Mozartschen Requiem* (Vienna, 1826).

Türk, D. G., *Klavierschule* (Leipzig, 1789; 2nd edn. Leipzig, 1802); facsimile reprint of 2nd edn. (Kassel, 1967).

Tyson, A., ' "La clemenza di Tito" and its chronology', *The Musical Times*, 116 (1975), 221–7.

—— 'The Mozart Fragments in the Mozarteum, Salzburg: A Preliminary Study of Their Chronology and Their Significance', *Journal of the American Musicological Society*, 34 (1981), 471–510.

Volek, T., 'Über den Ursprung von Mozarts Oper "La Clemenza di Tito" ', *Mozart-Jahrbuch*, 1959, 274–86.

Wardale, W. L., *German Pronunciation* (Edinburgh, 1955).

INDEX OF WORKS BY
MOZART QUOTED

Numbers in square brackets refer to the 6th edition of the Köchel catalogue, ed. F. Giegling, A Weinmann, and G. Sievers.

GENERAL INDEX